Real Stories of
HADASSAH
LIFE CHANGING
MOMENTS

thin threads®

Real Stories of

HADASSAH
LIFE CHANGING
MOMENTS

COMPILED AND EDITED BY

STACEY K. BATTAT and ELLIN YASSKY

kiwi·publishing

WOODBRIDGE, CT

Thin Threads® Real Stories of Hadassah Life Changing Moments

Copyright ©2012 Hadassah, The Women's Zionist Organization of America, Inc.

Published by: Kiwi Publishing, Inc.
Post Office Box 3852 Woodbridge
CT 06525 in-
fo@kiwipublishing.com
www.kiwipublishing.com
www.hadassahstories.com
www.thinthreads.com
Telephone: 203-295-0370

ISBN-10: 1935768158
ISBN-13: 978-1-935768-15-9

UPC 0 9103727286 7 First
Edition: July, 2012 Printed
in the United States

Cover and book design by Lori S. Malkin
Editorial Director: Ellin Yassky, Medici Editorial Services, LLC.

—— ✦ · ✦ · ✦ ——

To honor the Hadassah of yesterday.
To thank the Hadassah of today.
To inspire the Hadassah of tomorrow.

✦ ✦ ✦

Acknowledgments

We'd like to extend a special thank you to Joyce Saltman, Shomrei Chayim and Hadassah Life Member. Joyce was a major force and heart behind the initiative to produce this book. Our editorial interns, Emma Stein of the Jewish High School of Connecticut and Nancy Rogalski of New Haven, CT, worked tirelessly to gather important details and do follow ups and interviews when necessary. Lori S. Malkin's classic book design made the presentation of this celebratory volume particularly elegant and memorable. Nina Riccio, with her eagle-eye proof reading skills, combined with a love for oral histories, was an invaluable member of our team.

And a special thank you to everyone who submitted a story and was a part of this amazing project. Here's to many more Hadassah Thin Thread life changing moments!

✦ ✦ ✦

Table of Contents

Foreword By Ruth Gruber, author and photojournalist

Hadassah has held a special place in my heart for more than seventy years. And now that we are both celebrating our centennial year, I look back with fondest memories at the year I spent with the Hadassah nurse, Raquela Prywes.

I had been given an assignment by the Reader's Digest to find a woman whose life would define what it meant to be a "Woman of Israel." I began a long search. In the end, it was Dr. Kalman J. Mann, the Director General of the Hadassah-Hebrew University Medical Center who said, "I think I have a candidate for you. She's a ninth-generation Jerusalemite. A nurse and midwife. She delivered most of the babies born to the illegal immigrants in the British camps in Athlit and Cyprus. She worked in the Hadassah Hospital during our wars. And she was so beautiful that every man in Jerusalem wanted to marry her."

Traveling with Raquela and following her example of a commitment to Israel, I found my own commitment. Through my books and photographs, I was able to help refugees.

Writing *Raquela: A Woman of Israel* inspired my life and made me understand Hadassah's important mission.

✦ ✦ ✦

A Few Words from the Co-Editors

We are honored to present to you almost 100 years worth of stories of the women of Hadassah. It can be said that the stories of Hadassah began with the one story we read each year as the spring season draws near—*Megilat Esther*. As we celebrate the Jewish victory over the evil plots of Haman, we also study and reflect on the heroine, Esther, whose given Jewish name was Hadassah (the Hebrew word for myrtle). The myrtle releases its herbal fragrance only when it is crushed, in other words—under pressure. Esther was coaxed into her position of leadership in our history by her uncle Mordecai: "Do not think that because you are in the king's house, you alone of all the Jews will escape. For if you remain silent at this time, relief and deliverance for the Jews will arise from another place, but you and your father's family will perish. (Indeed,) *who knows but that you have come to your royal position for such a time as this.*"

More than a thousand years later, during another tumultuous time in our history, another legendary leader of the Jewish people emerged—the creator of OUR original Hadassah story, Henrietta Szold. In difficult, even "crushing" conditions, Henrietta Szold emerged a true heroine. Under her leadership of the organization

by Stacey K. Battat and Ellin Yassky

that was to be named Hadassah, two nurses were sent to what was then called Palestine to provide pasteurized milk to infants and new mothers, and to eradicate trachoma, a curable eye disease, that was robbing thousands of sight. By 1918, Hadassah had sent an entire medical unit, composed of forty-five doctors, nurses, dentists, and sanitary workers, to bring American-style medical care to serve all, regardless of race, creed, or ethnicity.

The momentous occasions when both Queen Esther and Henrietta Szold were inspired to rise and fulfill their destinies are an example of what we consider "thin thread" moments. These are the moments in our life when we must make a decision that can change the entire trajectory of our lives and the lives of others. What makes these real life Hadassah stories so poignant is the acknowledgment that we rarely know or can anticipate what is hidden along life's path. More often than not, these are the events that create the most important moments in the fabric of our own life's journey.

We Jews are a people who highly value stories. Some of the stories contained in this beautiful book reveal unexpected personal miracles that occurred at our beloved Hadassah medical center. Other stories are about love, romance, and the deep, often undervalued miracle inherent in women's friendships. Many depict the bonds that tie these women in unexpected ways, not only to Hadassah but to new aspects of themselves and their inner essence or leadership, just like Queen Esther and Henrietta Szold.

These stories convey the rich tapestry of Israel and its significance in the Jewish world as reflected though the eyes of many of the storytellers. Within these pages, you will read stories recalling Hadassah's first graduating classes of nurses, and stories of individuals who fought to build the State of Israel as orphan survivors of the Holocaust. Many stories evoke intense emotion and love for our homeland—a safe haven for Jews around the world. Some depict the universal healing and support provided by moms and dads of all religious backgrounds during crisis times— all occurring in the hallways and rooms of Hadassah hospital. While the universal city of Jerusalem is known for great history and conflict, here, nestled in the mountains of Ein Kerem and high on Mt. Scopus, the science of medicine and the foundation and structure of cooperation and medical advancement, are a bridge to peace in the world.

As we collected stories over the last year for this very special centennial edition of *Thin Threads: Real Stories of Hadassah Life Changing Moments,* we found that each story wove an original and colorful thread into this tapestry of Hadassah women. From discovering the essence of our inner strength to exploring a side of us yet undiscovered, the stories embellish the commitment, funding, and volunteerism of Hadassah members to enroll people in this institution of friendship, leadership, and healing.

We hope these stories will help you recognize how the sisterhood of Hadassah embraces people at their most fragile moments, when they are in need of healing and love, and how Hadassah connects us through our love of Israel and our fight to help it thrive. We hope these stories will inspire you to uncover the hidden "Hadassah" in you!

KADIMA B'shalom,

STACEY K. BATTAT, Co-Editor

My family's connection to Hadassah goes back to before 1948, and to Chaim Yassky, the Director General of Hadassah who was killed, along with seventy-eight other medical personnel, when their convoy was attacked while en route to Mt. Scopus. I was a child of the 60s and therefore never met Chaim Yassky, but my parents had become close with his widow, Fanny, and our family hosted her during her visits to the United States. My mother was a passionate supporter of Hadassah, as was her mother before her. I became a third-generation Hadassah Life Member when I became a Bat Mitzvah. My daughter, Zoe, became a (fourth-generation) Life Member in Israel at the Abbell synagogue when she was only ten years old. She proudly displayed her Life Membership pin that was presented to her under the flowing warmth and refracting colors of the Chagall windows.

Stacey's call to me to work on this book was done completely without any knowledge of my family's dedication to Hadassah or the hours I spent as a child accompanying my mother to Hadassah meetings or sorting through donations at our local Hadassah thrift shop. When she called to tell me about this book, I thought, *Beshert ... beshert.* A Thin Thread? A not-so-thin thread? What a pleasure and tribute to the remarkable women who forge ahead and embrace Hadassah's mission every day, week, month, and year, adding up into what has become a century of passionate dedication. If this is what we've accomplished during the past 100 years, can anyone even posit what will come with the next century?

B'Shalom,
ELLIN YASSKY, Co-Editor

✦ ✦ ✦

Hadassah Celebrates 100 Years

To put a fine point on it, we are the People of the Story. The Bible, from which we derive the more common description as The People of the Book, has meaning because of its collection of inspiring stories based on events, personalities, and divine guidance.

So it's no surprise that the Jewish people have given not only a spiritual foundation to much of the world, but have also had a disproportionate impact on the literature—the storytelling—in every country they have called home.

Hadassah is one of the great stories of the Jewish people. At a time when women in America didn't have the right to vote, Henrietta Szold and the women around her organized themselves into a critical part of the Zionist movement. They helped build the future state of Israel, establishing the foundations of its medical and educational systems. In the process, they also transformed themselves. Half a century before anyone had heard of "women's power," Hadassah was practicing it.

As Hadassah's Centennial approached, we knew it was time to tell the story of this great organization. This year we are recounting the Hadassah saga in many ways and in a variety of media. Our story, of course, has been told before, but viewed from the standpoint of 100 years, it takes on new resonance and teaches new lessons.

One of those lessons is that just as the Bible is a big story built around many smaller ones, so does Hadassah's grand, collective story of building hospitals, schools, and many other programs and institutions include individual stories that we rarely, if ever, hear. One building at the Hadassah Medical Center may result from the support and energy of thousands of members, each with her own unique story (or perhaps many stories) about how she came to be involved in the greater effort.

This volume, *Thin Threads: Real Stories of Hadassah Life Changing Moments*, presents 101 of those individual stories. Like the individual strands which, when wound together, produce an unbreakable cord, these stories are the basic materials of Hadassah. This collection includes tales of experience and inspiration, of connection and identity, of struggle and joy. They speak from the point of view of childhood, young adulthood, and maturity. They cover experiences from America, from Israel, and around the world.

These stories represent a small collection from a much larger universe. Consider that since its founding in 1912, Hadassah has had more than a million members. To put it on a more human scale, the next time you go to a Hadassah meeting or event, look around you: every woman there has a story to tell of how she came to Hadassah, what moved her, or what the defining moment was that made her realize the centrality of Hadassah in her life.

This is not a book about people you will never meet, but one about those close to you. If you read this volume from cover to cover, we encourage you to go farther. Talk to the women around you about their Hadassah experiences. There are good stories that can inspire, even if they never make it into print.

Hadassah is Jerusalem's largest non-governmental employer and has a high profile on the skyline. We also have a permanent place in the Israeli imagination and in the consciousness of the American Jewish woman. These stories are the particles from which everything else flows. Like snowflakes, no two of the stories are alike, but together they provide a beautiful cover to Hadassah's Centennial landscape.

MARCIE NATAN, *Hadassah National President*
MARLENE POST, *Centennial Co-Coordinator, Past National President*
FRIEDA UNGER ROSENBERG, *Centennial Co-Coordinator*
ROSELLE UNGAR, *Thin Threads Chair*
MELANIE NASBERG, *Thin Threads Committee*

✦ ✦ ✦

1

Her Journey Started on Friederichstrasse...

By Ruth M. de Sola Mendes

A favorite tradition at our Westchester Region May Conferences was the late-night pajama party for the delegates at which stories and experiences were shared. For many, these proved to be inspiring and moving memories that lasted a lifetime. Some of these experiences became favorites and were requested at many conferences. My mother, Margarete Wasser, was almost always asked to retell an encounter that created in her a life-long commitment to Youth Aliyah and to Young Judaea.

Born into an aristocratic German Lutheran family, she enjoyed a life of privilege. But her family stressed a code of personal responsibility and civility, which was alarmingly disappearing in the Germany of the 1930s. Several times she had witnessed the Brown Shirt thugs accosting Jews freely.

One evening at the railroad station at Friederichstrasse, she observed a small group of children huddled in a corner of the platform with a few adults. Curious, she approached one of the adults with the group and asked where they were going. At first he tried to ignore her but then, reluctantly, he responded that they were going on a trip. When she gently but persistently asked about the kind of trip, he must have sensed that hers was a sympathetic ear and quietly answered that they were being sent to safety. When she returned home and asked her mother what this meant, my very wise grandmother explained that these must be Jewish children who were being sent away from Germany by their parents.

My mother became involved with other young German friends in helping Jewish friends and neighbors leave Germany. My father was one of these Jews, and she helped him escape to America. From America, he wrote to her and, as they came to know each other, they fell in love. With only his "first papers" toward citizenship, he returned to Germany and, through a number of hair-raising episodes, the two of them miraculously succeeded in arriving safely in America. She soon converted to Judaism and they married.

My father, a committed Zionist, joined ZOA, so of course my mother joined Hadassah! As she became familiar with Hadassah's projects, she realized that those children on the Friederichstrasse railroad platform, so deeply etched into her memory, were Youth Aliyah children.

The connection between her and Youth Aliyah was so strong that to this day, those who knew her will recall her devotion to Youth Aliyah and how everyone at those late night sessions hung tearfully on her every word.

When my sisters and I were born, Mom's commitment to Jewish youth expanded to Young Judaea and she was the chairman of Young Judaea in Westchester Region for over twenty-five years. She worked with many Young Judaea directors over those twenty-five years in the Westchester region, including Bernie Weissberg and Mel Riesfield (who still remembers her with great affection as "Mrs. Young Judaea"). She used to joke that she had trained "her" directors very well!

Her love of Judaism and Israel were always tied to her dedication to the children of Youth Aliyah and Young Judaea. For my sisters and me, this is the precious legacy that we all share and treasure.

✦ ✦ ✦

2

Hannah Dagan: The Hadassah Nurse

By Bilha Ron

Hannah was the beloved nurse in my school at Hod-Hasharon, Israel. She lived with her husband Rafi and a son and daughter in a small community established by German Jews who had immigrated to Eretz-Israel (Palestine) during the 1930s. We were dear friends and continued our relationship, even after our family moved to Ohio.

In 1984, I received a call from Hannah asking if she could stay with us in Canton, Ohio for a short time. Hannah said that she needed to heal from the tragic death of her beloved grandson, Iddy Eyal. This twenty-year-old was an officer in the Israeli army and was killed while clearing unexploded mines.

My husband and I met Hannah at the airport. On the way to our home, a very emotional conversation developed. I knew that she had arrived in Israel from Germany as a teenager and I asked about her experiences at that time. She was surprised and said that

I was the first person who had ever expressed interest in her former life. During the two weeks of her stay, she shared many intimate details with us. The following is Hannah Dagan's story as I remember it now. It is a story of Hadassah, Youth Aliyah, and the amazing leadership of Henrietta Szold. It tells the roles they played in the rescue of thousands of children from the murderous hands of the Nazis all over Europe and the effort to rebuild the lives of suffering and traumatized children.

My family, Neiman, was very wealthy and well known in Germany. In 1935, as Hitler came to power, my parents responded to the call from the Jewish Agency. It had hastily embarked on a project to rescue Jewish adolescents and to bring them to Eretz-Israel. This was the major project of Hadassah Youth Aliyah, under the leadership of the American Zionist, Henrietta Szold.

At the age of fifteen, I was taken to a train, separated from my loving parents, and sent to a strange land far away. My younger sister was sent into the arms of strangers in England. Along with a group of other German Jewish teenagers, I was settled in a kibbutz (like a commune) in Northern Galilee. Each of us was bewildered and frightened. We faced a new language, culture, and lifestyle. Many of us were confused and depressed.

I remember that when I sent my clothes to the kibbutz laundry, everyone teased me about my fancy silk underclothes. The stress and alienation was so great that one boy from our group committed suicide by hanging himself.

(I later married his brother.) At that time, the reality of our stress was finally taken seriously.

Shortly after that event, we were told that a great lady was coming to find ways to help us. That visitor was Henrietta Szold, the first president of Hadassah. I will never forget how this gray-haired, beautiful, older woman, with remarkably engaging eyes, spoke to each and every one of us.

She asked me why I was so stressed and how I saw my future. She also asked me how Hadassah could help us. Tearfully, I replied that I wanted my parents and that I wanted to study to be a nurse. This caring woman hugged me and said, "When the war will be over, we shall search for your family, but now I plan to take you to the Hadassah Nursing School." That is how I became a Hadassah nurse. As a school nurse, I was able to repay my debt to Hadassah.

One promise could not be fulfilled. Our parents perished in the killing fields of Europe.

I married Rafi Dagan. He became a musician. We rebuilt our lives and established a family. I can say that we had a good life.

Now that I face my most tragic and terrible challenge, my spirit fails me. Our fantastic grandson, the joy of our lives, was killed in the army, and our son lost his arm in the war. (Hannah's son later became a well-known physician at Hadassah Hospital.) I came to you to rest and recover.

This was Hannah's story. As we celebrate the 100th anniversary of Hadassah, it is time to remember the important role this organization has played in the rebuilding of a nation and the saving of lives.

On a personal note, I was born in 1930 at Hadassah Hospital in Tel-Aviv. In 1947, I started to date my future husband of sixty-two years. I met Sam when he was a wounded soldier in Hadassah Hospital and I was a nursing aide. He is also a child survivor of the camps in Poland and came to Israel as a Youth Aliyah leader.

✦ ✦ ✦

✦ 3 ✦

My Hadassah Roots
By Muriel Haber

The year was 1936. I was a seven-year old growing up in Park Slope, Brooklyn. There were very few Jewish families in my Catholic community when a Jewish, Zionist family moved into the area with a daughter, Ruth, just my age. I was no longer the only Jewish child in the class.

Ruth's mother invited the few Jewish girls in the area to a club meeting in her home. She told us we were Hadassah Buds and we would meet together and learn about Palestine, sing songs, and learn about our history. On my block and in school, I was subject to verbal and physical anti-semitic attacks, but I looked forward to each meeting of the Hadassah Buds where we'd mix fun and education. I felt special being Jewish for the first time! At these meetings I was with the "in group." How I needed that!

In the spring, we took a long walk into Prospect Park and planted a tree in honor of Henrietta Szold. There was a plaque in front of the young tree with her name on it. It was such a revelation to me that we were allowed to plant a tree honoring a Jewish woman in this public park where everyone could see it. We could be proud of our religion.

To this day, I have never forgotten how much that moment has affected my life.

I thank Hadassah for allowing me to see the value of being a Jew. The group gave me the strength to stand up and be counted as a Jew and a woman in the Jewish world.

✦ ✦ ✦

Hadassah Love Affair

By Nancy Leavitt

Where and when did my love affair with Hadassah begin? It began in the Bronx, New York in 1940 when I was seven years old. My mother became a member of the Jessie Sampter Group of Hadassah and began her lifelong dedication to this organization. She took my sister Ruth and me along with her, and my father to a lesser degree.

My first in-house fundraising lesson came from watching my mother fill out forms in duplicate (remember carbon paper?) and sending them off to the Curtis Publishing Company in Philadelphia. Mother's first fundraising effort was selling magazine subscriptions to every person she passed on the street. She was determined to raise not only the $18.00 in donor credit needed to attend the annual Bronx Chapter donor luncheon at the Waldorf Astoria Hotel, but she was determined to raise $54.00 so she could take her daughters with her.

Hadassah to us was a day home from school. We dressed up in our spring suits, had a chance to wear our white gloves, and check out the hundreds of women in beautiful hats. Magazines didn't take up room in our four-room apartment, but when mother started to sell boxes of assorted greeting cards, that was another story. A parade of Hadassah ladies marching in and out of our apartment was commonplace. Next was Baur's Peanut Brittle. Calls to Mr. Herter brought cartons of brown and tan tins to the apartment. It was the most delicious candy and there was constant traffic of Hadassah ladies picking up their orders. By the time everyone's teeth were probably totally rotted away, my mother found Mr. Marmer, who was in the umbrella business.

During wartime, the fundraising item was umbrellas. Finding umbrellas with sixteen ribs was a real coup. I think she met that year's quota on umbrellas alone. My father arrived home from work one night with cartons of 100% wool men's argyle socks. Where did he get them? He refused to tell us his source and took that secret to his grave. We knew something was funny because mother didn't have to fill out forms for these. My sister and I designed a sign to hang over the cartons. It read, "Your feet will never be cold in Daddy's Hot Sox!" They sold like hotcakes!

Every year, the Bronx Chapter of Hadassah held a three-day bazaar in the grand ballroom of the Concourse Plaza Hotel. Everything was manufactured in New York in those days and the merchandise just poured in. The Bronx Chapter rented a store on Valentine Avenue, several months in advance of the bazaar, to store the tons of merchandise that arrived daily. Mother was at it again. She was marking, labeling, and pricing the merchandise when cartons of brassieres arrived. As the hotel did not have dressing rooms, it was decided that they just couldn't sell those at the bazaar. Guess where they wound up? Yes, you guessed it. This is how my sister and I received our sex education and a lesson in anatomy. There were all shapes and colors and sizes of bras. We couldn't believe that there were chests in all varieties to fill them. We quickly learned there were, because all the Hadassah ladies were trying them on in our apartment. Any hour of the day you could catch a fitting going on. We never made a sign for these, but we sure had a few good laughs from this venture.

Time marched on. By 1959, my family had moved back to the old neigborhood in the Bronx after spending two wonderful years living on an Air Force Base on Cape Cod. My daughter Amy was two years old. I was nine months pregnant and my husband was taking his anesthesia residency at Columbia University, coming home only every third night and every third weekend. To make life more interesting, we lived in a fourth-floor walkup apartment (fifty-eight steps).

Mother was still Hadassah'ing. I suppose she thought I was bored and needed something to do. She informed me that the Bronx Chapter of Hadassah was having a membership drive and that I should get all my friends who were also pushing carriages to join Hadassah. How could I say no to my mother? I signed up fifteen new members and won first prize, which was a pin and dinner for two at the Waldorf Astoria hotel. My sophisticated contemporaries informed me that we would have to give the maitre d' and the waiter big tips. We never went for the dinner, but I do still have my pin.

Over the next 30 years, Hadassah continued to be a constant companion. Eventually, after moving to New York City in 1999, I became active in the Sharon Chapter, where I still continue as the chapter's treasurer.

Why? Why do I do this? What's in it for me? Where is my payback? My efforts trickle down to Hadassah's projects and have helped build the most up-to-date hospital in the Middle East. I'm sure I will never receive any treatment there. I support the stem cell research being conducted in the hospital labs. It is unlikely that I will see a total breakthrough in my lifetime. I remember my mother talking about the Alice Seligsberg School where women in Palestine were taught sewing skills. Their efforts showed up at those Hadassah luncheon fashion shows. That training school led to Hadassah College Jerusalem where now not only trades are taught, but masters degrees are issued. No one I know has or will attend that school. The Youth Aliyah villages that housed Europe's refugee orphaned children in my mother's time now are providing safe havens for children at risk. I will never meet these children. I have visited two wonderful Young Judaea Camps and watched the children having a wonderful camp experience. None of my children, or grandchildren, has attended Young Judaea camps.

So what's in for me? I'll tell you what's in it for me. What's in it for me is you. Through Hadassah I have developed friendships that get stronger every day. I have friends that I know very little about. I will never meet their families. I don't know where they grew up. I don't know if their mothers were as committed to the Zionist movement and the survival of Israel as my mother was, but that really doesn't matter. My connection to you is that we are all here for the same purpose. There are children and adults with needs. If we don't help our people, who will? As long as what is in my head still works, I will continue to wear a hat that will hopefully do some good.

Now, as we celebrate one hundred years of Hadassah's commitment to improve lives, I will take off my hat long enough to thank all of the dedicated Hadassah volunteers. I know we can be counted on to continue the work that needs to be done. Happy Birthday Hadassah!

✦ ✦ ✦

— ✦ 5 ✦ —

Young Judaea in the 1930s

By Sybil-Frances Kimbrig Levin

Try to imagine how exciting it was for an eight-year-old girl, daughter of the only Jewish family in Hauppauge, NY (population: 200 souls) to find herself in a Young Judaean group! Such a delicious surprise to meet other Jews from the area. Miraculous.

That Young Judaean group in the 1930s was formed under the auspices of the Kings Park Jewish Center in Long Island, a congregation founded by my Uncle Sam Patiky and his family. School teacher Ida F. Kimbrig became the inspirational Young Judaean leader.

True, we had always collected money in the little blue box for the Jewish National Fund (Keren Kayemet L'Yisrael) to buy land in Palestine for the Jewish people. But by about 1936, there was a new sense of urgency regarding British Palestine, our ancient homeland Israel.

Many families in the surrounding rural towns were reading *Mein Kampf* by a virtually unknown man named Hitler and their understanding of the need for an "Aliyah" of European Jewry became magnified. Love of Israel was effectively intensified and the desire, in our tiny, isolated Long Island American Jewish community, to become more activity affiliated with Zionism became an imperative.

Perhaps, in part due to the vigorous German Bund activities in our area, Jewish parents became ever more acutely aware of the dark clouds hovering over Europe. We were galvanized and grateful to be able to affiliate with the "Youth of Zion" group of Young Judaea, under Hadassah's umbrella. From the initial spark that Young Judaea ignited, I and many others, became active in Junior Hadassah. We burst with pride over the many opportunities for personal growth which Hadassah provided: Some of us even went on to meet, marry, and encourage wonderful Hadassah Associates!

✦ ✦ ✦

6

How I Got Tied to Hadassah!

By Joyce M. Saltman

I was born the day before my mom's fortieth birthday, into the American family personified—a fifteen-year-old boy, an eleven-year-old girl, a dad who was a dentist, and a mother who devoted herself to volunteer work. On Mondays, my mother worked as a volunteer nurse's aide at the Brooklyn Veterans Hospital; other days she worked hard for the sisterhood of our local Orthodox synagogue, and served on the boards of several other worthy causes. But her first love was always Hadassah, and rather than giving up her involvement to stay home with a young child, she began taking me to Hadassah meetings at the East Midwood Jewish Center when I was just two years old.

In those days, I could be quiet for long periods of time; I would sit on the floor with a coloring book and crayons, and never make a sound. The only time I stood up was when Pearl Schwartz was called up to the podium to sing Hatikvah—The Hope. As young as

I was, her lovely soprano voice, accompanied by the piano, entered my soul, and to me, that song symbolized "Hadassah." In retrospect, I realize that back in 1946, the idea of a Jewish homeland was still a dream, and although I was too young to grasp the impact of those gatherings of bright, concerned women, I inherently knew that this song would be the most important melody of my life.

Sixty-five years have passed since those early memories. I have helped create two chapters in Connecticut, activate one in Delray Beach, and have served on the boards in each of the three (and as president of two!). The ages of members and their interests have been very different and even the demographics were dissimilar. But one element has been the same, largely due to my insistence: every Hadassah meeting, no matter where I am, begins with Hatikvah. The hope of our people has always been in our promised land, and Hadassah has 300,000 women throughout our country committed to keeping Israel healthy and strong. The thinnest thread—those early strains of an unfamiliar tune—have bound me to Israel and Hadassah forever.

✦ ✦ ✦

— ✦ 7 ✦ —

The Courtship: Thanks to Hadassah

By Gertrude Schloff

At my age of 88, people still ask, "How did you meet?" When they hear that I, a young woman from Portland, Maine, ended up marrying a man from Newark, New Jersey, they can't help but think what a long journey that was back in those days. Let me tell you how.

It's July 1946, and as president of my Portland Maine Chapter, I am an excited delegate to the Junior Hadassah convention at the Breakers Hotel on the boardwalk in Atlantic City. Can you picture the scene? Hundreds of young women from every state in the United States are gathered for kosher meals, learning, and love of Hadassah. A gala dance is one of the weekend events. The only challenge is that the ratio is twenty girls to every man!

Lo and behold, I was asked to dance and his nametag read "Milton Schloff." My first impression was that he was somewhat bald and wore old-fashioned rimmed glasses. That was all forgotten when he led me to the dance floor. Milton loved to dance and I later learned he was an Arthur Murray graduate.

Milton was fascinated by the fact that I came from a kosher home in Maine and was devoted to Hadassah. He asked for my address, hoping we would become pen pals. Within a week, I received my first letter from this stranger, Milton Schloff. His letters were well written, interesting, and funny. I assumed he had a dictionary at his fingertips because there was never a misspelled word.

This correspondence went on for two months and I felt it was a waste of time. But Milton wasn't giving up! He sent me a two-pound box of taffy kisses from Atlantic City and wrote that he was so proud to know a Junior Hadassah President. This sweet gesture deserved a thank you note, and so our letter writing began again.

A few months later, Milton boarded the *State of Maine*—an eight-hour overnight train ride to Portland (There was no Acela then!) He was a sightseeing addict. I saw more of Portland and the surrounding islands through his eyes than in all of my twenty-two years. Of course, I proudly showed off our Jewish Community Center, where I led Hadassah meetings. Needless to say, Milton charmed my mother and three sisters. After many one-day visits to Portland (Heavens! He would never have stayed over in those days!), Milton won my heart. The taffy kisses became real ones. After a short long-distance courtship, we were married on November 10, 1946, in Boston.

I once saw a plaque on a park bench with the caption: "Let's grow old together for the best is yet to be." Milton and I celebrated our 48th anniversary the year before he died. His last note to me was dated February 14, 1995. It read, "Dearest Gertrude, I went bananas the moment I met you! Milton."

On that hot summer day in 1946, the two loves of my life, Milton and Hadassah, became one. I still have and treasure every letter, card, and note from Milton. They are safe in my drawer, along with my Woman of the Year Award from Hadassah.

Rest in peace, dearest Milton.

And thank you Hadassah, for being my lifetime inspiration and bringing Milton along, of course.

✦ ✦ ✦

— 8 —

Ida Gnieslaw—How I Got to Know Hadassah
By Kathleen Hyman

We fell into the Hadassah arms of Youth Aliyah. We joined as a group of orphans, at Kibbutz Ein Hahoresh. There we had the honor to meet briefly the lady with the hat—Henrietta Szold.

That is how Ida Gnieslaw, one of the "hidden children," and a young Belgian woman who had survived the war, sums up the turning point in her life, the point when Hadassah stepped in as her surrogate family, providing, caring, comforting, teaching, and giving her and the other orphans an opportunity to begin a new life in Israel.

Ida was born in December 1929 in Brussels, Belgium. Like many Europeans, she speaks several languages: Yiddish, French, Hebrew, English, and Flemish. She was one of the early members of Kibbutz Nirim, established in 1946. Ida, along with about twenty

more young people from Ein Ha Oresh, came down as reinforcements to protect the kibbutz in 1948. As Nirim is directly opposite
the Gaza strip, during the War of Independence she defended the
kibbutz from the Egyptian army. Ida's story is typical of many of
Israeli pioneers, those whose lives prior to arriving in Eretz Yisroel
were filled with unimaginable challenges, any single one of which
would be considered too daunting to carry on. Yet, when young
women like Ida were introduced to the support of Hadassah,
especially during those pivotal years of Israel's early formation,
miracles happened every day.

Ida was born in Brussels into a traditional Jewish family of
immigrant parents from Poland and Lithuania. Her father started
out working in a coal mine while learning to speak French. Her
mother was a corset maker. Yiddish, rather than French, was the
language of the household. Every Sunday, Ida's father read aloud
the stories of Shalom Aleichem. Eventually, Ida's father taught her
to sew, and together the family established a small store.

Ida's parents were active in the local Brussels' Jewish community
where their home was often open to less privileged people. At an
early age, she witnessed the beginning upheaval that came with the
rise of Hitler and the sudden influx into Belgium of fleeing German
Jews, many completely destitute—some selling their last belongings
in order to survive.

In May 1940, Germany invaded Belgium. Anguish pervaded the
lives of the Belgian Jews. Carefree childhood was lost as the Nazi
noose imposed its gradual restrictions upon Jews: special listings,
the "J" on public documents, curfew at 8 p.m., the end of attending school, and no access to public places like swimming pools

and parks. Store windows were plastered with posters indicating a Jewish enterprise, yellow stars were mandatory on all clothing, and Jews were forbidden to have a radio.

Years later, people would ask Ida, "Why didn't the Jews flee? How come so many of you didn't do anything and went seemingly willingly to the slaughter house?"

How can you explain terror combined with no place to go? How can you explain being trapped?

Ida explained that many people of her parents' generation didn't have great financial means. And of course, there was the denial. No one, in their worst dreams, could imagine a "Final Solution." The anguish was too much, and so it was easier to hope that this part of their lives would pass.

People still saw a future for their children in Belgium and had become attached to their country.

In September 1942, marching papers began to arrive. Rumors began to circulate about unknown destinations. Eventually, reality sunk in—there would be no cure for these nightmarish days. The only means of survival was to go into hiding. To just disappear. When the deportation notices arrived, Ida's parents did not talk much about their thinking or planning. They didn't have to. Their lives became pervaded with fear. And so, Ida's mother made the unthinkable arrangements to entrust her "little treasure" to people she had never met. Can you imagine the courage it took to save the life of your child?

The act of separation for Ida and her parents was short and abrupt. She was told she was going on a "little vacation" on a farm. Her mother removed all the yellow stars from her clothing, and put her hand into the hand of a stranger. Together, this stranger and the child Ida walked away into the darkness.

Ida remembers that as she walked into that dark night, one hand on her little suitcase, the other held by this stranger, she missed her yellow star that had been part of her identity. She often found herself reaching for the place where the star had been—that inner place.

On the farm, she ate her first non-kosher meal. She can still see that plate of potatoes and green cabbage topped with a slab of bacon. She knew she was under scrutiny and her life depended on it. She had to empty the plate even if she felt like she was was going to "platz." But despite the anguish and fear that resided within this little girl, she did not "platz." She ate. She grew. She was safe.

The years at the farm presented other challenges that needed resolution: the curly hair that could have identified her as a Jew was tamed into omnipresent braids. She was the model child, never crying, showing anger, and was always obedient. Along with the metamorphosis came the need to learn a new language—Flemish, a language that, to Ida, bore similarities to her mamaluschen, Yiddish.

The war ended, yet everyone still continued walking on eggs. The people who had hidden Ida knew that her parents had been deported, although they never told her so. Ida still waited for her parents to come and reclaim their treasure. Every day, Ida would stand for hours on the road, waiting for her mother to walk down and come to get her. Slowly, her hopes faded. No more dreams of seeing her mother light candles Friday evening. No more hugging. No more having a home to return to. She understood the blackness behind the words, "never again."

One day, a lady from a Jewish organization came to pick Ida up and return her to Brussels, barely giving her the opportunity to say a proper goodbye to the people who had saved her, at the risk of their own lives.

Concentration camp survivors began to return to their cities, presenting a nightmarish site of walking skeletons, trying to reconnect with a lifesource. Many orphaned "hidden children," like Ida, made daily pilgrimages to the train station, searching in vain for returning family members. There was no common measure to dare claim their own sense of pain.

The English army had a contingent of the Jewish Brigade stationed in Belgium. Many of them were kibbutznikim. Before the war, Ida had belonged to the Hashomer HaTzair Youth Movement. The Jewish soldiers tried to regroup Ida and other youth in order to make arrangements, legal or illegal, for them to reach Israel. And that brings us back to the beginning of this story, how Ida Gnieslaw found her way from war-torn Brussels, to a kibbutz in Israel, and a meeting with Henrietta Szold, "the woman in the hat."

✦ ✦ ✦

That Brief Encounter

By Betty Samuels Seidel

When I was a very young child, it was not at all unusual for my dear mother, Anna Naomi Samuels (Nechama), to take me to a Hadassah meeting, but this one was special. We were invited to meet a lady by the name of Henrietta Szold, who would be speaking at the home of her sister Bertha Szold Levin. Upon arrival, it was suggested that the children go outside and play while Miss Szold spoke to our parents about her experiences in Palestine. "No. No!" exclaimed Miss Henrietta, the name she was called. "I want the children to hear my message. They are our future." So, we were invited to sit on the floor, in front of the assembled Hadassah ladies, at the feet of Henrietta Szold. Now, as I approach my ninetieth birthday, I can recall her every captivating word as though it were yesterday.

Miss Henrietta spoke of the unsanitary conditions she had encountered in Palestine: no clinic to provide maternity and infant care; unpasteurized and unrefrigerated milk, delivered from containers strapped to the backs of donkeys; flies surrounding the eyes of children with the contagious disease trachoma. Funds were desperately needed to address these medical concerns. As we listened, spellbound, to this plain, gentle, but determined lady, my life was forever changed. Her inspiration at that moment in time, that brief encounter, led me on the path that I would follow for the next eight decades. I had not recognized it then but came to realize that Miss Henrietta's concern for children on that fateful Baltimore afternoon foreshadowed the role she would play in the rescue and resettlement of thousands of Youth Aliyah boys and girls. The immediate response to Miss Henrietta's plea was a Mother/ Daughter fund-raising Milk Luncheon, a frugal mound of cottage cheese atop a peach half.

Our home was ever welcoming to youth of Young Judaea and Junior Hadassah, for whom Mother was the organizer and advisor. I am always deeply moved when graduates recall these early influences that inspired them to actively participate in Hadassah.

Little did I know, as I sat at Miss Henrietta's feet on that memorable afternoon, that I was in the presence of one of the world's greatest humanitarians. Nor did I realize the historic significance of the actions of her heart and mind. I knew only that I was moved and determined to help. Studying her life, her character, and her accomplishments, I learned that in 1877 she graduated from Western High School with the highest scholastic average ever achieved—over 99%. Soon after that, at the age of sixteen, she temporarily substituted for the principal who was ill. Henrietta was instrumental in forming the Western High School

Alumni Association, which she served as its first president. Since this school is my alma mater also, it was of particular interest to me as a Hadassah volunteer to participate in a breast cancer Check-It-Out event at which a portrait of Henrietta Szold was dedicated.

I have progressed through the leadership ranks, holding offices and portfolios in Hadassah Groups, Chapter, and Region, including fund raising, membership, program, education, and public speaking—the many facets that are the essence of our magnificent women's Zionist organization. My visits to Israel always include our Hadassah Hospitals where my late husband Mishel and I had the opportunity to donate a Microbiology Laboratory in the Moshe Sharett Institute of Oncology, and where many of my family members are memorialized in the Chagall Synagogue.

I had the privilege of associating with Henrietta's nephew Jastrow Levin. His lectures about Henrietta, with excerpts from her letters, gave us an intimate glimpse into the challenges, struggles, and sacrifices our founder confronted daily.

When the Jewish Museum of Maryland presented a retrospective exhibit featuring the life of Henrietta Szold, I was invited to recount my memories of her life in a film distributed nationally. Professionally, as the Public Relations Officer of CARE, the Baltimore City Commission on Aging, I produced *A Woman's Place* television series. This provided the opportunity to devote a program to the growth of Hadassah and to its founder Henrietta Szold, in which a knowledgeable past Chapter President Jackie Cohen participated.

I reflect upon the many wonderful friendships that might never have occurred but for that brief encounter, that thin thread woven into a tapestry that formed the fabric of my entire life. Today, as I approach the venerable age of four score and ten, I am president of my Business and Professional Group, co-chair of Senior Groups, Hadassah liaison to the Federation of Jewish Women's Organizations of Maryland, and board member of Israel Bonds Women's Division. Proudly, I wear my multi-generational Hadassah Life Member pin. With great joy and sense of fulfillment, I recall my childhood inspiration Henrietta Szold as I try to emulate her advice: "Dare to dream…and when you dream, dream big."

Whenever I face a portrait of Henrietta Szold, with her eyes looking toward the future, I am aware that her influence has been a life-changing thread that forever ties me and my family to Hadassah, to Israel, and to Am Yisrael!

✦ ✦ ✦

10

Hadassah—A Part of Me

By Diane Paige

Hadassah came into my life when I was just twenty. I watched my mother and father becoming working members of this organization. My father was always handy, and whenever Hadassah had a program, he would help behind the scenes. He would put up posters or adjust a microphone, or do whatever was needed. Both my mother and I became Life Members.

My husband moved around a lot because of business, so my children and I experienced living in different states, meeting different people. Wherever we moved, it seems Hadassah entered our lives.

I was working as an R.N. in Englewood, New Jersey, when we moved to Deal, New Jersey. My husband purchased a lot in a new section of town and I ended up designing a house from scratch. This is where Hadassah came into my life again.

A program chairman from the area approached me for permission to use my home for a luncheon. The program was varied and quite successful. They were expecting about seventy-five people and were shocked when 200 showed up.

This event changed my career. I resigned from nursing and became an interior designer.

Years later, I retired to Florida. A neighbor invited me to a board meeting and I soon became program chairman. The following year I came down with a rare, but aggressive, cancer. After nine hours of surgery and thirty bouts of radiation, I survived. A year later, I was nominated as president of our chapter. While one voice in my head said "You are not strong enough," another voice said, "G-d saved you. It's pay back time."

This year, I will be reaching my eighty-third birthday and my third year as president of Turnberry.

Hadassah will always be part of me and I will forever be grateful to have had the opportunity to give of myself to an organization that has accomplished so much for so many years. HAPPY BIRTHDAY HADASSAH 2012.

✦ ✦ ✦

11

A Plea for Help

By Tamara Greenspan Bennett

In 1947, the family of a high school student in Queens, New York, received a letter from a man named Henry Ramet. The return address read simply, "Jewish Camp, Hallein bei Salzburg, Austria." Hallein was a displaced persons camp. The author of the letter wrote that he desperately needed help to save the life of his newborn son and ailing wife.

While letters like this from survivors of the Shoah in Europe to American Jews were not unusual during this time in history, this one was. The Greenspan family in Queens had never heard of Henry Ramet.

In Poland, Henry Ramet had been a businessman, and his wife was a medical student. Then came the horrors of war. At the time he wrote the letter, the war was over and he and his family were living at a displaced person's camp, where he served as the camp teacher. One of the few treats there was access to *The New*

York Times. One day, the *Times* printed a list of New York State scholarship winners, and Henry, who knew little English, carefully chose one young man's name and address. He was looking to find a Jewish family to ask for help.

Many letters of this type were written to American Jewish families; so many, in fact, that there were organizations to investigate these letters for authenticity. After checking the validity of the Ramet family's needs, the young student's mother made a decision. She and her mother-in-law met with members of their Hadassah chapter at the Jewish Center of Forest Hills West in Queens, New York. Under their guidance, they collected and sent baby formula, diapers, infant items, food, clothing, medical supplies, and other necessities needed for survival to the Ramet family. Eventually, they sent supplies to others in the camp. If Henry asked, they responded. That's what Hadassah women do.

The Ramets and other families survived the horrid conditions of the DP camp, but the camps were temporary, and decisions had to be made. Those who had survived the war only to find their salvation in a DP camp, needed a new place to live. Israel was a choice. Many went. Others wanted to go to the United States or Canada. But those quotas were quickly filled.

Australia was accepting refugees, and in 1950, the Ramet family immigrated to Melbourne, Australia. As Henry wrote, "Some thought that Australia had milk flowing in the rivers and streets paved of gold." Henry knew better. Life was very hard there and the Hadassah women continued to send supply packages to Australia and Israel as needed.

As time passed, Henry's letters continued and the two families grew to become one. The Ramet's little boy was now in school and wrote letters to "Dear Auntie." He wrote to his "cousins " as well— they were his only family.

In 1975, almost thirty years after receiving the first letter to her scholarship-winning son back in 1947, Flora Greenspan fulfilled a dream. She flew to Australia to meet the Ramet family for the first time. The baby whose life she and her Hadassah sisters saved was now 28 years old. Flora had saved every letter Henry had sent over the years. Their friendship would continue past that emotional meeting, many years into the future. In 1987, Henry passed away, followed by his wife in 1993. Their son, Simon, his wife and children, remained in Australia, where they live today.

On February 22, 2002, Hadassah Southern California, San Diego honored my mother, Flora Beethoven Greenspan on the occasion of her 100th birthday, for her commitment to Hadassah, and for saving the lives of the Ramet family and many others at their time of need. It was Flora's request that when she died, all of Henry's letters be buried with her. She passed in September 2003, and her great-grandchildren honored her wish. It was truly a beautiful sight.

✦ ✦ ✦

12

My Road to Hadassah

By Helen Gordon

In 1950, I was a participant in the Second Annual Summer
Institute to Israel. The impetus for my joining the group was an
address given by Ruth Gruber in the fall of 1949 at Webster Hall in
Pittsburgh, Pennsylvania. Her talk—and columns written by Molly
Lyons Bar David for Hadassah publications—described a place so
different from how I lived that I felt I had to experience this place
for myself.

It was a summer that changed my life. The group was housed
in Rehavia Gymnasia in Jerusalem where we used linens given by
Hadassah members from the States and towels given by people
in my own community. It hit close to home to see how much the
people in Israel truly needed, appreciated, and used the things that
Hadassah was able to provide for them. We took our meals at the
Alice Seligsberg School while in Jerusalem. . . and what meals they
were! As a Hadassah member I was proud.

As an occupational therapist, I was particularly interested in the Hadassah Hospitals and visited every one of the five in Jerusalem as well as several other institutions. In a fund-raising talk I gave on my return, I spoke of the Hadassah hospital on Mt. Scopus, which was inaccessible to everyone but the Arabs:

> "They [the hospitals] are housed temporarily in Jerusalem in buildings which are inadequate, but you hear few complaints. In one Hadassah clinic I saw examining rooms that were so small that with one doctor and one patient they'd be crowded and there would always be more than two people there. Doctors crowd around one sink to scrub under a tiny stream of water."

How could I not want to help?

I visited Meir Shfeya, the children's village being supported in part by Junior Hadassah at that time. Hadassah had moved to Shfeya in 1923, caring for orphaned and needy children. During and after World War II, it became a haven for many European children, providing them with a stable environment and activities designed to offer outlets for their many problems. Over the years, it has changed to help the acculturation of Ethiopian youngsters as well as others.

One of the activities most prized by the children was caring for their cow. This was the beginning of the agricultural schooling it now provides. In 1950, I spent a night in one of their houses; the children were eager to entertain Helen, the American woman who spoke practically no Hebrew. The children made sure that I felt like part of the community: we conversed in Yiddish, pidgin English, and pidgin Hebrew and got along beautifully. They were curious about America, my Kodak camera, movie stars, and anything I could tell them about my country. I was even able to hear a few of the children's stories. All of us know of the miraculous escapes a few children had from the horrid deaths their families suffered. How could I not want to help these youngsters?

By weaving together these threads, I arrived at the conclusion that I needed to become active in Hadassah and to do my part to insure that its work would continue and prosper.

On my return to the States I moved to a new city. My first foray into the Jewish community was presenting a resumé of my summer to a Junior Hadassah group. Sixty-one years later, I am still a committed member of Hadassah, helping out when I can. My husband, son, and grandson are all Hadassah Associates and my daughter, granddaughter, and I are all Life Members. One of my prized pieces of jewelry is my mother's Three Generation Life Membership pin, which she gave to me before her death. Hadassah is, and always will be, a major part of my life.

✦ ✦ ✦

13

Teaching Tzedakah

By Cissy Lacks

One of my childhood recollections is of a blue and white tin box that was in my mother's top dresser drawer. The paint was chipped, the box was dented, and the lettering worn; yet, for my mother it seemed an object to treasure.

Every so often, I'd pick it up and the coins inside would jingle against the metal. "That's my tzedkah box from Hadassah," my mother would say when she saw me handling it.

"What's it for?" I'd ask, interested in whether I was going to benefit from the money because, as far as I was concerned, we didn't have enough for ourselves.

"I put loose change, leftover change, in there. And then every year, I open it and send the money to Hadassah. They send it to Israel where they do a lot of good things there with this money and money from other peoples' tins. They built a hospital. Some people think tzedakah means charity, but it actually means 'justice,' an obligation to make things right in the world."

"Do you want a tzedakah box?" she'd ask me every time I showed interest.

"Not really," I'd answer, and put the box back.

Perhaps she thought I'd change my mind when I was an adult, especially the first time I returned from a trip to Israel.

"Did you go to Hadassah Hospital when you were in Israel?" she asked me.

"I went to see the Chagall Windows," I answered. "They were magnificent."

"Remember my tzedkah box from Hadassah?" she asked. "That money went to help build that hospital. Maybe you want to join Hadassah now that you're an adult?"

She never gave up trying.

"No. It's not for me," I said.

When my mother moved into senior housing, she organized a Hadassah chapter there. For memorials and for simchas, she collected donations and sent out Hadassah tribute cards.

I was forty, and no matter how hard she tried, I still never joined or contributed to Hadassah. Then, on my forty-fifth birthday, I got a tribute card in the mail from Hadassah. "Lenore Lacks has given you a Life Membership in Hadassah." It turned out she gave one to my sister as well.

"You're a lifetime member so you don't have to make annual contributions or pay membership dues, but I want to know you're part of Hadassah," she said to both of us.

The money was no small amount from her limited income; and even though I didn't want to disappoint her and tried to be appreciative, I knew the effort would be for naught.

But I surprised myself when I saw a hand-painted, wooden tzedakah box at an estate sale and immediately took it in hand and brought it home. At first, I started dropping in loose change. Then, I began to fold up one-dollar bills and open the bottom to stick them in. For my sister's fiftieth birthday, I gave her a pewter, hand-sculpted tzedakah box.

"I think every year we should give the money to Hadassah because it's so important to mother," I wrote on my card. And diligently, every year, I donated the money in the box to Hadassah and sent my mother a tribute card in honor of her birthday.

"What took you so long?" my mother asked, after getting one of the acknowledgements. "You should have made us lifetime members earlier and you should have had a prettier tzedakah box," I joked.

Actually, I was embarrassed that it had taken so long and that it took her the gift of lifetime membership to get me to realize that carrying on a family tradition would mean so much.

And I had missed why it was so important. My baba, my grandmother, had a tzedakah box because even poor Jewish immigrant women in the United States wanted to be a part of Israel, and Hadassah was one way of participating. They could give their coins and it would mean something. My mother felt the same.

Now, the efforts had borne fruit, and they were proud, proud enough to make sure their children carried on the tradition. Sure, there were lots of charities to give to, but this one was special to my mother, and she tried everything to make it special to me.

What I'm glad about is that before she died, she knew her strategy had worked. When we cleaned out her apartment, I found her old Hadassah tzedkah box in a bottom dresser drawer. She never traded it in for a newer one, and she didn't want a prettier one. The connection she hoped to make for her daughters with Hadassah wasn't for her. It was for us to learn about charity, about Jewish justice, about continuing family traditions, about being part of my mother's past and her hopes for the future.

Last year, I talked with my sister about the two of us giving her daughter a lifetime membership to Hadassah.

"Ask Jennifer first," my sister said. And so, I did. "It's not my thing, Aunt Cissy,'" she told me.

We haven't done it yet, but I'm pretty sure Jennifer's going to get a card in the mail from Hadassah on one of her birthdays.

Another lesson learned from my mother.

+ + +

✦ 14 ✦

A Sacred Purpose

By Florence Kaplan Nathanson

I was born in Brooklyn in February 1926 and, when I was eighteen months old, my father died. As a result, my mother had to work very hard to support my sister and me, particularly during the Great Depression. My mother impressed on both her daughters that we needed a profession so that we could be independent and escape the poverty in which we found ourselves. I entered nursing school during World War II in 1944, and because there was a shortage of nurses in the U.S., the government paid my tuition with the understanding that I would go into military service when I graduated. However, by the time I graduated, the war was over and there was no longer a need for my military service. Instead, I went to work at Jewish Hospital of Brooklyn. It was there that I saw on a bulletin board a Hadassah poster describing the urgent need for nurses in Israel.

Over the strenuous objections of my mother, I sailed to Israel along with five other nurses, to work in a transit camp for new immigrants established by Hadassah at Rosh Ha'Ayin. We were young and knew little of what Hadassah did, but we were idealistic, and so we joined hands and made our way to Rosh Ha'Ayin, which was then a small, arid patch of land near Petah Tikvah, about ten miles due east of Tel Aviv. My mother and sister wrote me that they could not find Petah Tikvah, let alone Rosh Ha'Ayin, on the map. Israel had a huge snowfall that year, the first in thirty years, and it had turned everything to mud. I have no idea how Hadassah got the whole thing organized: posting notices in hospitals, getting us prepared for the ocean crossing, seeing to it that we got our shots, and gently nudging us to our day of departure, January 10, 1950. (By an interesting coincidence, my eldest son was born on that day, five years later.)

My job was to care for Yemenite children who were refugees of the ancient Yemenite Jewish community, which had been languishing in dire poverty and threatened by extreme danger from Arab backlash in the wake of the 1948 War. Their overnight leap from a primitive, tribal way of life to a modern society demanded extraordinary faith and perseverance. They arrived at Rosh Ha'Ayin with not much more than the clothes on their backs. The operation, "Magic Carpet," that flew between 40,000 and 50,000 Yemenite Jews to Israel was led by a man, Robert F. Maguire Jr., who David Ben-Gurion is said to have called "the Irish Moses." Over the door of each aircraft was painted an eagle with outstretched wings, inspired by Exodus 19:4: "You have seen what I did to the Egyptians, how I bore you on Eagles' wings and brought you to Me."

We worked out of two Quonset huts; one served as the hospital and the other as our dormitory. Ours was a pediatric hospital quickly set up for the children from Yemen who were malnourished and sick with life-threatening illnesses: diarrhea, dysentery, tuberculosis, and meningitis. Trachoma, an eyesight robbing disease, was also prevalent. The children were scared and withdrawn. The American and Israeli nurses at Rosh Ha'Ayin were the first close contacts these children had with Western women. We could not speak their language, Arabic, so communication was done by a hand lovingly placed upon a head or by caressing a cheek, or by smiling when you felt like crying because of the pain in their eyes. We spoke softly to them in a language they could not understand, but they were still comforted by the sound of our voices. We lacked everything: medications, food, and clean linens, not to mention soap and hot water. Keeping things hygienic was a constant battle, but we improvised. During the sandstorm that accompanied the Hamsin (the hot east wind), we soaked cheesecloth linens in cold water and draped them over the cribs to keep the sand from choking and smothering the babies.

Staffing was done as best we could and work hours were long. We learned "medical Hebrew" on the fly. I still recall one word: "Shilshul" (diarrhea) because all the children suffered from that, which was followed by dehydration and often death. The parents were suspicious of Western medicine. Their methods of healing were primitive. For example, small burns were made around the child's belly button to chase out the spirits that made the child ill. It took a good deal of patience and competent negotiations on the part of the Israeli nurses, who spoke enough faltering Arabic, to convince the parents that we wanted to help and not harm their children.

I served there for nine months before returning to the U.S., where I resumed work at the Jewish Hospital. I have been a Life Member of Hadassah for more than half a century and will always remember my time at Rosh Ha'Ayin with gratitude that I could be used for such a sacred purpose.

✦ ✦ ✦

My Favorite Rubin

By Marion Lipsitz

As a transplant from Connecticut to Missouri, I embraced St. Louis, and soon afterwards, Hadassah. That was the beginning of seven decades of passionate involvement.

You can imagine the excitement of my first trip to Israel with my mother-in-law in July, 1951. It began with an on-site visit to our hospital at Mt. Scopus, the Straus Health Center, Brandeis Vocational School, Alice Seligsberg's High School for Girls, all followed by a private visit to Golda Meir's house for tea.

One evening, Hadassah hosted an evening at Meyer Weisgall's house (head of the Weitzman Institute). There on the walls, were the most beautiful paintings I had ever seen. I knew nothing about art at that time, but I knew I wanted one of those. As coincidence would have it, the next evening the artist, Reuven Rubin, gave a talk. I went up and spoke to him, and he flirtatiously invited me to his studio "to see his etchings." I wrote in my diary, "It was an experience of a lifetime. . . he was fascinating and his studio had all sorts of artifacts. I knew when I saw his Safed landscape, I had to have it." My diary continued, "The painting did something to me; I was captivated." Through that trip, I acquired a painting that is my treasure to this day. Rubin signed the piece, "To Marion, with love" and it has adorned my living room since 1951. My very first piece of art through this Hadassah connection greets me every single day. At 92, I still remember how it came into my life. The painting and Hadassah are now synonymous.

As I reflect back on the years of my dedication to Hadassah, I realize we are almost the same age, and I am only a mere symbol of the worth of the outstanding and life-changing work that has been done. Hadassah has been the mainstay of our national and international accomplishments through the local levels. I remain active on the St. Louis board to this day. The famous words that Henrietta Szold spoke in 1912 to her study group always bear repetition: "If we are Zionists like we say we are, what is the good of meeting and talking and drinking tea? Let us do something real and practical. Let us organize the Jewish women of America and send doctors and nurses to Palestine." One hundred years later, we are still that practical organization. Zionism is the conscience of the Jewish people. Without this, Hadassah would be just another fundraising group.

Those words really resonated with me. In the 1940s, the tenor of American Jewry was a lot different because we were imbued with the realization that there might actually be a State of Israel, and people banded together under the banner of Zionism. In those days, it was no big deal to have 600 to 1000 people gathered in support of Youth Aliyah in the Khorassan Room of the Chase Hotel, which was the biggest venue in the city at the time. I organized those events, as well as house tours, and occasions where I encouraged husbands to make their wives Life Members. Even after the State was created, Israel needed a great deal of help because of the recurrent wars. Hadassah was the backbone of the health industry of the country, the only hospital system in the country at the time—a nursing school, a medical school, both in their infancy.

I was 22 when I started my relationship with Zionism through Hadassah. Although I have lived a life of philanthropy, it seems there is no end to all the needs. Wherever I go, I still recruit new Life Members, adding to my list that is now too long to count. Today, we live by the cell phone, the clock, the calendar, the computer, and the Internet. People who live only for themselves come to regard time as an enemy, but those who use their time in the service of others discover, with each passing year, a rich accumulation of purposeful and worthwhile experiences. When we attach ourselves to ideals that transcend our own personal needs, our lives take on a depth of meaning, and maybe even, an aspect of eternity. This is what Hadassah has done for me. To this day, as I revel in each Hadassah milestone and marvel at each strategic accomplishment, I am a better and happier person for my involvement. The honors I have received are not mine; they belong to all of us—those who have come and gone and those who will carry on tomorrow. In my heart and mind, Hadassah does us all honor.

Reuven Rubin corresponded with me for the next ten years. He came to New York for a gallery showing when my husband and I were also there by happenstance. He had created a new medium of pen and ink drawings and came to launch the new series of his works. Of course, I bought a second painting, which also graces my home next to my wall full of Hadassah awards and citations. Hadassah has really defined me–my interests and the creation of my lifelong passion. Rubin's works, Hadassah and I have moved together into the future.

✦ ✦ ✦

---+ *16* +---

The Power Of One

By Lydia Krieg

The tomorrows belong to the young, and the young belong to you, for you to mold and temper for great deeds.

—Henrietta Szold, Founder of Hadassah

I was born and raised in the multi-cultural East New York neighborhood of Brooklyn, New York. As a child of a mixed marriage, I had an understandable confusion about religion. My father was of Italian Catholic extraction, and my mother was Jewish. The area I lived in was comprised mainly of non-Jewish families, and my few close friends in my pre-teen years were not Jewish. The Jewish families lived in another part of East New York, and I didn't come in contact with them until I entered high school.

Holidays were celebrated in both my Catholic and Jewish families' homes. Both families celebrated Christmas, Chanukah, Easter, and Passover with equal fervor. The High Holy Days weren't as important, since my Jewish relatives weren't synagogue attendees, and there were no Passover Seders. Growing up in the close, loving environment of both families left me insecure as to what religious direction to take. My parents' separation and eventual divorce when I was a teenager really left me at loose ends.

My grandmother, along with my aunt and her family, lived only a few short blocks away from us, in what was a totally different ethnic world. It seems strange now but that short distance was a bridge to a totally Jewish neighborhood. The stores, the people, and the schools were all slanted toward Judaism.

One weekend, while helping my aunt by babysitting her children, I met Marilyn, a friend of my aunt and leader in Young Judaea. In conversation, Marilyn casually asked if I was interested in learning more about my Jewish heritage, meeting some young people my own age, and doing some very interesting things. Of course, I was intrigued, and that was the beginning of Young Judaea and my Jewish life.

Marilyn told me about Young Judaea's programs, activities, and values. She helped me join Kadimah, a Young Judaea club, and I started on a road that led to where I am, emotionally, today. I became interested in the Zionist movement's ideals of a Jewish homeland, and I began to associate more and more with Jewish people while I learned about my religion. In Kadimah, I learned about the Jewish Holy Days and what they stood for. I learned about Jewish culture and its ideals, Hebrew, and Israeli music. I learned to celebrate Shabbat. Ultimately, I learned to make a difference.

Several Young Judaea chapters formed an Israeli folk dancing group. We were invited to perform at many Hadassah chapters throughout Brooklyn, and I developed a deep understanding and love for these dedicated Jewish women. In conversation with Hadassah members, I realized that the need for a Jewish homeland for all Jews was an imperative. I made up my mind to work in some manner to support the new State of Israel.

But back to Young Judaea. Due to my family's financial situation, I would never have been able to attend a Young Judaea camp. Through the generosity of the Hadassah women who supported Young Judaea, I was able to spend a summer at Camp Tel Yehudah. There, I met young Jewish girls and boys of my own age and was able to experience a camaraderie I never knew existed. It awakened a spirit inside me that still burns today.

My lifetime passion continues to be Hadassah, and I have devoted my charitable efforts toward that end. Young Judaea, the Zionist Youth Movement of Hadassah, was instrumental in helping me discover myself, who I am, and lead the way to my love of Israel. The importance of Young Judaea cannot be overestimated, and the support you give cannot be measured in dollars or time. The far-reaching impact of Young Judaea is immeasurable because we can never know who we have reached and how we have changed their lives.

Thank you, Hadassah!

✦ ✦ ✦

$$\relax \text{--+ } 17 \text{ +--}$$

Hadassah—My Finishing School

By Leona Brauser

In 1954, Hadassah was forty-two years old and I was twenty-three. I was a brand new mother, living fifty miles away from where I was raised. I was delighted to be asked to come to a meeting of something called "Hadassah." I did not know what Hadassah was, but I knew there would be other young Jewish women attending this meeting in Hauppauge, New York, and I happily attended. Wow, that was my lucky day! Not only did I make new friendships, but my Zionist soul was stirred, and learning about Israel added a whole new dimension to my life.

As it happened, that evening a brand new chapter was created and I became its first recording secretary. The woman who came to speak to us was Bernice Salpeter, and many years later, when she was Bernice Tannenbaum, she became National President. I thank her for being my mentor and my inspiration to become a leader. Three years later, I was the president of what was then known as the

Ida F. Kimbrig Chapter of Hadassah, and my husband and I made our very first trip to Israel.

What a thrill it was to stand on a hill overlooking the town of Ein Kerem and see the outline structure of what would then become our Hadassah Hospital at Ein Kerem. Today, having visited Israel at least twenty-five more times, I have not only seen this wondrous hospital grow, I have been privileged to see the land of Israel turn from brown to green, to see towns become cities, and to finally see the thriving land of Israel, although diminutive in size, grow to become a major hub for all kinds of industry and resources. Hadassah has been my "finishing school" and added great depth and knowledge to my life.

As a leader, I served five separate terms as president of groups and chapters. I have learned to speak publicly and have traveled to many cities promoting Hadassah and its life-saving work. We are a totally involved Hadassah family—my husband and my three sons are Associates, all of my daughters-in-law are Life Members, as are all of my eleven grandchildren. I have had the opportunity to attend dozens of conventions and leadership training courses and to meet the physicians, nurses, teachers, and social workers who are involved in our healing, teaching, and social welfare programs.

My commitment as a volunteer these past fifty-seven years has given me confidence and personal fulfillment, but one of the greatest bonuses of my relationship with Hadassah is the friendships that have been formed in these past decades . . . friends who shared years of growing together and "growing Hadassah" with our monetary and personal support. These friendships have lasted through the years and, along with my family, my Hadassah friends and colleagues have enriched my life.

What Hadassah has meant to me most in all these years is that I have a personal responsibility and the obligation of tzedakah— the responsibility of making life easier, safer, and better for my fellow man, woman, and child. I have never felt burdened by the hours and obligations necessary for a leader to function. My Hadassah work has never taken me away from my other family responsibilities; rather it has given me a dimension that has made me feel proud and productive, without which I think I would be less of a human being.

So, thanks to the memory of that very first day I heard about Hadassah in March 1954, and thanks to the over 300,000 members who support our good work. Hadassah was my finishing school. But at eighty, I tell you . . . I am not finished yet!

✦ ✦ ✦

— 18 —

Young Judaea—A Thread that Binds

By Shirley Krick Michalove

I n 1955, many of my friends had elaborate parties for their "sweet sixteen" birthdays. Instead, I chose to participate in Young Judaea's Summer-in-Israel program, and celebrate my birthday in a very unique way and place—Israel.

Our experiences there reflected the very early years of the new state of Israel. Our group spent time volunteering on a kibbutz, working on a moshav, and traveling to watch the Hula swamp being drained. In order to get a view of the Kotel, we had to climb to the top of the YMCA building and look over the barbed wire, just to catch a glimpse.

Fast-forward thirty-five years. It is "pay back" time; I am now the president of the Southeastern Region of Hadassah. At a National Board meeting, I saw a woman sitting across the room who looked very familiar, but I could not place where I had seen her before. There is a break, and I began playing Jewish geography with her. Of course, it turns out we were both in Israel on that same Young Judaea program, thirty-five years ago.

As we catch up on each other's lives, Ruth Wasserman de Sola Mendes told me that another alumna from our group was also on the Board. I look around the room, but could not recognize anyone else. Ruth told me that Barbara Holland Tirschwell was on our trip also, and at once I remembered the name.

Subsequently, at the National Convention in Atlanta, we handed out copies of the Young Judaea group picture from our trip more than three decades ago and asked the National Board to pick out the three members who were in the picture. I don't think anyone correctly identified all three of us!

Ruth and I were both on Hadassah's Solidarity Mission in 1991, during Operation Desert Storm. We reminisced about how different Israel is from when we first visited, as we walked the same streets as grown women that we had once walked together as teenagers. It was on that mission that Rose Matzkin, of blessed memory, told me, "Every trip to Israel is a first trip, because the country is different every time you visit." It was a wonderful and emotional experience. In contrast to seeing the Old City thirty-five years ago through the strings of barbed wire, we were able to touch and kiss the Kotel. We visited Hadassah Hospital and felt we were a vital part of the Jewish people.

In 1968, as the education director of a new congregation in Atlanta, I worked closely with our Rabbi who had grown up in Pennsylvania. As prospective members came into the office, I knew so many of them and asked them how their families were. This roused the Rabbi's curiosity and he asked, "You grew up in Atlanta,

George Stern is from Nashville, Ben Landey is from Valdosta (Georgia), and you act like you all grew up together. How is that possible?" Each of us had the same answer: Young Judaea.

The South was filled with many small Jewish communities. Our parents thought nothing of letting us travel to other locations to meet Jewish contemporaries. A bus would start in Memphis, travel to Nashville, Chattanooga, Atlanta, Macon, and Valdosta, picking up Judaeans in each city to finally end the journey in Daytona Beach for a YJ convention.

We did this so often that we knew all about each other. We visited each other's homes and got to know parents and siblings. We became a family—a Young Judaea family. It is a small Jewish world indeed, and Young Judaea is a thread that binds.

I recently attended the installation of a new Rabbi in our community. The Rabbi who came from Houston to install him had a name that was very familiar, but I couldn't place how I knew it. In his introduction, it was mentioned that Roy Walters grew up in Memphis, Tennessee. At once I knew that he was a former Judaean.

Following the service, many people went over to tell him how much they enjoyed his remarks. When it was my turn, I told Roy that I was going to ask an "off the wall" question: "Were you in Young Judaea?" He could have answered with a simple yes or no, but instead replied, "What was your maiden name?" As soon as I said Shirley Ann Krick, he began singing a parody that I didn't even remember, and he said he had not thought about in more than fifty years.

Hadassah women have become my closest friends, and I have become the person I am largely as a result of the bond of friendships I made during the connecting events in my life. All of this just goes to prove that once a Judaean, always a Judaean, and no matter where you go, someone will remember you and reconnect.

✦ ✦ ✦

—✦ 19 ✦—

Hadassah, a Life-Changing Thread
By Joan W. Sacarob

During my teenage years, living in Annapolis, Maryland, I was in love with Palestine. As a very young bride married to a Naval officer fresh out of the United States Naval Academy, I (as did my husband Don) knew that our Jewishness and Zionism would play a major role in our marriage from the very beginning. When Don went to sea, I turned to the Newport Rhode Island Chapter of Hadassah. It was where I was able to be with the few Jewish friends I had made. Being a Navy wife was lonely, and being on my own for the first time in my life was daunting. Hadassah was my thing.

In 1957, out of the blue came orders sending Don to Washington, D.C. on temporary duty. The question became, where to live? Being sick and pregnant made matters worse.

At that time, I had a cousin living in Arlington, Virginia, who suggested that we move there, as they had a fabulous Hadassah chapter and this would make the transition easier. From the week that we moved in and I made that first Hadassah call, a whole new world opened up to me. These women of all ages became my extended family and remain so to this day. My first chairmanship was as Card Chair, and from there I moved up the ladder, from group to chapter to region president to Hadassah's National Board, eventually becoming a national vice president. Today, 39 years later, I am still serving the National Board with a portfolio. After all those years, Hadassah threads have blanketed my life and been interwoven into our family's very being. Our children and grand-children have been greatly influenced by Hadassah. They, too, travel back and forth to Israel and are steeped in Jewish traditions, Zionist causes, and know the meaning of tzedkah. They give of their time to help the Jewish people.

My very own successful business as an event planner, becoming known as the grand dame of Washington planners, came as the result of chairing and planning so many local Hadassah events. (In those days, I even catered the meals myself with the help of all my volunteer peers).

Perhaps my proudest moments were the creation of the Washington Special Program, known today as "Day on the Hill," and the eventual opening of the Washington Action Office. As the Washington representative, I met with many top government officials. I served, under Frieda Lewis' presidency, as the local chair for Hadassah's seventieth anniversary, held in our nation's capital. How many National Board members can recall a breakfast on Capital Hill with Senators Ted Kennedy and Scoop Jackson wooing the crowd? The day included the unveiling of Henrietta Szold's portrait at the National Portrait Gallery of Art, tea at the White House with Nancy Reagan, and a visit to the Israeli Embassy, where each and every one of us felt so happy to be "home."

I have had a lifetime of wonderful experiences made possible through Hadassah, both nationally and internationally. Visiting almost every state for Hadassah as a speaker was an eye-opener. To have attended two world Zionist congresses and to have been to Israel for highlights, dedications, as well as wars and bombings, has given me greater insight into who I am, and into the real Israel.

As we plan our Centennial Dedication gathering in Israel in October 2012, I am able to see how the Hadassah thread has blanketed my life, a lifetime of fulfilling the dreams and aspirations of a young Jewish woman searching for a cause dearest to her heart. As a wife, mother, grandmother, friend, Zionist, political activist, and Jewish traditionalist, I have been blessed with a world of opportunities and achievements as a daughter of my people.

Thank you, Hadassah, for the thread that has been the fiber of my life.

✦ ✦ ✦

── 20 ──

Eleanor the First Lady

By Sarah Harris

I was program chair of Baltimore Hadassah in 1958. Its president at the time was Helen Greenfeld. I invited Eleanor Roosevelt to be the guest speaker for our Baltimore Chapter opening meeting. She accepted the invitation and took a plane to get to Baltimore. I went to the airport to meet her and pick her up, bringing her back to my parents' house to join us for breakfast. Eleanor Roosevelt told us that when she traveled to the Middle East, the Arab countries were dark but Israel was light.

As she was such an important guest, my husband wanted to bring our children home from school to meet her. He called their school and asked the secretary to send the children home and explained the special circumstances. When the principal heard that Eleanor Roosevelt was at my parents' house, she said, "What? Are you kidding me?" and agreed to send them home as long as she could come with them. My husband took all of the pictures that day. The picture of the principal, my children, and Eleanor Roosevelt was given a place of honor in their school.

The next year, I had to come up with another speaker who could top Eleanor Roosevelt, so I invited Helen Keller to present to our chapter. I picked up Helen Keller and her aide at the bus station and took them to the Lord Baltimore Hotel. When we walked in to the lobby of the hotel, Helen told me that she could smell the flowers. Over dinner that evening, Helen ordered a full glass of rye whisky. She asked me if I wanted a glass, but I declined. Helen informed me that she made yearly trips to the Mayo Clinic, and they recommended this drink to her. She said the same thing that Eleanor Roosevelt said to me about Israel—that when she was there, she could sense that everything was light and bright, but the Arab countries were dark. I remember that there was a piano player at the Hadassah meeting, and Helen Keller could feel the vibrations of the piano.

The third prominent speaker that I invited to Baltimore Hadassah was Hubert Humphrey.

The Baltimore chapter really liked our speakers.

(Sarah Harris celebrated her 100th birthday in 2011).

✦ ✦ ✦

21

What Hadassah Did for this Holocaust Survivor

By Esther Gastwirth

Before I joined Hadassah, I was a lonely and unhappy woman. As a Holocaust survivor, I did not have any friends and always felt inferior. I was full of anger, and the memories of my tragic youth never left me. I was depressed and had nightmares. Even though I took care of my home and children, there was a personal emptiness in my life and I felt isolated from everyone.

One day, a neighbor invited me to a Hadassah meeting. My reaction was, "What do I have in common with these American women?" After I refused her offer, she shamed me: "You of all people should belong to Hadassah." And so I went to a meeting and found out that it did relate to me, as I cared about Israel very much. Caring for the sick and helping the young survivors who had come from Europe got my attention, and the members showed genuine interest about my experiences. Within no time, I became involved.

I knocked on people's doors and collected money. We organized bazaars where I watched with fascination how some of our members' husbands drove up with goods from their factories or stores. We all donated second-hand clothes or dishes. I enjoyed the hustle and bustle of the market and found out that I was a very good saleslady (later in my life, that experience would help me find a job in retail sales). We were all happy with the money we made and knew that it went to heal people in Israel, regardless of their belief or race. I was not shy anymore. I started to believe in myself, made new friends, and admired our leaders. I remember sitting at an educational meeting and watching an old lady writing and listening. She looked so alive and interesting that I thought, "This is the way I want to grow older." I met a lot of interesting and intelligent women and admired some who wrote the plays that we put on. There was always a part for me: a woman with an accent. I changed. I made new friends and learned new things. I had fewer nightmares. The second year, I was chosen as a membership chair and attended education classes for leadership, which I enjoyed very much.

One day, I was invited to speak at our regional meeting. The theme was "What Hadassah Did for Me." It was held in a theater in Brooklyn, New York. Before me was a lady who spoke about her retirement as a principal of a school. Instead of facing an empty life, her days are filled with Hadassah activities. If someone would have told me a year ago that I would get up and speak before such a big crowd of people I would tell them that they were crazy. Now, thanks to Hadassah, I could do anything. I got up and said:

"I am a Holocaust survivor who was always depressed and unhappy. Getting involved in the activities in Hadassah changed all this. For me, Hadassah is a springboard; it changed hate into activities. Israel is very important for all Jews. If the Jewish people had had their own country, there would not have been a Holocaust. Hadassah for me is the college that I was never able to attend. Through Hadassah, I have learned so many new things."

My speech was received with much applause. I brought in many more members to our organization. My family was very proud of me and was happier because I was now a better mother and wife. Together, we all read and enjoyed the beautiful Hadassah magazine, which made me feel as if I were a part of Israel. It gives me a very warm feeling. I also was very happy to hear that my son collected money for Israel in his school. I insist that for my birthday or for Mother's Day, I don't want gifts—I want a donation made to Hadassah, and I enjoy the certificates I get!

Because of what I learned from Hadassah, I was able to form the organization, Holocaust Survivors of the Palm Beaches, about twenty years ago. Hadassah taught me how to be a leader, how to encourage people to join our organization, how to make speeches, and how to plan events. Hadassah also gave me the courage to speak in schools and universities about my Holocaust experiences. My message is that no country came to our rescue. If we had had a homeland of our own, the Holocaust would have never happened.

Through Hadassah, I learned that anything is possible. I interviewed Holocaust survivors and wrote and published a book of my poetry and our tragic stories, *Determination, Courage, and Destiny*, which is catalogued in the Library of Congress.

Today, I am a Life Member and reside in West Palm Beach, Florida. We had two chapters in our Century Village, but now we have only one, and with people dying we have fewer members. We are still active and are members as long as we are alive.

Thank you, Hadassah, for the opportunity you gave me to become a better, happier, and more productive person.

✦ ✦ ✦

$$ \longrightarrow 22 \longleftarrow $$

My Mom—One of the first Hadassah Nurses

By Lucille Tarant

I could feel the energy of the hospital as we drove up to its home, where it sits cradled in the Jerusalem mountainside, on Mt. Scopus. It was the first time I had ever visited Hadassah Hospital, although I grew up with its stories pulsing through my veins.

I always knew I would visit the hospital, although I had no idea what was truly in store for my family and me that particular day, during our very first visit to Israel.

We took a tour of the hospital, and made it a point to speak to the guides about my familial connection to Hadassah. I mentioned that my mother had been one of the founding nurses of Hadassah, and they connected me to the Office of Archives and History. There, I opened a very special book. It was the fiftieth anniversary book with photos from Hadassah's history. As my fingers flipped through its glossy pages, I came across a page that instantly took my breath away. It was a page of photos of Hadassah's first nurses.

There, right in the center of the page, was a shining photograph of my mother, Sonia Henkin Toskar, from the first graduating class of Hadassah Nurses Training School in Palestine. I gazed at her, beautiful and radiant in her Hadassah uniform. I was overcome with a wave of emotion. Hadassah was my history, but I, too, was a part of Hadassah's history. Tears began streaming down my face as I realized how deeply connected I felt to this organization, to these people, and to this country.

The nurse who had been my guide told me I could have the book as a gift, and I clutched it to my breast the rest of the day— and metaphorically—for the rest of my life.

My mom had escaped from Russia's pogroms and left for Palestine in her late teens, to join her brother Yohaskel Henkin, who was one of the founding members of Hashomer, the first Israeli defense force! Sonia (my mom) graduated from the nursing school in 1921 and continued her nursing career until her beloved brother Yohaskel was ravished by the yellow fever epidemic and died. This turned my parents' lives around, because my father also had yellow fever. On the advice of their doctor, they left family and friends for what they thought would be a short while and ended up settling and staying in Brooklyn, N.Y. Here, she raised me and my sister, but yearned to return to nursing. When we were more self-reliant, we helped her study for her New York State boards. We watched with admiration at how hard she worked, and when she graduated and became a certified New York nurse, my sister and I were bursting with pride. She returned to her much-beloved career in nursing, and was loved by all who were touched by her heart and hands. She rarely slept and always found time to help friends and neighbors as well. One of those neighbors had a very handsome son, and we just celebrated our sixty-second wedding anniversary in January, 2011.

My mother died in 1953 of breast cancer, but her legacy lives strong. Her name is carried forward by two grandsons, and her ideals and commitment to public service have been passed on to her children and children's children. We have embraced careers in nursing, teaching, counseling, and social work, and are proud of our two medical doctors in the family. My mother would be very proud of her family.

But back to the "Hadassah" moment. That moment when I saw my mother printed in ink in Hadassah's history will forever stay with me. It was then that my emotional connections to Israel, and to Hadassah, were solidified. Today, I contribute to the neonatal unit at Hadassah hospital, along with my son who is a neonatologist. I have learned the importance of the equipment that can mean the difference between life and death, and am proud to be a part of that. I am a Life Member of Shira Hadassah Chapter in Delray Beach and I hope that my small contribution to Hadassah will continue to propel and support Hadassah's important work into the future.

+ + +

$$\longrightarrow 23 \longleftarrow$$

Hadassah Gives Life

By Bonnie Saban

I came to Israel in 1964 to study Hebrew, live in Jerusalem, and work as an English teacher. I had accomplished those goals by studying Hebrew in Jerusalem at Ulpan Etzion, and then teaching English at The Berlitz Language School while giving private lessons. By 1965, I was married and ready to begin a new and exciting life in Jerusalem. My partnership with Hadassah began in 1966, when I started to work as an English secretary at the neurophysiology department of the old medical school in downtown Jerusalem. I worked there on a grant for over six years.

My first son was born on June 18,1967, right after the Six Day War. I spent several nights and days in our air raid shelter during the War. Our apartment was directly on the way to Hadassah Hospital and the Knesset, two of the big targets during the War. We could see and hear each of the bombs directed toward their targets. Luckily, Joel, my son, decided to wait to be born at

Hadassah instead of in the shelter. Even then, all major operations were still being performed underground at Hadassah. It had taken many hits, but was still functioning as a major hospital for the many wounded soldiers and civilians. Life was difficult at this time, but we survived and rebuilt both Jerusalem and Hadassah.

On February 10, 1971 (Tu B' Shevat), my second baby was delivered at Hadassah in Ein Kerem. Hooray, it was a girl—Miriam (or Mia, for short). Times were somewhat peaceful and the experience was much easier. The next day, as I was waiting for Mia to be brought to my room, her doctor came to see me. He told me that she was born with a TEF (tracheosophagel fistula—her esophagus was wrapped around her heart and not connected to her stomach). She needed immediate surgery. I was very upset with this news. I had a very beautiful little Sabra who would now have to fight for her life after major surgeries. I was then told that I was fortunate that the head doctor had just returned from Boston after two years of studying how to perform this surgery and the aftercare needed for survival. Dr. Schiller, who later became head of the pediatric department, and his team of doctors and nurses were going to make Mia their first baby to successfully have this operation. Previously, all babies born with this problem were not as fortunate.

Dr. Schiller and his team gave her one year to come through the operation and post-op procedures before she would be considered well. Mia became the darling of the pediatric ward and was treated like royalty. She spent five weeks at Hadassah undergoing many surgeries and having good days and bad days. Finally, we were able to take her home, but only to return weekly, then monthly, for tests, procedures, and evaluations. All of this was hard on such a little girl, but she was a fighter. After all the tears, she had a smile that would melt any heart.

After one year, she was progressing very well. She would still continue to visit the clinic for several years as this study progressed. On her first birthday, we made Mia a party. She had a doll cake that was made especially for her. The doll was in the middle of the cake and the lovely green and white dress was made of butter frosting. She was so excited. We invited all of the doctors and nurses from Hadassah to celebrate this milestone in her life. Everyone came, and our small apartment was filled to overflowing. All were wishing Mia "L' Chaim," to life for the years to come. With the Grace of G-d and the skilled and loving work of Dr. Schiller and all the doctors and nurses from Hadassah, Mia was given a chance for life. Yes, Hadassah gave my daughter her life as she became a teaching example for others.

✦ ✦ ✦

24

A Hadassah Legacy

By Linda S. Goldstein

I had the good fortune of having a mother, Yetta Fried, *z'l*, who had joined Junior Hadassah as a young woman. My father, Benjamin Fried, *z'l*, had recently returned from the Army and saw a sign in Manhattan that read, "Junior Hadassah Dance." He went in, said he saw my beautiful mother counting money (she was treasurer), and asked her to dance. They were married two weeks later! I grew up with both my parents being ardent Zionists. My parents were first of what are now four generations of Life Members and Associates.

One day, I had just come home from a Hillel House event at college, and told my parents I saw a flier advertising a Junior Year in Israel on the American Student Program at The Hebrew University of Jerusalem. I told them I would like to be a part of that program. The year I would go was June 1966 to July 1967. My parents were totally supportive.

We were a group of 150 college students who sailed from New York to Haifa on the SS Shalom cruise ship. I attended ulpan at Hebrew University and pursued studies in mathematics and Judaica. I had a background in Hebrew, as I graduated eighth grade from a Modern Orthodox Yeshiva in New York and then took Hebrew as a language in public high school. Both schools, as well as family, imbued me with a love of Zion, and a longing to go to Israel. I will never forget landing in Haifa. Our landing made the Israeli newspapers.

We toured Israel for two weeks straight, then settled down in new dorms at Hebrew University to begin our ulpan. One of the places we toured was Hadassah Hospital in Ein Kerem (we did not have access at that time to Mt. Scopus). I saw the Chagall windows in the synagogue. They were so beautiful. This introduction to Israel was so important. David Ben Gurion came to speak to our group! I wrote to my parents about what I had seen and heard.

However, the winds of war were in the air and Israel was mobilizing for the confrontations ahead. I must have taken a dozen first aid classes. They were given in Hebrew and I wanted to make sure I fully understood. We were being trained to rescue casualties from the front. It was then that I finally realized the entire country is on the front! My dorm was to be turned into a hospital and so I volunteered to help there. Thinking back, the students who taught the first aid classes on campus were probably trained at Hadassah.

One day, shortly before the war, I was walking on campus. It was eerily quiet, as most of the students were either in the Army or went home. I saw a tour bus, a rarity at that time, as tourists were leaving Israel, not arriving. It was a group of Hadassah women from Miami Beach!! I lived in North Miami Beach. I spoke to them and proudly told them that my mother was active in Hadassah in Miami and asked them to please tell my mother I was all right when they arrived home (and they did).

I finally left Jerusalem to visit distant relatives for Shabbat, first in Tel Aviv and then Herzliah. I awoke early Monday morning, June 5th, in Herzliah, and was told the war had broken out. I quickly dressed and left for Jerusalem. I felt a need to honor the commitment I had made as a teenager to help out in my dorm, which was to be converted to a hospital. I stopped in Tel Aviv, helped my relatives put up blackout curtains, then went to the central bus station and started my journey to Jerusalem. On the road to Jerusalem, a jet flew above us. The bus driver told us to get out and spread out in the nearby field. Thank G-d it was an Israeli Jet. We re-boarded the bus and continued to Jerusalem. I was sitting next to a young student/soldier, who had to get back to his dorm and get his uniform and report to duty. We had to walk the length of the campus to our dorm. We barely started walking when a bullet barely grazed my eye, but thank G-d, missed. We ran to take shelter at the end of the road. Jerusalem was under attack by the Jordanians. After a short while, he left the shelter and soon after I also left and ran to my dorm. We were gathered in the basement and sometime later that afternoon/ evening we were told to go to a nearby dorm, as the soldiers needed to use our dorm. I found a bed in one of the dorm rooms and quickly fell asleep. My friend had to wake me up from a deep sleep, as we were being shelled. We left for the shelter and heard the false news reports from Europe that Tel Aviv and Jerusalem were taken. Jerusalem was reunited on the third day of the war!!

The shelling subsided and I took a walk on campus. On the way back, a soldier in an army jeep stopped me and asked if I wanted to see the Western Wall. I must have flown into the jeep. We approached the Mandelbaum Gate and were told to turn around, as there were still snipers shooting and there were civilians in the jeep. The driver's female cousin begged him to drive into the Old City and he did. The desire to see the Western Wall was overwhelming. We made a quick trip in and as we came out through Mandelbaum Gate, the Chassidim were shouting "Kol HaKavod!!"

Shortly after the war, I went to Hadassah Hospital in Ein Kerem. The hospital was full. Women were nursing infants, people of all ages were in all manner of dress according to their culture. I wrote home to my mother to report on the important, vital work Hadassah was doing.

Shavuot came soon and we spent the night going from one professor's home to another, studying. Early in the morning, I had the privilege of being in the first group to go up to the Western Wall as a Jew.

Before I left Israel, I took one of the first tours to the Old City. We stopped at Hadassah Hospital on Mount Scopus. I sang to myself the song, *M'Al Pisgah Har HaTzofim Shalom Lach Yeruhalayim*. I felt the sadness of seeing firsthand the terrible state of disrepair that the hospital was in, but the joy of knowing it would now be back in good hands.

I soon left Israel and over the next few years, my mother became a chapter president and then treasurer of the Miami Region. A few years later, I became president of one and then a second chapter of Hadassah in North Miami Beach, and I am now treasurer of the

Greater Miami Region. My three children grew up listening to stories of my experiences in Israel and our connections to Hadassah. My daughter Esther became a chapter president in Miami and later, living in Atlanta, won the prestigious Judith Epstein Young Leadership Award. Her three children are Young Judaeans. My son Len went to Camp Judaea and Hadassah's College Summer Program. My son Mark attended high school in Israel program, as did my daughter, Esther.

Years later, my husband, Dr. Burton Goldstein, and I went on the Hadassah CEM Mission. We toured our beautiful state-of-the-art hospital on Mount Scopus. Barbara Goldstein had given me the privilege of leading a prayer at the graveside of Henrietta Szold, as she had heard of my connection to Jerusalem and to Hadassah. It seemed that I, as well as Hadassah, had come full circle.

✦ ✦ ✦

✦ 25 ✦

I joined Hadassah in Israel

By Shelley Sherman

I grew up in a passionate Zionist household. The centrality of Israel to the Jewish people and to each of us in our family was a guiding value. However, unlike all of the other issues of the day that were hotly debated or discussed at the dinner table, NO critical remark about Israel, or even one that was too questioning, was tolerated. My father had been in the Army and had arrived at a concentration camp shortly after its liberation. He saw the crematoriums and never needed to see or think about anything else. For him and for my mother, the existence of Israel was essential to Jewish survival and they were not willing to entertain any questions that even suggested ANYTHING about Israel was less than perfect. I felt a true connection to Israel and participated in the march to Washington and other activities, but I was still frustrated that open dialogue was forbidden.

My parents' Zionism was largely manifested through their support of Hadassah, and I grew up watching skits, eating tuna fish, and stuffing envelopes. My mother was a president and they were both loyal and proud donors.

I was a child of the '60s—a political and civil rights activist and a great challenger of authority. To me, nothing was off limits, and I had some real questions about the establishment of the State of Israel that needed responses. I went off to study political science in Washington, D.C. where my anti-war, feminist, and generally liberal agenda continued to be honed. Coupled with the stage of life of automatically questioning the tenets of "the establishment," which included my parents, of course, I was actually embarrassed about their strong lobbying efforts.

Nonetheless, the summer before I started law school, I decided to backpack through Israel and see for myself what it was all about.

My first jolt was when the coast of Israel came into view through the airplane window, and tears ran down my cheeks. When the plane landed and we descended the stairs onto the tarmac, I was overcome with emotion.

And yet I still vowed not to let my emotions be my only guide to learning more about Israel. I joined up with some other young people I met on the plane, and traveled the country from east to west and north to south, which at that time included the Sinai Peninsula.

No one reading this will be surprised to hear that this summer in Israel transformed my life. I spent time with an Israeli friend on a kibbutz in the Galilee and volunteered long days and watched my Israeli peers stand guard duty all night. The women my age had just finished their military service and we spent hours talking about the differences between my anti-Vietnam war activism and their pride in bearing arms for their country. As I traveled, I met people from the four corners of the world—it really was the ingathering of our people. People spoke French, Yiddish, Arabic, and halting Hebrew. I also saw many people with numbers tattooed on their arms, and thought of my father's experience. I was most struck though, by the neighborhoods where Arabs and Jews lived side by side, patronized each other's shops, and greeted each other with *Shalom Aleikham,* and *Salaam.*

In my travels, I passed a sign to a Hadassah Youth Aliyah village and to my great fortune was provided with a very short tour. The residents were not that much younger than I was and the young man leading me around had been a resident there himself as a teen. Although I had heard the story of Henrietta Szold welcoming the children rescued from the Shoah many times, hearing it from this animated young man while standing in a village that was created from her dream stirred me to my core.

I realized that I could not leave Israel without visiting Hadassah Hospital, and so I trekked up to Ein Kerem, which seemed a very long way from Jerusalem. There, too, I received a tour and as many of you have experienced, I saw the entire demographic of Israel in the halls and waiting rooms of the hospital.

When the tour was over, I asked the guide if there was someplace I could join Hadassah. She led me to the volunteer office, where I filled out the membership form and even paid my dues! I was presented with a pin that reads "I joined Hadassah in Israel because I saw." It is one of my most precious possessions.

As proud as I was at that moment to align myself with Hadassah, the organization that had done so much to help build the magnificent nation I had just spent the summer falling in love with, I never realized how many more proud moments I would have being a part of Hadassah. I have returned to Israel with family and friends many times, but when I come with Hadassah, it is with family and friends and always very special.

It was with great joy that I returned to my parents and showed them my new pin. At that moment, all the differences melted away and we were bound to each other, to the Jewish people, and to Israel with no need for debate or explanation. I am grateful that they introduced me to Hadassah, which has become my way of living my Zionism as well.

✦ ✦ ✦

26

A Healthy Family
By Patricia Levinson

Hadassah's cutting edge research gave me my family!

It was 1968, we were living in Israel, and I had just learned that I was pregnant. My husband, Lionel, was a doctoral student in physics at the Weizmann Institute in Rechovot, and I was working at the Institute doing biochemical research, looking at the early stages of embryo fertilization and placental formation.

We were overjoyed to learn that we were going to have a family, but we were also very concerned. During the Six Day War, I had become a blood donor, and discovered that I am RH negative. This meant that the chances were very high that our baby would be RH positive, and that due to the mingling of blood during the birth, my body would start to develop antibodies that would prevent me from carrying and delivering a healthy baby in the future.

We knew that an anti-RH factor serum had recently been developed in the United States which, when administered within seventy-two hours of the birth, would prevent the mother's body from developing antibodies. But we were living in Israel and had no access to it. What were we to do?

One day, Lionel came home with wonderful news. He had learned that Hadassah was doing cutting edge research on the RH factor! Through connections at the Weizmann Institute, he was able to contact a doctor at Hadassah Hospital who was doing work on the RH factor, and had developed anti-RH factor serum on an experimental basis. If we agreed to participate in his research, Hadassah would make the serum available to us.

We readily agreed, and both went through blood tests that showed that Lionel was in fact homozygotic RH positive. In order to show as blood type RH negative, I had to be homozygotic RH negative. That meant that any child that we had would have one positive and one negative RH factor gene, and because it is a dominant trait, all our children would be RH positive. I would absolutely need the inoculation if we were to have any children in the future!

Immediately after the birth of our healthy baby Ronnen, Lionel drove from Rehovot to Hadassah Hospital in Jerusalem (in those days it took over two hours), returned with the precious vial of anti-RH factor serum, and I received the life changing injection.

Three years later, we were living in the United States when my second healthy son, Jonathan, was born. By that stage, anti-RH factor serum was standard treatment. But I never forgot that it was the cutting edge research at Hadassah that enabled us to have a second child, and to be the grandparents of two happy and healthy grandchildren today.

+ + +

27

The Summer of '69

By Ruthanne Warnick

My Hadassah "thin thread" began long before I was a member of Hadassah and long before I had any idea of the role Hadassah would play in my adult life.

My mother, Jackie Rubenstein, was introduced to Israel, Zionism, and Hadassah by a simple invitation to a program. It planted a seed that blossomed into a leader, and my mother ultimately became a group and chapter president and region board member. You might jump to the conclusion that my story is about how I grew up in Hadassah, but that's not it at all. My mother's involvement in Hadassah led to my eventual connection to and leadership roles in Hadassah, from a very different path.

Because Hadassah connected my mother to Israel and Zionism, she and my father took their first trip to Israel in the summer of 1968. For that, I will always be thankful to Hadassah. The following summer, after a few camp friends and I had outgrown the camp scene, my parents gave me an opportunity that would change my life in ways that I didn't realize at the time. They sent me to Israel, at age fifteen, to spend six weeks with my peers. I had never been on an airplane, and that gigantic 747 took me to a place that changed my heart forever. That experience was a milestone in my life. It began my love affair with Israel—the people, the land, the culture and the history. It ultimately led me to Hadassah, and because of my experience, my husband and I encouraged our two children to visit Israel at young and impressionable ages as well.

I returned to Israel two summers later to work on a kibbutz and then spent a semester in Jerusalem during my college years. As a young adult, I was not a "joiner" of organizations, but when I was a young mother and our family moved to a new community with a small and welcoming Jewish community, I wanted to connect with other Jewish women. Joining the Hadassah chapter there became the way to connect with those women, combine Judaism and Zionism in one place, and ultimately develop a passion for Hadassah's mission. A long-time leader took me under her wing, and when I became the chapter's membership vice president, my Hadassah leadership "career" was launched. Over the past twenty years, the journey has led me from that small chapter to a much larger chapter, many group, chapter, and region positions, and now, region president.

I have given countless volunteer hours to help fulfill the mission of Hadassah, but I never imagined what I would receive in return. Hadassah has given me the opportunity to save and change lives, to play a role in Israel's future, and to contribute to *tikkun olam* in a tangible way. Through Hadassah, I have been empowered and have empowered others. The skills and personal growth I have gained, the mission I have passionately supported, and the women I have come to know as friends and as mentors are gifts that I cherish.

You could say that my Hadassah journey began in that small community where I first joined Hadassah, but I believe it really began in that summer of 1969—my long, but thin thread.

✦ ✦ ✦

✦ 28 ✦

Coming Home

By Sheila Horvitz

I grew up in New York City in the 1950s and 60s in a very traditional, orthodox, Jewish home where "Yiddishkeit" and Jewish rituals were practiced and valued. I was surrounded by a loving extended family of bubbies, aunts, and uncles who had fled the pogroms of Russia to make new lives in America.

But like many in my "Vietnam" generation, as a college student and a young married woman, I faced a crisis of confidence in traditional institutions, exploring many other philosophies and values, rebelling a bit and slipping away from my roots. But then, the defining moments and decision points of our lives come into focus when we have to become responsible adults and parents and define our values for ourselves and for the next generation.

For me, it happened one night in the cold, hard winter of 1970, in the small Jewish community of Colchester, Connecticut. My husband and I had moved there with our one-year-old daughter to begin our lives as parents and young new professionals. A new friend had encouraged me to accompany her to a Hadassah meeting. I was familiar with Hadassah, having been a member of Junior Hadassah for a time while I was in high school in New York.

As soon as I walked into the meeting room in the basement social hall of the synagogue, I felt it and knew it. These impressive and devoted women were my bubbies, my aunts, my history and my traditions. I had never really lost my roots and feeling for my Jewish heritage, values, and Israel. They were always inside of me, waiting to be inspired and reawakened. Over the last forty years, Hadassah has inspired me to be a proud Zionist, Jewish activist, and student of my heritage.

And so, on that cold, but very warm, evening in February 1970, in Colchester, Connecticut, I came home.

✦ ✦ ✦

✦ 29 ✦

A Dark and Stormy Night

By Anne Lowe

know you aren't going to believe this, but it REALLY WAS a
dark and stormy night! It was raining cats and dogs, a real
toad strangler. And there I was, straining through the windshield
wipers, trying to glimpse house numbers on a suburban street in
Sacramento, between sheets of solid water that were hitting the
windshield with titanic force. I glanced at my watch and groaned.
I was almost twenty minutes late. I had been driving, all alone,
for over an hour and a half, going to some lady's house for, of all
things, a Hadassah meeting! It would be crazy to turn around and
go back. Besides, I was desperate to find a bathroom!

As I slowed to a halt at a stop sign, I regretfully remembered the
call to my mom, Florence Susman, who lived in Saratoga Springs,
New York, that I had made two weeks before. It was 1971, and my
husband was in the U.S. Air Force and overseas in Thailand, supporting the Vietnam War. We had married in 1969, and had ended

up in Yuba City, California. I had taught school, and now I was seven months pregnant with my first child. My husband was a lieutenant in the Air Force. When he was deployed, I was lonely, and I knew there was a lot missing in my daily life. It lacked yiddishkeit. There were only six other Jews on Beale AFB. I missed my Jewish family.

So I had called my mom. She had been a Hadassah chapter president, and one of my earliest memories was as a little girl, accosting anyone who came into our home in Saratoga, to put a coin into my Youth Aliyah quarter book. I was determined to fill it up before my brother or sister did. When my mom (to her utter delight) heard me ask if there was a Hadassah chapter somewhere in northern California that I could join, she told me to stay put, and she would get right back to me. She would do some phoning. And after all, she was a reference librarian! (No Google or PCs in those days!)

She rang me back in just fifteen minutes. She had called National Hadassah in New York City. She gushed over the 3000 mile phone connection to me, "Guess what! There's a Hadassah chapter in Sacramento. And it's only fifty-five miles from Beale AFB, where you live!" Then she proceeded to give me the phone number and name of the chapter president.

So I called that lady. By that point I was in too deep to disappoint my mom. No doubt, from the minute she hung up on me, she called all her Hadassah friends in Saratoga to tell them the great news: L'dor v'dor! (From generation to generation!)

The president of the Sacramento Chapter was thrilled to invite me to an upcoming meeting, and she gave me the driving instructions (No GPS in those days!).

So here I was, dying for a bathroom, and late for the meeting, somewhere near Sacramento, in the downpour of the century. Finally, I found the house, extricated my big belly from behind the steering wheel, and ran to the stoop of the home, getting thoroughly soaked. I rang the doorbell, and the door pushed open to warm greetings, hugs, and exuberant chatter. It was as if I had come into the home of a dear aunt, with cousins and relatives galore. Everyone made a fuss over me, my pregnant stomach, and my rain-soaked hair and clothes, and it felt as if I had known them all my life. It felt like home.

I joined Hadassah that night, and when a lady called two weeks later to ask if I might want to be a Life Member, I said, "Yes, of course." (I think it was all of $150 then.)

That thin thread of connection that was formed that evening has lasted me forty years. I have been a chapter president in Princeton, New Jersey, and Milwaukee, Wisconsin, and am currently on my second chapter presidency in Tucson, Arizona. Along the way I was a region president of the Great Lakes Region of Hadassah, and therefore, a member of the National Board for four years. I have been on the Camp Young Judaea-Midwest Committee for nigh on thirty years, and all three of my children have been Young Judaeans (clubs, camps, Israel programs). And when I was the Princeton chapter president, I went to Israel with my mom, both of us for the first time, for the first National Hadassah Convention in Israel, in 1978.

I hope that over the years that I have been in Hadassah, I have made at least one more woman feel as connected as I was that dark and stormy night in northern California. Hopefully, that thin thread will never break.

✦ ✦ ✦

✦ 30 ✦

Full Circle

By Lee (Emily) Pinchuk

The smartest thing I have ever done was to join Junior
Hadassah when I was fifteen years old. The leaders were
very nurturing and we were so proud to tell everyone that we
supported a children's village in Israel called Meir Shfeya. When
I moved to Smithtown, New York, as a young woman with two
small children, Hadassah became an integral part of my life.
My first portfolio in the Smithtown Chapter was Young Judaea.
Shortly after that I become chapter president and chair of the
Suffolk Youth Commission. I attended many Young Judaea
functions with the person who most inspired me, Ruth Popkin,
who later became Hadassah's eighteenth National President. I
always looked at her with love, admiration, and respect.

I felt such joy when Ruth asked me to join her and twenty-nine
others on Hadassah's first Youth Study Mission to Israel in 1971. A
farewell party was held at J.F.K. International Airport with the entire

staff of the Youth Commission, as well as many members of the staff of the American Zionist Federation. In Israel we were greeted at the airport by representatives of the Jewish Agency and the Tsofim. Our guide turned out to be none other than the inimitable funny, friendly, well-informed Avraham Infeld, who today is a popular educator and former president of National Hillel. In a speech at the 2010 Hadassah Convention he stated, "Our mission is how to ensure the continued, significant survival of the Jewish people. The Jewish world was not created to support Israel. Israel was created to ensure the continued, significant survival of the Jewish people." We visited youth villages, Kibbutzim, schools in deprived areas, community and day centers. We attended lectures that emphasized our youth program in Israel. This gave us an invaluable learning experience that offered us insights into aspects of life in Israel never offered on any regular tour. On our tour, we were taken to all of Hadassah's installations, and we traveled through the beautiful countryside of Israel, visiting the major cities and historic landmarks. It is such an overwhelming feeling to walk on the land we call our own.

I came home with a greater understanding of our youth movement and its needs for the future and an understanding of the motivation that prompts our young people to go on Aliyah.

How ironic that after fifty-plus years I have come full circle and am now working once again for Young Judaea.

As a young impressionable woman, this trip left an indelible mark on me and made me see Hadassah and Israel in a different light. Once again, I thank Ruth for being my friend and my mentor, and giving me the once-in-a-lifetime opportunity that has enriched my love of Hadassah, Israel, and our people.

✦ ✦ ✦

31

My Golden Hadassah Thread

By Carolyn Gray LeMaster

L ife is truly a tapestry, and it is woven with many threads. There is one golden Hadassah thread that intertwined with mine. This happened in 1972 and led me to what would become my life's purpose. I would never have dreamed that a chance query and comment by a Hadassah colleague would have such far-reaching consequences.

At the time of this member's comment, I had been associated with Hadassah for more than twenty years. As an evangelical Christian, I had been introduced to the group through my mother, Erma Gray. She had begun an in-depth Bible college course in 1942 and was fascinated by Biblical Jewish history. To better grasp the teaching of the Tanach (Old Testament), she contacted the two local rabbis, one Reform and one Orthodox, who helped tutor her. Her genuine interest evidently was a topic of conversation between the rabbis and their spouses, for when a local chapter of Hadassah was being formed in 1944, the Orthodox Rebbetzin invited Mother to be an honorary member. Mother delightedly agreed and later became a Life Member. I was a teenager at that time and Mother took me with her to some of the Hadassah meetings. I was affected deeply by one of its programs, which included an early film showing the Nazi's wanton slaughter of the Jews. At that age, I could not comprehend how or why one group of people would do that to another group, especially the Jews, whom I had come to respect through Bible stories.

Hadassah remained a significant part of my life, even after I married in 1947. It was reinforced in 1950 when a bright Hadassah thread intertwined with mine. After the birth of my second daughter, I awoke in a hospital room and learned that my roommate, Sylvia, was a Hadassah member. We hit it off very well, and over the years became like sisters. After the birth of my fourth child, a second son, my home duties kept me from meetings, but my interest in what was happening in Israel was kept alive through *Hadassah Magazine*, which I read each month from cover to cover. In the 1960s I became an active Life Member, serving variously as Hadassah bulletin chairman, program vice president, education vice president (during the latter office, I ordered every item, book, or pamphlet that the Hadassah Education Department offered), and as Zionist affairs chairman.

After conducting one education program that dealt with the Jewish/Arab conflict (using Hadassah's publication, *Historic Confrontations Between Jew and Arab*), the golden-threaded Hadassah colleague I mentioned above approached me and asked, "Why don't you become Jewish, since you know so much about the Jews, Judaism, and Israel?" I was rather taken aback, but I did say that I would gladly convert if allowed to still acknowledge Jesus as the Messiah promised in the Tanach. Her reply to that would soon change the course of my life. She said, "If you knew the original Hebrew, you probably wouldn't believe as you do."

A year or so later, I noticed a small news item in a local newspaper announcing that the University of Arkansas at Little Rock would offer a course in Biblical Hebrew for the fall semester. After pondering the opportunity and thinking back to my Hadassah friend's comment, I enrolled, taking just the one course. I dearly loved the study and continued for a second semester. By that time, I was hooked! I took a third semester that fall, along with five other courses. (I had married young and often regretted not getting a college degree.) By the end of the third semester, I enrolled as a fulltime student with a double major in philosophy and journalism, graduating magna cum laude in 1977 as the outstanding graduating senior.

During my last spring semester, another thread impacted my life, when I happened to take a course in expository English. Our professor, the author of a number of books on the American Indian, had each class member choose an ethnic group in Arkansas to research and write about. With my background, I naturally chose the Jews. My mentor was the Reform rabbi who had tutored Mother. He had come to Little Rock's Congregation B'nai Israel in 1926 and was acquainted with the state's rabbis and congregations. During my research, I found this topic to be an extraordinary (and overlooked) section of Arkansas history. At semester's end and after the good review my professor gave, one event after another led me to the realization that a book on Arkansas Jewry must be written—the data was too fascinating and historically valuable to be more than a footnote in our state's history. I began in late 1981, at the American Jewish Archives in Cincinnati, encouraged and helped by a strong thread, Dr. Jacob Marcus, AJA's founder and director (who had been a college schoolmate of our Reform rabbi). I then spent twelve years traveling to 126 Arkansas cities and towns and to ten other states, interviewing hundreds of present and former Jewish citizens, tracking down and writing to several hundred former Jewish citizens, inventorying all the state's Jewish cemeteries, and later copying thousands of obituaries, photographing and duplicating photos, compiling histories of the Jewish congregations, all without benefit of the Internet. The end result, *A Corner of the Tapestry*, was published by the University of Arkansas Press in 1994. This 622-page book chronicles a history of Arkansas Jewry from the 1820s to the 1990s.

Although this project took great effort, in emotion, time, and funds (it was written during my second daughter's illness and death from breast cancer and my own battle with the same malady), it was a joy for me to see it brought to fruition by the UA Press. As a student of world history, which includes knowledge of the off-repeated deplorable treatment of Jews by Christians-so-called, I have considered it a mitzvah to show, for all to see, how our state has been blessed by its Jewish citizens, just as G-d promised in Genesis 12:3. I trust the book will, in some miniscule way, help offset evil with good.

So, to that golden thread, my dear Hadassah colleague who piqued my interest in Biblical Hebrew and prompted my college days, and who has long since passed away, I can only say "thank you" for your comments that Providence used to guide me these past forty-plus years.

✦ ✦ ✦

32

Coffee, Seders, and Legacies

By Millie Fain Schneir

I'm 94 years young, and have been an active member of L'Chayim Plantation Chapter of Hadassah for more than thirty-five years and president for three different terms for a total of twenty-three years. When I moved to Florida in 1972, I was already imbued with the Hadassah spirit, having started a chapter in my hometown of Caldwell, New Jersey. The Caldwell Chapter of Hadassah was chartered with forty-five members and quickly grew to be a wonderful and productive chapter that thrives to this day. When I moved to Plantation, I was a sad widow. I joined Hadassah, B'nai B'rith, and the Lauderdale West Women's Club organizations that were already up and running in my community.

As a relatively new member of L'Chayim Plantation Chapter, I was surprised when the chair of the nominating committee turned to me at a general meeting and asked if I would serve as chapter president. Well, I was flabbergasted and very honored. I said I would think about it. I knew this was a big job, but I always enjoyed challenges and service.

When I came home, I told my new husband, Milton Schneir, that I was asked to become president of Hadassah. His response was, "Ridiculous!" After a reflective moment, I commented, "You're right. I can't accept because the president's husband makes the coffee." After a few minutes, Milton turned to me and said, "So, I'll call Abe Sneider and ask him how to make the coffee."

My life took on a new mission as I became energized and passionately involved with Hadassah. I read every piece of literature I could get my hands on, and the more I learned, the more focused I became on the good works of Hadassah. Milton became an Associate and helped whenever and wherever he could. My daughters, granddaughters, and great granddaughters are Life Members. Over the span of thirty-five years, my passion has never diminished. One of my life's pleasures is knowing that this passion is both understood and appreciated by the family. Additionally, the lasting friendships I have made through Hadassah have enriched my senior years. Hadassah friends are my second family.

Each year at our family Seder, to which some close Hadassah friends are always invited, my son makes a fuss about hiding the afikomen. Last year, my great grandchildren negotiated a high price for returning the afikomen, and then they turned to me and said, "GG, we want to give you all this money for Hadassah." Everyone around the table clapped, but I said to myself, "G-d bless these children!"

From generation to generation – L'Dor V' Dor!

✦ ✦ ✦

$$\cdot\ 33\ \cdot$$

Hashem Has a Plan
By Edith Barr

My grandchildren have a wonderful CD that I love to listen to, with songs for each of the parshas in Bereshit. My favorite song is about the life of Joseph. The refrain is "Hashem has his plan. We don't always understand." As I have lived my life, this refrain has become more meaningful, and Hadassah has been a truly transformative part of it.

I moved from New York City to the Boston area when I married. My husband was a graduate student there. I thought I was moving there because of marriage, but Hashem had other plans. The lack of Judaism around me made me take an active role to create that environment for myself, so I joined Hadassah in order to meet other Jewish women. That, in turn, introduced me to a lifetime of Jewish learning through Hadassah Jewish study groups. Everywhere I have moved throughout my life, Hadassah has always been there to welcome me and integrate me into the community, even when we lived in Israel for a few years.

My involvement in Hadassah led me to learn about Hadassah's youth movement, Young Judaea. I couldn't wait until my children would be old enough to join. We chose the location of our home in New Jersey because it had a Young Judaea club. But the Young Judaea leader in our community had to move to Florida, and if I wanted Young Judaea for my kids, I had to become the leader. I had no experience as a youth group leader, but I spent the next eighteen years as a Young Judaea leader of five clubs, designing experiential activities to give unaffiliated kids Jewish experiences.

When my kids were old enough, I decided to go back to work. I had been a computer programmer but had not worked in fifteen years. I wrote a new resume, including the work I had done for Hadassah, and with that background, started a new career as Director of Recreation in an assisted living facility. In this new role, I used all the experience I had gained from my work in Hadassah, which had taught me how to program events, design educational experiences, teach, manage a budget, speak in public, and deal with different personalities. I would never have imagined that I would ever pursue such a profession.

Hadassah had changed my life. As I begin 5772, I will be studying in a seminary in Jerusalem for the fall semester. This is the culmination of my quest for Jewish learning that was awakened by Hadassah. I will be commuting to Jerusalem with a neighbor in Ramat Beit Shemesh who works at Hadassah, Ein Kerem. Hadassah will now physically be my portal into learning as well as my spiritual one.

✦ ✦ ✦

→ 34 ←

Hadassah, My Partner for Life

By Barbara Strauss Heyman

When my son, David, was eight years old, he joined
Young Judaea. From that moment on, Hadassah became
my partner for life. It didn't make a difference that as a single
mother I was unable to afford all the activities. Hadassah stepped
up and provided my children with scholarships. They never
missed an event.

Perhaps the most amazing part about this is that my children
were the only Jewish children in our town and school system in the
small Pennsylvanian town of Conway, where we lived. Although
my son became more involved than my daughter, Lisa, she became
a member of the Young Judaea (YJ) dance group in Pittsburgh.
Lisa also attended the YJ camps where she found one of her closest
friends, Beth, as a result of the relationships she made through this
incomparable organization. Today she is proud to be a Life Member
of Hadassah.

When David began high school and wanted to attend a Young Judaea event that was far from the house, he wouldn't let the distance stop him. He would take three buses to attend a meeting. During his high school years he became a counselor and subsequently made several trips to Israel, leading a group from Hadassah's Camp Tel Yehudah and working in Israel with the Israeli Scouts. David attended Year Course and after returning, attended the University of Pittsburgh for one year, but decided to leave the university and make aliyah. Without the involvement of Hadassah and its youth programs, he would never have had the connection to his Judaism that led him to a life in Israel. Today, his family is settled in Modi'in. I have visited Israel many, many times over the past thirteen years, and this past summer I attended my grandson's Bar Mitzvah at the Kotel and in the Synagogue.

How do you say "thank you" to an organization like Hadassah? Of course, financial support is vital, but so is volunteerism. And because Hadassah was so kind to me and my children, I have served as president of my group for twenty-eight years, always making our quota. I only just stepped down this year and am extremely proud that my name is inscribed on the Keepers of the Gate Wall in Jerusalem.

✦ ✦ ✦

35

A Hadassah Doctor for Life

By Suzanne Libenson

In 1975, when my daughter was nine-months old, my mother gifted us both with Hadassah Life Memberships. I had been a member for a few years by then, having first joined because of the book discussion group sponsored by my local chapter. Hadassah became increasingly important to me as a young mother in suburban Long Island eager to interact with adult women on intellectual, social, and philanthropic levels. Those were the days before college-educated women went back to work after a few months of maternity leave; the thought of working while our children were young never crossed our minds. The creative opportunities offered by Hadassah enabled me to contribute to Israel and my community and to be a part of something important, when life would have otherwise been quite circumscribed by daily routine.

It was a proud day when I brought my baby daughter, dressed in frills, to the Myrtle Wreath event at which we received our

Life Membership pins. We had made a life-long commitment to Hadassah, thanks to my mother's gift, and soon we would be a Hadassah family when my husband and son become Associates. I rose up through the local chapter's ranks and eventually took on a regional board portfolio. This brought me into contact with some very impressive and inspiring leaders, who later went on to national roles. Little did I imagine at the time that my Hadassah activities would provide me with some much-needed credentials for my C.V., after fifteen years out of the working world.

I also didn't realize on that memorable day that, in less than ten years, I would be living in Israel. And even less imaginable was that my daughter would study to be a medical doctor at the Hebrew University-Hadassah Medical School. Today, she is a family practitioner at a community clinic in a suburb of Tel Aviv, and the mother of two.

How many Hadassah Life Members are graduates of its medical school? I personally know of only one other.

I am so proud to be a member of Hadassah and know first hand how doctors who are educated in this amazing institution are quietly treating patients and saving lives in hospitals and clinics throughout Israel.

✦ ✦ ✦

— 36 —

To the Promised Land
By Bonnie Lipton

In 1975, my husband Alan and I began our first journey to the Promised Land in a less-than-expected way . . . but what a journey it turned out to be.

It was shortly before Shabbat when the phone rang. A voice said, "I am calling from El-Al Airlines to tell you that a strike has been declared. Report to Sabena Airlines when you reach JFK tomorrow night. You will be flying to Israel via Brussels."

"You must be joking," I responded. "Really, who is this?" The line had already gone dead.

Like us, almost 2,000 participants from across the United States were heading toward El Al stand-in airlines: Alitalia, British Air, Iberia, Swiss Air, Air France, and every other airline that could be mobilized to carry Hadassah women, their husbands, and their families to Tel Aviv. The airlines were responsible not only for bringing us to Israel, but for bringing us to Jerusalem in time for the opening ceremonies of the 1975 re-dedication of Mt. Scopus Hospital, Hadassah's first hill of healing.

Despite the unconventional change in our plans, we arrived on time for what would be the most unforgettable Hadassah experience of our lives.

Atop Mt Scopus, the flags of all fifty states and Puerto Rico lined the walkway approaching the entrance; along the way, nurses wearing caps, aprons, ankle socks and wooden clogs greeted us with open arms.

Try to imagine us seated in the courtyard in front of the home of the late Chaim Yassky, former Director General of HMO. (In April, 1948, Yassky, along with seventy-eight other nurses and doctors, were massacred when their convey bringing them to Hadassah Hospital on Mt. Scopus was ambushed by Arab gunfire.) Feel the intense heat of the sun. Take a sip of the tepid water from the common ladle that was shared by one and all. Glance up at the rooftop and count the soldiers responsible for our security, young, alert, and armed with weapons.

We heard distant music and suddenly we stood as one, arm in arm, until the words of the "Hatikvah" filled the mountain and valley. Prime Minister Yitzhak Rabin rose to speak. He compared Hadassah to a symphony orchestra with strings and brass, harp and piano, wind instruments, and drums blending together under the direction of the conductor.

My heart beat faster. I was overwhelmed by, well, everything. In a single moment, my destiny was sealed. I knew I needed to be a part of that orchestra. When the time came years later, I drew strength from the memory of those moments as I accepted the baton of leadership and became the conductor, the twenty-second National President of Hadassah, the Women's Zionist Organization of America.

✦ ✦ ✦

→ 37 →

The Interconnectedness of Two Firsts

By Ellen Hershkin

When I was very young, it was understood that I would get to Israel "some day," but not until I was much older — maybe not until I was sixty-five!! What do kids know about "age" and predicting the future anyway?

I invited my parents to attend the Closing Banquet of Suffolk Region's Spring Conference in 1977, to share my pride in receiving the honor of "Woman of the Year" from the Dix Hills Chapter. Our then region president, Rose Novick of blessed memory, closed the event by reciting the phrase we use to close the Pesach Seder, "Next Year in Jerusalem." It was apropos, since the first Hadassah National Convention in Israel was going to take place in September 1978. My mother turned to me and said, "And you will be there!" I wasn't really sure I heard correctly, but I had, and the excitement I felt was almost impossible to contain.

There were so many arrangements to be made. My husband,

Joel, who would probably have preferred going to Hawaii, agreed to come with me so we could both share "the first time" we saw anything or participated in something that we would remember forever. We spent more than a year taking care of everything. It wasn't just a matter of filling out the registration form and going! We needed to get passports, make arrangements for our two young children (both my mother and mother-in-law were full time working women), Joel needed to secure the time off from work—and we had to write a will!

The day finally came and we were off on our most significant journey. The security personnel at JFK asked why we were going to Israel and with all the pride I could muster, I said, "I am a delegate to the Hadassah Convention in Israel." The response was, "You are going to call everyone grandma!" Joel almost went home!! Thank G-d he didn't!

It was our first trans-Atlantic flight. It was long and uncomfortable and we were both exhausted. Looking out the window with the full realization that it was Israel I was seeing, when Hatikvah came over the speakers and the plane actually touched down, the veil of involuntary tears that flowed from my eyes became the "garment" I proudly wore for the next two weeks.

The Convention was spectacular. I was in Israel and Israel was "home," and I didn't want to leave. I soaked up everything I saw and heard, smelled, and tasted. I was given the opportunity to touch the land and its people and they touched me. My first trip to Israel as part of Hadassah's first National Convention in the Holy Land was, without a doubt, a life altering experience.

There was so much to absorb. We traveled the length and breadth of the country and I loved every minute of seeing the sites of Israel and Hadassah's impact through its projects. I was SO proud to be a part of the wonder of Hadassah in the home of my ancestors.

A "defining moment" for me was when I first saw Henrietta Szold's office in our Mt. Scopus hospital. I felt her spirit touch me. I vowed to come home and do my best not just to recruit members and solicit donors, but to share the pride and the passion that erupted in me as a direct result of having seen with my own eyes the miracle that is Hadassah—Hadassah in Israel—the Hadassah that is inextricably intertwined with all the "threads" of Israel. Hadassah "weaves" a pattern of diversity into one incredible tapestry. I am very proud to be one of the many "thin threads" that comprise the "fabric" of Hadassah.

✦ ✦ ✦

✦ 38 ✦

And It Is All Because of Hadassah . . .

By Barbara Spack

In 1975, when I was the Jewish education chair of the Southern
New Jersey Region, we joined with the Pennsylvania, Northern
New Jersey, and Westchester regions for family *kallot* at Camp Tel
Yehuda. I was new to the National scene, so it was exciting to eat and
learn and pray with Judith Epstein and Ruth Popkin, Tamar de Sola
Pool and Miriam Freund Rosenthal, all legends in their own time.
Our children, Beth, Paula, and Rachel, grew up sitting at the feet of
these great women and learned how to become leaders in their own
right, not to mention what their influence did for all of us!

For me, these family weekends did two things. First, they created
a new family structure for my husband and me—our Hadassah
family, which is still so strong to this very day.

But most importantly, I began my spiritual journey in a way
I am confident would never have happened without Hadassah.
My dear friend Barbara Goldstein, now Deputy Director of

the Hadassah office in Israel, was the Region President and a driving force for these *kallot*. We prayed in the same synagogue in Metuchen, New Jersey, Neve Shalom, where her beloved husband, Mordy, *z'l*, was our Hazzan. She knew that I could lead a service as *hazzanit* if asked, and that frequently happened. And so began my personal spiritual journey. When I stood before the congregation of new and old friends, our children, and our Hadassah leaders, something entered my soul that has never left thirty-eight years later. I felt the history of the Jewish people in my own *neshamah*, bursting forth in song and praise of G-d. I began to realize the power of the music and the words and it moved me beyond anything I had ever felt before. In the late 70's women in the Conservative movement were not permitted to lead services since, in most congregations, they were not yet counted in the *minyan*. While our congregation was at the forefront of this brave new world, I had some limited involvement, but not with the same sense of profundity as I did at Hadassah. It was with a heart full of joy that I read Torah, led services, and experienced an elation that I had never experienced. And it was all because of Hadassah!

As the years progressed, I became a Region President and then moved on to the National Board. Once again, when we met at pre-convention meetings, I was blessed to be able to lead Shabbat services. By then I was a fully accepted *shlihat tsibbur*, spiritual representative of the community, in my *shul*, even leading services on *Rosh Hashanah* and *Yom Kippur*. But nothing can compare to leading a service of mostly women who come together to pray and to sing and to commune with G-d in the midst of all of our other deliberations. When we finished the service I would be on a high that kept me going for quite some time. And it was all because of Hadassah!

As Jewish education chair, I was privileged to respond to a request from the convention chairs, Barbara Goldstein and Leah Reicin, to initiate a Bat Mitzvah program for our National Convention in Miami. For a year before that convention, and for four years following, I worked with many hundreds of women who wanted to read Torah, who wanted to change their Yiddish names to Hebrew names so as to remember a loved one or looking for new meaning for their own spirituality while creating a book of their *divrei Torah,* their words of Torah, about their experience or the *parashah* for the week of their Bat Mitzvah. Even today, when I am at a National meeting or speaking in a community, there are women who come up to me and say, "You Bat Mitzvahed me and I was so proud! I learned so much and even continued to study with my group afterward." What better words could an educator hear? And it was all because of Hadassah!

Hadassah changed my life from a young leader, just starting out, and with each portfolio that I have held for over thirty years. I have raised my own family, I have grown as a woman, I have matured in my years, but I will never forget that my spiritual journey was enhanced, was molded and shaped, strengthened and actualized in the vineyards of the organization that I love with all my heart. There are no words of thanks that can suffice for this experience, just praise for an organization that takes sisterhood to the highest level, gives wings to its members, and then becomes the wind beneath those wings so we can soar!

And it is all because of Hadassah!

✦ ✦ ✦

$$\longrightarrow 39 \longleftarrow$$

The Wedding Planners,
By Peg Elefant

"You fools," chuckled the Rabbi. And with that, the story of how Corvallis Oregon Chapter of Hadassah came to be wedding planners, begins.

It was 1978. I was new to Oregon, and I had been reunited with my b'shert two weeks after my arrival to this small, university town in the heart of the Willamette Valley.

For the two of us, it had been instant love; we decided to marry in January 1979, agreeing that we would invite immediate family only, since it was a second marriage for us both.

That November, with our invitation list in full agreement, we attended our first Hadassah function together—a Blintz Brunch Factory where Hadassah women were to make more than 2500 blintzes for sale for the upcoming Hanukkah fair. Why did I drag my soon-to-be husband, Steve, along? Because I couldn't cook (still can't) and he could (still does, thirty-two years later).

With me stationed at the rolling station and Steve at the stove, the work began. Ruth took one look at Steve's beard and cocked a questioning eyebrow at Selma, who turned and gave a shrug to Milly, who turned and said, quite loudly to Mimi, "Who's that?"

Each woman turned her eyes to Steve, and, not trusting his expertise with the crepes, examined each one with an eagle eye toward quality control. Me, they left alone. . . for a bit.

Pretty soon, Steve had them smiling, laughing, and kvelling over his ability to turn out the perfect crepe—four at a time.

Attention shifted to me, the roller. Selma said, "Try it this way." Milly peered over my shoulder. Ruth took her turn, too. Mimi just said, "How ya doin'?" not really expecting an answer.

The hours passed. Suddenly, Steve is shooting angry stares my way. 'What? What?' I thought.

Selma announces, "I'm making the salmon mold."

Ruth: "I'm bringing cookies."

Mimi: "I'm making the challah."

Suddenly, all thirty-five Hadassah women, none of whom we had invited to our wedding, are announcing what they are bringing to the simcha.

Steve is accusing me. I deny it all. No, I have not broken our holy agreement. Two hours later, we're in the car for a rather stony, silent ride down to Rabbi Kinberg in Eugene – our very first visit with the rabbi.

The conversation with the Rabbi went somewhat like a good Jewish joke:

Us: Rabbi, what are we going to do? All these people think they're invited to our wedding. They're most definitely not!

Rabbi (chuckling): You fools! Don't you know? When there's a Jewish wedding, which seldom occurs in a small Oregon town, there's no such thing as an invitation? *Everyone* is automatically invited!

And, so it was. Corvallis Hadassah put on our Jewish wedding thirty-two years ago. We were blessed by community and Hadassah.

✦ ✦ ✦

✦ 40 ✦

We Were Like Dreamers

By Bernice S. Tannenbaum

There was a period when the first stirrings towards peace in the Middle East were evolving. It was a time when a bold Arab statesman called Anwar Sadat came to Jerusalem on a mission, which led in time to the first peace agreement between Israel and Egypt. Psalm 126 says, "We were like dreamers." During this period, we, the leaders of Hadassah who cared about Israel's future, dared to dream that there could be a time of peace. And the people of Israel dared to be guardedly optimistic.

In 1979, as president of Hadassah, I was in Israel when the president of the United States came to Israel to address its parliament. Prime Minister Begin invited me to join a party of twenty-five American leaders on the field at Ben Gurion Airport to greet President Jimmy Carter as his plane landed on the runway. It was a brilliant sight—red carpet was thrown on the tarmac and the two presidents stood together in close embrace. Then, Prime Minister

Begin welcomed President Carter with the words, "I greet you from the eternal City of David, the capital of Israel, the indivisible Jerusalem."

Just a short time later, I flew to Washington, D.C. to close the circle of this experience. The White House lawn was jammed with people who came together for this festival of peace and hope. The huge crowd became silent as the two solemn heads of state, Prime Minister Menachem Begin of Israel and President Anwar Sadat of Egypt, signed three versions of the peace treaty (English, Hebrew, and Arabic), after which the third member of the triumvirate, President Jimmy Carter, added his signature as witness. Then the silence exploded into sound, with an almost hysterical audience applauding thunderously. With tears of joy running down our faces, we hugged each other, whether stranger or friend. Fathers held children on their shoulders and told them to remember this moment. All of us vowed never to forget that dreams could actually come to fruition.

That night, under a huge orange and yellow tent set up on the White House lawn, Jews and Egyptians broke bread together and began to reach out to one another, and the first real steps toward peaceful co-existence began!

There was a level of exhilaration and joy that evening in Washington, D.C. that, until the next peace celebration in the Arava Desert Crossing, has not been replicated for me.

As I look back at the texture of these events, I am awed by the fact that time and circumstances came together, permitting me, as a leader of Hadassah, to be witness to and a participant in great events in the life of our people.

✦ ✦ ✦

41

Yad B'Yad, Le Dor v'Dor: How I Became a Hadassah Third-Generation Life Member

By Linda Ettinger Lieberman

On Father's Day, 1980, my beloved maternal grandmother, Gussie Langer Burstein, was in the hospital. My husband and I went to visit her before we spent the day with our immediate family.

While visiting her, Grandma Gussie handed me a wrinkled handkerchief, inside of which was nestled a Hadassah Life Membership pin. She whispered to me, "I've made you a Life Member of Hadassah." We took the pin, not quite understanding the meaning of Gussie's gesture, as we didn't have a chance to talk about it with her— she passed away while we traveled home that evening.

After shiva was over, I contacted the Brooklyn Region (New York) to see if Grandma had indeed made me a Life Member in her chapter. There was no record there or at National. Grandma had made a literal deathbed legacy and had handed down her Life Membership pin from one generation to another. I told my mother that I wanted to officially upgrade from annual to Life Membership, but asked her to become a second-generation Life Member first. She did that through her aunt's chapter in Monticello, New York.

I became a Life Member in the White Plains New York Chapter, and proudly wore Grandma Gussie's pin, as well as a third-generation tree. I made my daughter, Shani Golda, named after her great-grandmothers Sheindl and Gussie (Golda), a fourth-generation Life Member on the occasion of her eighteenth birthday.

We proudly continue Tikkun Olam, as inspired by the members of our family. I made my husband an Associate on his sixtieth birthday, and became a Founder almost five years ago when I received a bequest from a relative's will. Hadassah is an every-day part of my life. I lovingly recall my grandmother taking me as a child to her meetings, luncheons, and other events. I loved her reading *Hadassah Magazine* to me when I was small. I hope to some day have a granddaughter to whom I, too, can gift a Life Membership.

✦ ✦ ✦

42

Myrtle Branches

By Carol Goodman Kaufman

We moved to Worcester in 1981 and began renovating our 1900-era house in a decidedly non-Jewish neighborhood. One day, while I was in the backyard with the landscaper, I asked him to identify the green vines growing on the back wall. He told me they were myrtle. I tucked that bit of information into my memory and promptly forgot it.

Several years later, I became the President of the Worcester Chapter of Hadassah and used my home office for chapter business. One late afternoon, while making supper, I got a phone call. On the line was an elderly gentleman who wanted to tell me that his elderly mother had recently died and, at her instruction, wanted him to make a donation to Hadassah in her name. (Having herself been an active Hadassah member, she knew that bequests would not count toward quota, and she had wanted her money to help the chapter reach its goals.) Because our chapter did not have its own phone number, this man called Hadassah's New York headquarters to get the chapter's contact information.

He said, "When they gave me your address, I got chills up my spine."

"Why is that?" I asked.

"Your house is the house I grew up in when my mother was the Hadassah Chapter President," he said.

Bertha Price Lyons had planted the myrtle—*hadas* in Hebrew. What were the chances that two Hadassah presidents would live in the same house? The following spring, I gave cuttings from that myrtle to all newly installed officers on our chapter board.

✦ ✦ ✦

✦ *43* ✦

Hadassah and My Influence on Government

By Barbara S. Keil

aving served Hadassah in many capacities, including being the chapter president when I was only 29, I was well equipped to seize the opportunity to have a positive influence on a member of Delaware's delegation to Washington, D.C.

My "thin thread" occurred in September, 1982, when Delaware's Congressional candidates were scheduled to appear at Hadassah's bi-annual forum, during which the Jewish community and the community–at-large were invited to meet the candidates.

This was no ordinary "Meet the Candidates" program, but our candidate did not know that yet. It fell to me, on the morning before the program, to help forge his feelings and his later actions toward Israel and other important agendas.

How did this happen? The candidate was born in 1947, thus he knew almost nothing about the Holocaust and the creation of the State of Israel. He grew up in the South and came to Delaware in order to continue his education after his military service. We met by happenstance when we both supported the candidacy of one of our professors in a previous election. I realized during that campaign that Tom might one day decide on public service and I mentioned my willingness to volunteer on such a campaign.

When Tom did phone and ask for my assistance, I was happy to join in the initial advisory stages. (It should be noted that my political "savvy" came from working with my husband, Charles K. Keil, on his successful campaign for State Representative, and numerous other civic responsibilities of his and mine over the years.)

Back to the 1982 election: Tom had expected to smile, shake hands, and do the usual things when meeting prospective supporters. In preparation for the Hadassah forum, he learned that he would be in front of an intelligent audience and that there would be many questions to answer. We spent several hours that day helping Tom to learn a lot about the background and creation of Israel, and about the importance of the connection between Israel and the United States. He easily understood the issues once they were explained, as he had been a naval flight officer and mission commander in the U.S. Navy.

Hadassah's forum is known locally as an important point in political campaigns. Tom did very well on the podium that evening. He went on to win the election, and I soon joined his staff. One of my responsibilities was to be his liaison to the Jewish community, where I arranged for him to meet the people who were then in active roles in our Jewish community, and to provide the historical and current prospective that would make his trip to Israel more productive.

Upon his return, I arranged for him to speak and answer questions at meetings of the major Jewish organizations. I accompanied him to the meetings and more than once he quipped, "Barbara Keil must know this talk by heart by now," which was a warm compliment and drew a laugh from the audience.

Thus, my career of volunteer service put me in a place where I could help to mold the opinion and action of a five-term U.S. Congressman (Delaware has only one), who is now Delaware's senior Senator, Thomas R. Carper. To quote David Broder of *The Washington Post*, "Senator Carper is a notably effective and non-partisan leader, admired and trusted on both sides of the aisle."

✦ ✦ ✦

44

Confessions of a Jewish Mother

By Deborah Rabinowitz Layman

*'Kol ode balevav p\'nimah, nefesh Yehudi homiyah
Ulfa\'atey mizrach kadimah, ayin l\'tzion tzofiyah...'*

I sang along in the hotel ballroom as the ladies of my mother's Hadassah chapter stood for the Israeli national anthem at the start of the fund-raising luncheon. I was then a young student in my twenties. I could feel her pleasure at having me there, and her pride at being able to show off to her friends that I knew all the words to Hatikvah. I was glad to give her a reason to kvell. I loved pleasing her.

Today, more than forty years later, she would be pleased to know that I am now a Life Member of Hadassah, the organization she so believed in and served with such enthusiasm and commitment.

My road to Life Membership was not a typical one. After college, I married an Episcopalian boy from Birmingham, Alabama, who swept me off my feet with his good looks and Southern charm and who sealed the deal by agreeing with me that we should raise our children in the traditions of both of our families. And so we have.

We moved from the Northeast to Alabama over thirty years ago, shortly after our first son was born, and I was welcomed warmly into my husband's family. We settled about thirty miles from Birmingham, in a roomy house on a country road where our three boys grew and thrived. Along with exposing them to the liturgy and practices of the Episcopal Church, I taught my sons everything my parents had taught me about being Jewish. I was aware that there was a Jewish community in Birmingham, but we were far from the city, and life was busy in the country.

The years passed and lo and behold, the children were grown and gone, my work schedule lightened, and I had time on my hands. So I reached out to a Jewish educational organization in Birmingham and got involved in a project. Again, I was welcomed warmly. I discovered that my particular "skill set" can be put to good use in Jewish community projects, and I love being involved.

Last year, I became a member of Hadassah. This year, I jumped on the $100 Life Membership Centennial Anniversary Offer, which is a deal my mother, the consummate bargain-hunter, would have approved of wholeheartedly. I'm excited and proud to now stand alongside my mother and the other women of Hadassah who have made a lifetime commitment to an organization whose good works have made a difference in so many lives.

I feel I've fulfilled a calling of a sort. I began to ponder this after a conversation with my daughter-in-law-to-be, a lovely African-

American girl who has added a new cultural ingredient to our personal family melting pot. One day, when the two of us were alone, I brought up the subject of getting to know each other better, which is a desire of my heart. She's a quiet girl, and I couldn't easily discern if she wanted to keep her distance or if she wanted to get closer. I told her I wanted to get as close to her as she would like. "I'm a Jewish mother," I explained, "and I'll be a Jewish mother to you if you want me to be." There was a long silence after which she asked, "What does a Jewish mother do?" "Oh, honey," I thought. "Where do I begin?"

I responded, "Well, there are a few stereotypes associated with Jewish mothers, like being pushy and overbearing. Then there's the whole guilt thing, like the Jewish mother who gives her son two ties for his birthday, and when she sees him wearing one, asks, 'So you didn't like the other tie?' Jewish mothers have elevated this kind of logic to an art form."

But there's much more to being a Jewish mother than just the stereotypes, and I wanted to offer a real answer to my son's betrothed. I thought a moment. "At heart," I said, "we're family women. We want to be close to our families and involved in their lives."

There was another pause, during which I wondered if I had scared her. Then she replied, "That sounds O.K." And so, we're building our relationship, my daughter-in-law-to-be and I.

We're family women, we Jewish mothers. If we push or meddle or interrogate, it's because we want to be on the inside with the ones we love. We want to be more than connected; we want to be intertwined.

There's another important element to being a Jewish mother: We want to help. We want to make a difference and we want to make things better, especially where our family is concerned.

For the Jews, our commitment to our people is profound and complete, and the magnitude of our family is as large as we will make it. Hadassah makes our family very large indeed, by innovating health care for a nation and equipping the children of the land to continue the legacy of education and progress that sets Israel apart.

I am proud to be a Life Member of Hadassah and I hope to carry on the tradition of service and friendship exemplified for me by my mother, Molly Siegel Rabinowitz, who taught me to be a family woman.

✦ ✦ ✦

45

Becoming a Zionist
By Sharon Schneider

I t was 1967, and I was a junior in high school. My radio alarm clock went off at 7 a.m., just like any normal school day, but what I heard on the radio was anything but usual. Israel was at war on three separate borders, with Egypt, Jordan, and Syria. I frantically woke my parents, and ultimately stayed home from school and joined my mother, then president of the Bronx Chapter of Hadassah, at the chapter office. By the time we got to the office, people were lined up at the door. They were scared and anxious. Some were crying, holding their heads in disbelief. That day, I watched people coming off the streets, emptying their pockets and pocketbooks, writing checks, throwing it all on Mom's desk in an effort to ensure the survival of Eretz Yisrael. Their fears, their worry, and their passion had a powerful affect on me.

Twenty years later, I was president of the Lower New York State Region of Hadassah on my first trip to Israel as a member of the

National Board. I remember standing on the tarmac at Ben Gurion airport, while passengers were disembarking from a plane from the Soviet Union. Young and old alike, they were carrying all of their worldly possessions and so many musical instruments. As they came off the plane, they bent down and kissed the ground. Suddenly, they joined hands with us and together we began dancing the hora right there on the tarmac.

Although we did not speak the same language, we shared the same tradition. I realized that if my grandfather had not come from Russia to the United States many years earlier, it could be me and my family coming off that plane. We were *mispacha*—family. It became clear to me that as American Jews, it was our duty to protect and strengthen the Jewish homeland. With that experience, I became a passionate Zionist.

+ + +

46

The Power of A Story
By Selma Kron

During my marriage, I had no time for interests other than raising my five children and running a skilled nursing facility in suburban Philadelphia. However, my daughter was to give birth to our first grandchild in Florida. While waiting for the birth of the baby, we bought a condo in Bellaire Beach that we considered to be a vacation resort. I was still busy in Philadelphia managing our business and a busy home.

One day, while swimming in the Gulf of Mexico, I met an interesting gentleman. Dr. Alfred Schick and his wife, Lisl, soon became our good friends. Our best friend, Dr. George Stein, was a revered radiologist in Philadelphia, like Al, so we had much in common. However, shortly after our friendship developed, Al passed away. Norman attended his funeral in Florida. Whenever we visited our children, we called Lisl and took her to dinner.

One night, she told us a story of her experience with Hadassah.

Al was invited to speak at Hadassah Hospital, so Lisl joined him. On the day he was to give his speech at Mt. Scopus campus, Lisl was at Ein Kerem and found she had no transportation to get there to hear him. Someone told her that an ambulance was about to take off for that hospital, and she could hop on it. She found herself in an ambulance with two children as the patients, lying on cots with their mothers by their sides. One was an Arab woman while the other was Israeli. They were speaking to each other in a warm and friendly manner as if there was no hostility outside the windows of the ambulance. This impressed Lisl very much, for at that time, war existed between the two nations.

Norman and I were so touched by her story that I called Lisl the next morning to tell her that we would like to do something for Hadassah. Within three days, Prof. Shmuel Penchas, former Director General of Hadassah Hospital, and Bonnie Lipton, soon to be National President of Hadassah, were sitting in my living room in Florida while I was busy preparing lunch for them. They proceeded to tell us about Hadassah being forerunners in health care in Europe, and that presently they were building the Mother and Child Pavilion on Hadassah's campus. Within the building was to be the Gene Therapy Department. It was a very moving and impressive afternoon.

After they left, Norman and I thought that we would like to do something for Hadassah, and so we helped to build the Gene Therapy Department in the Mother and Child Pavilion. From that moment on, Hadassah became a very important part of my life. Norman and I flew to Israel to see how the building was progressing, and he reached his arms out with great pride on the

Gene Therapy floor and felt it was his contribution to Hadassah and Israel.

When we returned home, he felt content with his life and shortly thereafter he passed away, having suffered with cancer for several years. Bonnie Lipton gave a eulogy at his funeral.

Hadassah has played an important part of my life from that time to present.

+ + +

$$\text{\textasciitilde} \; 47 \; \text{\textasciitilde}$$

Mission Accomplished

By Ronnie Jo Sokol

While a member of Hope Hadassah, a group consisting of many single women, I won a sabbatical from my school and decided to spend it in Israel, becoming more fluent in Hebrew and volunteering at a home for abused children. Earlier that year, our Hadassah group had seen a photography exhibit at the Spertus Institute for Jewish Studies in Chicago. We all commented on an interesting photograph taken at a sage's hilly grave, "Amuka's Tomb," often visited by single women seeking husbands. Knowing I was leaving for Israel, my group asked me to visit the spot and pray for husbands for our single members. Challenged by an additional mission, I set about planning my journey. Little did I know it would turn out to be an adventure!

On December 15, 1989, a cold, damp, rainy day, I hiked through the sand dunes below Wingate to a particular bus stop near the ulpan where I was studying. It took four hours to reach Safed by way of Netanya and Haifa. Safed is the ancient site of the Kabbalah, or mystical movement, located in the rocky hills of the Golan. From the bus, I grabbed the only taxi I saw in the area and directed the driver to take me to Amuka's Tomb. The driver startled me by stating we should pray for a safe journey. I accepted his blessing and asked him how much the trip would cost. He told me we'd be on fifteen km of paved road and then a dirt road through the steep hills. He asked for 100 shekels, which was fifty dollars in those days. Seeing no other taxi in sight, I really had no alternative if I was going to complete my mission. Before we left Safed, the driver noticed a Hassidic rabbi in the street and asked him to come over to the taxi to once again bless my journey. I began to get anxious. Exactly how dangerous was this?

After traveling on paved road, we came to a sign that said, "Mitzpah Amukah," translating to "deep place." From there, we drove at a creeping pace down what had been a graded dirt road and was now a very uneven dirt path down a hill. Twice the taxi actually slid, and I said my own additional prayers for a safe arrival and return. At last, we came upon the tomb of the tzadik (righteous man), Yonaton Ben Uzziel. In a driving rain, I ran to the enclosure and prayed for good spouses for all single people who wished to marry. Having done my duty, I had the driver snap my picture— the necessary proof—and scurried back to the taxi.

Our first attempts to ascend the hill were hampered by the driving rain and slippery surface. I began to understand the importance of the blessings and fee for the trip. Giving up the possibility of traveling back up the same hill, the driver turned the cab back to look for another path out. Mercifully, he found one and we slowly ascended, sometimes staying off center to grab some traction from the grass on the hill itself.

Back home, safely tucked in my bed at the ulpan, I went to sleep, happy in the knowledge I had successfully completed my mission. Perhaps my prayers were heard. Of the women back in the United States, many of Hope's members who had urged me to make this special trip eventually married, moved away, and transferred to other Hadassah groups. What we do for Hadassah!

✦ ✦ ✦

48

The Promise

By Binnie Stein

The world was in flux in October 1990. Our soldiers were getting ready for Desert Storm. Questions regarding our basic safety flourished. Yet we were a resilient, unstoppable people who never let barriers stop us. With this as background, the thirty-one members of the first National Hadassah Mission to the Soviet Union, under the leadership of past National President Charlotte Jacobson, *z'l*, got ready to take off. We were guests of the United States.

While it was warm in New York that day, we knew that Moscow, our initial destination, was freezing. We dressed for that scenario and left. The trip was uneventful, save for getting to know and bond with the group even further.

We arrived toward the end of Chol Hamoed Sukkot, settled into our hotel, had a quick lunch, and went to the Adin Steinsaltz Academy Yeshiva to bring the students desperately needed medications. They met us in their well-stocked library, which burned down a few weeks after our visit.

We spent the rest of that afternoon acclimating to the city. As we traveled about, we saw long lines of people waiting to get food supplies from huge trucks. The people had nothing. The country was basically threadbare. We found the Arbit walking street and explored the stores. Be it the green market with its dehydrated looking fruits and vegetables, or the butcher, who featured scrawny feathered chickens, or the grocery, which sold watery borsht, bread, a few boxes of eggs, and some milk, the people could buy nothing. All of it was exorbitantly priced! We went to the G.U.M. Department Store and found the counters bare! As we walked along the street, there were people at tables featuring caviar, lacquer boxes, and matryushka (stacking) dolls. Others tried to sell their blue jeans and sneakers for funds, which would support them for a year! This unique scenario would be repeated in our hotel dining room each morning during breakfast. While it could have been comedic, it was really very sad!

Our first dinner replicated everything we saw on the Arbit that day. The people in our group were the only appetizing part of the experience.

The next day, we went to the American Embassy, where the ambassador shared his thoughts about world events. We continued to a Gan (a pre-kindergarten for Jewish toddlers) to meet the students and their teachers. They sang and danced for us and shared their rudimentary Hebrew. We continued to an Ulpan, where adults were preparing for Aliyah by studying Hebrew. We traveled on the subway and concluded the day with a visit to the Kremlin and its

Armory. Early that evening, we went to the Choral Synagogue for Simchat Torah services. There were thousands of people inside and they were matched by their numbers outside. We had the chance to interact with the congregants and share a host of gifts from the Golden Land: America! The best gift was a box of Marlboro cigarettes. Services included presentations by a delegation from Israel who brought a wonderful choir of Chazzanim with them. It was a totally meaningful experience. All of the people expressed their desire and dream to make Aliyah as soon as possible, and we promised to meet them in Israel the following summer. As we left the building, we were surrounded by the outside congregants who hugged us, sang and danced with us, and practically carried us to the bus. They reluctantly let us move away. We represented the reality of their dreams for tomorrow.

After another day of visits, we flew to Vilna, Lithuania and warm weather! Our first stop was the grave of the Vilna Gaon. Next to his resting place there was a grave containing 17,000 victims of the Holocaust. We visited numerous concentration camps and cemeteries, where we conducted services in memory of those people. We finally enjoyed a superb dinner in a highly rated restaurant. We traveled to Kovno Gebernia and were met by Mr. Zilber, a leader in the International YIVO organization and a former partisan. One of our travelers fought beside him in the neighboring forests. They hugged, kissed each other, and wept as they recalled those terrible times. Suddenly they began singing partisan songs and we joined them in song. Mr. Zilber addressed us in Yiddish regarding the devastating living conditions. Again we promised to meet those who went to Israel by the following July.

We continued to Riga, Latvia, where we went to a concert of music by George Gershwin and Leonard Bernstein. During the event, we learned that Mr. Bernstein had died earlier that day. We had the moderator announce the anniversary of one of our couples. We saw additional camps, mass graves, and Ulpanim. At least there was LIFE and the promise of tomorrow!

We flew to Leningrad, where we saw statues of Stalin, which would be knocked down during the eventual downfall of the government. We visited a social service agency and gave them supplies for their clients, who endured a devastating life. We saw several agencies like it throughout the trip and the story was always the same. On our first morning in the city, we went to the embassy and met the ambassador, who gave us a bottle of kosher wine to observe Shabbat. He invited us to sign the condolence book in memory of Leonard Bernstein. We continued to the Dutch Embassy, where the Soviet Jews were applying for permission to make Aliyah. The lines were endless and their dreams were limitless, but they were realistic. We gave them hope by repeating our promise to meet them in Israel the following summer. We saw the sites of the city, which, in part, replicated what we saw in Moscow. Suddenly, we found ourselves surrounded by unsavory people who selected us because we looked Jewish. We hid every symbol and traveled incognito. When we got ready to leave, we reiterated our promise to the people as together we chanted "NEXT YEAR IN JERUSALEM!"

In July, 1991, we went to Israel to participate in the Hadassah National Convention. While they were confronted with the Lebanon War and the huge Aliyah of the Ethiopian Jews, they also kept welcoming planeloads of Jews from the Soviet Union.

As we traveled about, we listened to stories of difficult living conditions. At one point, we actually met some of the former Soviet Jews we had seen during our trip to that country.

One night, we kept the most sacred part of our promise and went to the airport to welcome a planeload of Jews from Russia. The excitement was palpable. Each of us was handed an Israeli flag to give to an incoming passenger. Most people deplaned with a bag and a musical instrument. Others carried only bags. When we asked them what happened, they told us that they were pianists. They were amazed that a group of American Jews could speak Yiddish with them. We kept our promise to them as we welcomed them with hugs and songs. We even shared a *hora* with them. They left us with smiles and hope for the future. They proved to us that the thin thread each of us carries is united into a tapestry of Jewish life and tradition.

I lovingly dedicate this story to my mother, Esther Stein, who extended the entire event with me by sharing over two dozen lectures about our experience. May the thin thread keep going eternally.

✦ ✦ ✦

49

On the Right Path
By Diana Feld

I n 1950, I was granted a scholarship to attend The Brandeis Hebrew Art Institute for Music in California to study with some of the finest musicologists in the field. One of the conditions for receiving the scholarship was to do assigned volunteer work upon returning home.

I spent the summer engrossed in the most wonderful sounds of our people and enveloped in the warmth of feelings they evoked. Being taught by some of the greatest teachers and meeting other students who eventually became composers (Yehudi Wyner won a prize for his compositions, Jack Gottleib became dean of the School of Sacred Music-HUC), cantors, choir conductors, and soloists, was a dream come true. My life's path of being engrossed with our peoples' music was set.

Upon returning home, I received a phone call from the Manhattan Beach Hadassah Chapter in Brooklyn assigning me to be the "new" leader of their Young Judaea Group. "New," because the girls had already discouraged three other leaders. So, armed with a smile, good intentions, sweaty palms, and a beating heart, I went to face the "demolishers." What a surprise to find girls who were ready to learn, try new things, explore and, best of all, were not that far from me in age! That alone established rapport. We had a ball learning about everything. . . their appetites to know were peaked so I used my knowledge from my deeply involved Jewish background and studies in Yiddishe Shule, Talmud Torah, Israel, and Zionist organizations to wet their appetites. We entered contests, joined activities, and created projects in various synagogues, did our own volunteer work, and visited places of Jewish interest in New York City. I was truly sorry when the year ended, and we all hugged and cried. More tears ensued when, at a Mother's Day Hadassah Meeting, I was presented with a JNF certificate for five trees planted in my honor for being a good "mom" to the girls.

Being tapped by Hadassah for this first experience with the Young Judaea Group led to my involvement with many temple youth groups, which then prompted me to pursue studies in Jewish Education at Hebrew Union College and the Jewish Teachers' Seminary. After obtaining certification as a principal and religious school educator, I was appointed a Master Teacher by the Union of American Hebrew Congregations and the New York Board of Jewish Education. I enjoyed twenty years of teaching all subjects to all ages and, in my capacity as a Master Teacher and specialist in the arts, trained student teachers and faculty members how to incorporate music, dance, and art into the classroom curriculum. Not only did the outcome of the summer of 1950 fulfill my hopes, aspirations, and dreams of what I could accomplish, but set me on my path of being involved in the most precious of vocations—teaching Jewish children. And to think, it all began with Hadassah and a Young Judaea Group!

✦ ✦ ✦

$$\rightarrow 50 \leftarrow$$

An Incredible Journey

By Janice Greenwald

Before becoming involved with Hadassah, I had never even ventured out of my town by myself. I could never have imagined that from that very first exciting experience in Hadassah, when I flew alone from Pittsburgh to Boston, my life would be forever changed. At that meeting, I met one of our matriarchs, Judith Epstein. I listened to the story of Hadassah from a woman who actually knew Henrietta Szold. She instilled in me the passion that was to grow and grow over the next couple of decades.

The years that I volunteered for Hadassah were an amazing journey. Personally, I developed from an ordinary woman who grew up in a small town to an empowered woman who made a difference in the world.

It is impossible to choose only one experience that made this change. There are so many life-altering events that I could share with you.

My most memorable moment was when I spearheaded a drive to send medicine and other supplies to war-torn Sarajevo. We sent tons of supplies that actually made it through all of the obstacles, such as bribery and theft. It was a tremendous feeling of satisfaction to know that we really saved so many of these people's lives. They received much-needed medicine and clothing, formula for their babies, and so much more. In addition to aiding the people of Sarajevo, this project united Hadassah members all over the country. Men, women, and children asked for and collected the goods, then packed much of it with their own hands before it was sent overseas. It was a very proud moment in the saga of Hadassah. We reached out to people of all religions. It was truly the realization of the Talmudic quote, "Whoever saves a life it is as if he saved the entire world."

The health of women in the United States and in Israel was enhanced by the work that I was able to do under the auspices of Hadassah. I interacted with Jewish nurses from all over the country who belonged to the Hadassah Nurse's Council. They ultimately worked with their Israeli colleagues and created a Masters of Nursing Program at Hadassah. As head of the Department of Women's Health for Hadassah, I helped create programs and educated women in the United States and in Israel on good health habits and prevention of disease. I contributed to a Data Book for Women's Health in Israel with the Israelis, the first such book to be published in Israel. I actually had the opportunity to go to Israel and work with professionals, sharing our programs with them. My nursing background came in handy for this part of my Hadassah career. One time, I actually spoke at an Israel Medical Association meeting in Eilat, informing them of the work that we do at Hadassah.

It was an honor for me to have represented Hadassah at the United Nations for four years. I attended the very first Holocaust Remembrance Ceremonies at the United Nations and designed and facilitated workshops at the UN in New York City and at the UNESCO Headquarters in Paris. Through these workshops, people from around the world heard about the wonderful things that are happening in Israel in the fields of health and water and environment. I even presented a report on Hadassah's work with assisting women in the Middle East (Arab and Jew) to start their own businesses to empower the women and enhance the quality of life for their families. The details of the workshop that I organized with Jordanians and Israelis from the Arava Institute at Kibbutz Ketura on environmental issues appeared in the Jordanian newspapers, as well as in the Israeli press.

I have had the opportunity to travel the world and to interact with dignitaries as well as with women who still walk miles to fill a container of water for their families. I was a part of the Women's Conference in China, traveled to South America, Turkey, and many other places with Hadassah, and have been to Israel twenty-three times. I led missions with nurses, incorporating educational classes at sites all over the country with exciting touring.

Against the wishes of my children, but with the support of my husband, I did go to Israel during the Gulf War. After two days of Hadassah Board meetings in New York, a group of the National Board went to Israel, even as the Scud missiles were falling. Our Director General of the HMO met us as we arrived and were put on a bus at the airport. At that time, he handed us our gas masks.

He said it would be OK to lose your purse, but not to lose your gas mask. We actually had to go into the safe rooms on several occasions, gas masks in place, but I can't tell you how grateful the Israelis were that they were not abandoned at this time.

One moment sticks out in my mind. I went with Marlene Post to visit a friend of hers in Ramat Gan. This was where one of the Scuds had recently fallen. We visited the home of a handicapped woman. She had a small baby and another child. Because of her handicap, they could not sleep at night in their bedrooms because she could not make it down the steps to their safe room in time when the siren sounded. Instead, they spent the night, the entire family, in the safe room. This was a very small space that you could hardly call a room. But, in spite of all of this, the woman served us cake and tea, and even had a few flowers on her table. This was important to her. She needed to show some signs of normalcy in these terrorizing times. Her spirit inspired me more than I can say. To this day, I think about her and the courage that she and so many others showed during such difficult days.

I was in Israel with Hadassah at the time of the Sbarro Pizza Shop bombing. It was a very weird feeling knowing that only twenty-four hours prior to the bombing, I had been in that very same place. After the event, all of the members of the National Board went back to the hotel and we made sure that everyone was accounted for.

All said, it has been a most incredible journey. I pray that I will be granted the strength to continue to help Israel and the Jewish people through this vehicle called Hadassah.

✦ ✦ ✦

51

Gulf War—My Hadassah Experience

By Dorothy Lasensky

I t was January 1991 and the First Gulf War had begun. Having secured credentials from the Ministry of Health in order to work in Israel, I found myself on a nearly empty 747 flight ready to embark upon my volunteer experience as a nurse in the operating room at Mt. Scopus Hospital in Jerusalem. It had been a dream of mine for many years to work in an Israeli hospital, but I had not planned to fulfill a wartime need.

Upon arrival at Ben Gurion Airport, I was handed a gas mask and my personal protection kit containing various antidotes for chemical and biological attacks. During the ride from the airport to my French Hill apartment, my thoughts went back to the novel *Raquela* by Ruth Gruber. This true story details Raquela's career as a Hadassah graduate nurse during the many conflicts throughout Israel's history. Would I step into her shoes for a few moments during this new war? These reflections were interrupted by my arrival at the apartment I would call home.

Sleep came easily my first night, but I was abruptly awakened by the sound of the air raid siren signaling a Scud missile attack. I grabbed my gas mask and protection kit and ran into our secured, sealed room with food and water. I was grateful for my roommates' companionship and reassurance. I now could relate to every Israeli who had lived there during wartime. I was prepared for any future attacks, reassured that Jerusalem was safe. I had left the security of the United States to work side by side with my Israeli nurse colleagues.

The next morning, I walked to work on the "Hill of Healing," seeing in the distance the old city and the Dome of the Rock gleaming in the sunlight. At the entrance to the hospital, a staff member in front of me touched the mezzuzah at the front door before entering the building. This single incident was that "ah hah" moment!!! I had never worked at a Jewish facility. I found myself doing the same act with tears in my eyes. Here I was entering this sacred historic space greeted warmly by MY people!!! A flashback to the ill-fated 1948 convoy came into memory. Never again!!! This was a new day of a medical institution and its sister campus Ein Kerem where all individuals (Israelis and Palestinians, Jews and Arabs) are treated alike, whether in times of peace or war.

Once back home in California, I helped organize and charter the Los Angeles, San Diego, and Orange County Nurses Councils. Family members now make up four generations of Life Members. My late husband and I became Founders. This Quintessential Hadassah journey is still not over, as we soon celebrate our Centennial.

✦ ✦ ✦

52

Safe Landing

By Marcie Natan

E veryone over fifty likely remembers where they were when they heard the news, or watched on television, as Neil Armstrong took his first step on the moon. Everyone over fifteen remembers where they were when they first learned of or saw the terrible images of the 9/11 attacks.

Such moments of celebration or tragedy are a part of history. But each of us has indelible memories of personal events and experiences that changed our lives. I've made many trips to Israel, for example, but there is one in particular that stands out as a defining moment of my life.

It was in January 1991, during the first Gulf War, and missiles were already falling on Israel when a Hadassah mission lifted off at Kennedy Airport. I was then president of Hadassah's Eastern Pennsylvania Region and decided that I couldn't sit home and watch the news from the Middle East. I had to go.

The mission was planned before the first Iraqi attack and people I had spoken to about my plans—including some in my family— were divided into two camps. My son David represented the matter-of-fact wing: "If mom wants to go to Israel, let her go," he told my husband. "The truth is that if war breaks out, the ladies of Hadassah are not going to get on that plane."

The more emotional wing was represented by my daughter Heidi. "How can you do this to me?" Heidi asked. "It's too risky. What if something happens to you?"

There were also those who thought that however well meaning we might be, visitors in Israel during a war would only get in the way.

Late on the night before the mission left for Israel, I got a call from Heidi. "When you first said you were going I thought it was selfish," she told me. "But then I realized this is your way of teaching us what really counts, that you're going to stand up for your convictions and show us the way. I'm still worried," she added. "But go safely."

Twenty years later, I remember every detail of that mission, from the gas masks that were handed to us on arrival at Ben Gurion Airport, to the time we spent in sealed rooms during alerts of incoming missiles, to the ABC drill (the abbreviation for atomic, biological and chemical attack) we watched at Hadassah Hospital.

But one seemingly insignificant moment sticks in my memory. There came the moment when I wanted to call Israeli friends to let them know I was in the country. Those were the days when you still needed an operator to make a call if you weren't familiar with Israel's city codes. As always, my total lack of Hebrew made this a tense experience. With friendly operators in rare supply even in good times, what would I encounter at a time when the entire nation was stressed?

This time was different. As soon as the Israeli operator heard my American voice she said, "Thank you. Thank you so much for coming." I was so touched that I cried.

We heard much the same message from Prime Minister Yitzhak Shamir. He didn't think we were in the way. In fact, he came to meet with us in person. So did future Prime Minister Ehud Olmert, who was then mayor of Jerusalem. And so did future Prime Minister Benjamin Netanyahu, then the deputy minister for foreign affairs. They were among the parade of top officials who took the time to meet with Hadassah.

I knew from that trip, that above and beyond Hadassah's projects, I had a role as an American Jew in the Israeli story and it wasn't just as a potential immigrant. I learned from ordinary Israelis and the nation's leaders that our physical presence and emotional support were as important to them as the institutions we build.

I've told my Gulf War story many times, and often noted how it changed my life and even the Zionist dynamics of my family. When I got home from the mission, David gave his first significant donation to Hadassah. I may have been the one who got on the plane but, looking at the impact after all this time, it seems as if my family was with me on that mission.

That trip taught me a few additional lessons. People who have an important place for Israel in their hearts always feel anxiety when the Jewish state is threatened, and never more so than when it is actually at war. In those circumstances, going to Israel actually produces a feeling of relief. Suddenly, you are there in a country so dear to you and amid people you admire. From afar, you see only the threat; up close, the danger is one element in a rich landscape of determination, heroism, and solidarity.

A related lesson is about falling in love again. We all know that an intense shared experience with another person can strengthen the bonds you feel, even if they were already strong. It happens with countries, too.

My Gulf War experience is an important part of who I am. It not only bound me even more tightly to Israel, it also took my work in Hadassah to a new level. Assuming the national presidency of this great organization was certainly the result of many years of dedication and learning, but some days are more equal than others.

To paraphrase Robert Frost, there were other roads I might have taken in January 1991, but the road I took to Israel has made all the difference.

+ + +

✦ 53 ✦

From Sprout Lake to San Juan

By Lynn Ross Davidson

L ike many of you, I have been a Zionist since I first saw the
movie *Exodus* and truly "felt" the value of the Jewish state
in my heart, as this historical story took hold of my life's mission.
I can't deny that Paul Newman playing Ari Ben Canaan may have
had something to do with it.

And while the following is not a historical story to anyone
else, it has become part of our family folklore.

I had become an active Hadassah leader and, since 1991,
served on the Nassau Region Executive Board. My family knew
that my commitment ran deep and all of our visits to Israel were
with Hadassah.

When my daughter, Lauren, was eleven, she and I were truly at
odds. It seems to be the age girls turn into "the thing from outer
space," when they are being possessed by some strange force. She
and I needed a break, and *one* of us had to leave home for the

summer. As much as I would have enjoyed an extended trip, it was decided that Lauren would go away to camp. The choice of a camp was easy; Lauren would go to Camp Sprout Lake, a Hadassah camp not far from home in New York. She wasn't happy about this, as she would be going to a camp not knowing any other kids. She complained and even shed more than a few tears. However, this story continues to shape into a happy ending.

Lauren made great friends and, even her first time, had a good time at camp . . . so good, in fact, that she attended both sessions the following year.

Our "resistant" daughter went on to attend the teen Camp Tel Yehudah, and then Machon in Israel, and went so far as to do the entire Young Judaea Year Course in Israel. One of our trips to Israel was a wonderful mission as parents of Year Course participants, and we were able to see Lauren's joy at being part of this experience first hand.

But this is only part of the story. At Camp Tel Yehudah, Lauren became good friends with Daniel Hoffman, a camper from San Juan, Puerto Rico. Lauren's friendship with Daniel was platonic for a long time, cemented by their connection to Young Judaea, Camp Tel Yehudah, and Israel.

Over the years, their friendship developed into full blown love, and on December 6, 2009, Lauren and Daniel were married, surrounded by many of the friends Lauren met that first year at Sprout Lake, as well as friends of theirs from Tel Yehudah.

Lauren and Daniel live in San Juan, and she has met two new close friends through Hadassah. The Hadassah "love connection" has continued to keep us all connected to the Hadassah family.

What started as a summer "banishment" ended happily with a beautiful marriage and wonderful lifetime friends.

Hadassah continues to be my way of expressing love of Judaism and Zionism. Hadassah has given us rich and beautiful friendships that are taking us to the next generation.

✦ ✦ ✦

✦ 54 ✦

We Are All Mishpacha

By Renee Sidman

In Hadassah, we are all mishpacha. When we meet, we look for a connection of hometown or childhood friends and often find one. When I first met Haidi Appel in 1992, there was no reason to search for such a connection. She was a new chapter president from El Paso, Texas, and I was a new chapter president from Colorado Springs, originally from Seattle. We were assigned to room together at our first National Convention in Washington D.C. and hit it off immediately.

As chapter presidents in the far-flung Desert Mountain Region, we only got together a few times a year, but always made time to catch up. When we were in Colorado Springs or El Paso, we visited each other's homes and met each other's families. Four years passed. We became "old Hadassah friends." When Haidi's mother, Francine Raileanu, succeeded her as president, we realized that we shared a common Romanian heritage. More years passed until one day I was looking through my mother's childhood album and an old wedding photograph of my grandparents fell out. On the back my mother had written all about her mother, born Anna Kanner in Jassy, Romania in 1884, one sister Bianca, and one brother Jacques. This was nothing new as we had already well researched our family tree. But then she wrote, "Jacques often went by the name Raileanu." This was new!

This serendipitous footnote led to the discovery that Haidi and I are indeed cousins. Jacques, my great uncle, had one son, Marcel, who as a baby immigrated to New York City with his mother. My grandmother, who had come to New York in 1904, sometimes looked after them. Marcel later had a son, Jordan, and a daughter, Coralie. Jordan is Haidi's father and my second cousin. And, on closer inspection, Haidi's and my children do have a striking resemblance.

I still get chills when I think about two Jewish children born in a small, poor village in Romania well over a century ago and the series of random events that brought their granddaughter and great granddaughter together a world away, first as Hadassah colleagues, then friends, and now family. So, it's true. In Hadassah we truly are mishpacha.

✦ ✦ ✦

✦ 55 ✦

Hadassah Is Her Middle Name

By Jane G. Strom

We are a five-generation-family of Hadassah women, including four generations of chapter presidents and a National President. In one way or another, we had all dedicated a good portion of our lives to the work of Hadassah. My sister, Nancy Wiadro, has served on the National Board for over twenty years. Little did we know that Hadassah would enter into the life of our granddaughter, Mira, in a way that would not only save her life, but ensure that there might one day be a sixth generation of Hadassah women.

We owe Mira, our first granddaughter, to Hadassah in two ways: our daughter Rebecca met her future husband at a Hadassah International event in London in 1994. When their first daughter was born, they named her Mira Naomi Hadassah Trenner. Reason number two is more serious.

Rebecca and her husband, Justyn, were visiting Israel to celebrate the Bat Mitzvah of their friend's child. In quick succession, we received two emailed photos: the first showed them with a happy and smiling Dr. Dan Galon, a cardiologist and colleague of my husband, Joel. The second photograph was confusing. Why was my granddaughter, Mira, on a gurney in the Emergency Department? It turned out she was experiencing severe belly pain and their friend and Hadassah doctor, Penina Scherzer, who had been showing them around Hadassah Ein Kerem, suggested they let the CEM doctors take a look. Mira, age 11, was diagnosed with a grapefruit sized cyst on her ovary. Mira was at imminent risk of the cyst causing her fallopian tube to twist with the loss of blood supply to her ovary. She was admitted to the hospital and stayed for five days until her cyst was drained. Mira was placed with another young girl, and even though they shared no common language, they quickly became friends. Mira's brother and sister passed the hours waiting to know if their sister would be all right by wandering around the halls, looking for names of family members on plaques in the hospital. It was like a scavenger hunt of our family's history. Rebecca emailed updates, since by the time I got the news about Mira, I was attending my first Hadassah Convention as a region president.

Rebecca let us know that the doctors, nurses, and entire staff at the hospital were friendly and helpful—Mira got the best of care and we got an inside look at what goes on within the walls and halls of Hadassah Hospital. I realized that of all the places in the world where this episode could have happened with Mira, it was comforting that it was in Israel, under the care of Hadassah's doctors and nurses. I was truly relieved that she was at Hadassah and am grateful for her good luck to have been in the best place at the right time. In the end, Mira was conditionally released from the Bloomberg Mother and Child Pavilion and allowed to fly back to London on schedule. And I was allowed to breathe a sigh of relief surrounded by the support and caring of my Hadassah colleagues. My family has played a part in building the CEM, the Tower, and the hospital into what it is today. My feelings of connection were deepened further by knowing that she got the best of care in a place where my heart is.

I can never thank Hadassah enough for giving us our eldest granddaughter—twice.

✦ ✦ ✦

56

Hadassah International—
The Kiwi connection

By Lindy Davis

This is a story of the makings of Hadassah International New Zealand in the Antipodes, and just how far-reaching thin threads can be.

Kia Kaha is a New Zealand Maori expression. Its translation is "be strong, get stuck in, and keep going." This belief is what drove Valda Knight to establish the first branch of Hadassah International in New Zealand in 1996.

After recuperating from a lumpectomy procedure in 1995, Valda was vacationing in Israel; however, while there, she needed to be admitted to Hadassah hospital. She was so impressed by the care she received that she was inspired to return home to New Zealand and establish a membership that would support the worldwide organization.

She communicated her willingness to drive the leadership in

this island nation and set about establishing a committee of like-minded volunteers who would share her vision. Her three children and eight grandchildren became instant Life Members!

In 1996, the first of many fund-raising ventures was held for some much needed heated bassinets for the Mother and Child center. A magnificent walk around Auckland's coastline was to become an annual event. "Walking for a Better Future" was something that Valda found easy to promote, given that hiking was one of her favorite pastimes, and she was able to generate interest and enthusiasm from all age-groups. She even organized a first Hadassah children's walk. This led to many other successful fundraising activities over the next ten years that she served as president. This steady support grew and enabled the New Zealand branch to flourish into the thriving membership it has today.

Valda would often speak of her admiration for Hadassah hospital, promoting medicine that speaks one language of health and peace. Her many years of experience in voluntary work meant she understood the effort required to reach out to communities and convey the message of Hadassah in a way that people would understand.

Although New Zealand is a small community by international standards, the membership grew beyond expectation. The Hadassah New Zealand organization has become a life force within both the Jewish and wider secular communities.

An evening of opera and fine wine marked its tenth anniversary and raised $50,000 for the Hadassah medical center. More recently, a wonderful gift was given through the Guardian Trust on behalf of the Lady Marion Davis Memorial Foundation, which has been donated for the development of the Sarah Wetsman Davidson Tower. Valda's tireless work was honored at a cocktail reception for Hadassah International Keepers.

It was only as her health deteriorated that Valda reluctantly let go of her responsibility, allowing the very capable Jenny Leiman to take over the president's role. Her goal to see Hadassah New Zealand go from strength to strength has been realized with the dedicated and close knit committee that functions now in her absence.

Our memories of Valda live on with the establishment of an annual Hadassah New Zealand scholarship. This provides an employee from the New Zealand health sector with an opportunity to enhance their professional development and personal enrichment at Hadassah Medical Center. The hope is that this example of global peace by way of treating all patients equally will be adopted worldwide, "medicine without borders" being one of Hadassah's key initiatives.

A Nurses Charting Station was one of Hadassah New Zealand's main fundraising goals and will be realized in 2012 with the opening of the new Sarah Wetsman Davidson Tower. The New Zealand branch has chosen to honor Valda with a plaque in her memory.

Although Hadassah was very much her "baby" from the outset, Valda's enthusiasm magically spread to all who came into contact with the New Zealand branch. Her immediate and extended family embraced Hadassah with her, and even now, members of the family continue to support it in various ways. One of her grandsons, Jordan, will spend a month studying orthopedics as a house surgeon at Hadassah hospital in 2012.

Although the two countries couldn't be further apart geographically, they both share a commitment to a future of peace and empathy for all nationalities without prejudice.

Valda Knight was my mother. Her desire to ensure that Hadassah's vision would be perpetuated, and its commitment to reaching out to all people, has taught me more than she will ever know. As Joan Baez so eloquently put it, "You don't get to choose how you're going to die or when. You can only decide how you're going to live."

✦ ✦ ✦

57

Judy Turetsky: A Chance Reference Transforms a Legacy

By Alana Fodeman

Alana Fodeman, a second-generation Life Member of Hadassah, and president of the Fairfield Connecticut Chapter for thirteen years, retells the story of Judy Turetsky's amazing gift.

During my tenure as president of my Hadassah chapter, I have had many unbelievable experiences and have met a great number of people whose commitment to Hadassah is unsurpassed. I feel, however, that the story of Judy Turetsky, and how Hadassah changed her life, and consequently that of so many others, needs to be told.

Some years ago, Judy came to Fairfield Hadassah as a new member. Judy had come to learn about Hadassah rather late in her life, and in the beginning, her relationship with Hadassah was more of a way to establish social interaction and a connection with her community. You see, at the relatively young age of fifty, Judy had become an invalid as the result of a blood transfusion that resulted in her contracting hepatitis C.

An extremely intelligent and talkative individual, the ramifications of this disease were devastating. Judy was an accomplished librarian, at first serving as a medical librarian at the Albert Einstein Hospital, and later moving to a Connecticut law firm, where she assumed the responsibility as their legal librarian and de facto paralegal.

The isolation imposed upon her by her illness was overwhelming for this warm, gregarious woman. A good friend of Judy's convinced her that Hadassah could bring her back into the company of other intelligent and dedicated women, while giving her a meaningful job that she could do from her home. She joined Hadassah and was quickly given the job of being the "Card Lady" (taking the orders for the Hadassah greeting cards).

Around this same time, Judy was continuing her own research regarding her illness and began a correspondence with a doctor in Australia. This is where the thin thread begins its sinuous connection. From one end of the earth to another, this doctor put Judy in touch with Dr. Eitan Gallun, a liver specialist, at Hadassah Hospital. After a series of conversations wherein Dr. Gallun reviewed her existing condition and protocol, he put her on a strict, new regimen, which would require a full year of treatment. The result? She was completely cured of her hepatitis. Dr. Gallun, and the research he was conducting at Hadassah Hospital, gave Judy her life back. She was able to get out of her house; she traveled to Israel several times, meeting with Dr. Gallun as well as her brother's son, who had made aliyah. Her dogged research had led her to Australia, which in turn led her to Israel and the ground-breaking research being done by the doctors and researchers at Hadassah.

Judy had come to Hadassah at first seeking sisterhood and a way to be connected to her community. But the pull of Hadassah's thread now became even stronger. She wanted to make sure that others benefited from the opportunities that Hadassah's medical research had afforded her. She arranged through Mediscope (the program that brings Hadassah doctors to the United States for the purpose of lecturing and the sharing of medical knowledge) to bring Dr. Gallun here. Today, Dr. Gallun is head of the Goldyn Savad Stem Cell Research Center. Always invested in saving lives, Hadassah Hospital is proud to be at the forefront of stem cell research.

Several years ago, Judy passed away. In her will she left over $350,000 to Hadassah for research at Goldyn Savad, so that Eitan Gallun and his staff could continue their research on finding cures for diseases that effect the liver. What began as a search for Judy to help cure her own illness was transformed into a dedication to Hadassah for the last decade of her life, and to her promise to allow Hadassah to continue the healing of others into the future.

On a side note, Judy could smile at the serendipitous role Hadassah would play in the life of other family members: all of her nephew's five children were delivered at Hadassah Hospital.

+ + +

58

An American in Zurich

By Ellen Frick-Delman

I was born into the quintessential American Jewish family and grew up in the greater New York City area. My mother, grandmother, and aunt were all Hadassah members.

I studied in New York, received a master's degree in communication arts from Syracuse University, and have a professional background in marketing. I fell in love with Europe during my first visit whilst in college. After graduating, I did a short stint as a commercial and fine arts teacher, then public relations work in the New York City Mayor's Office of Economic Development. Finally, I landed my "dream job" as creative marketing director for an international art licensing company.

Destiny and marriage took me to Switzerland, and I've lived in Zurich since 1984. Shortly after moving to Zurich and following my passion for art, I founded my own art consulting company. I thoroughly enjoyed the expat experience as "an American in Zurich."

I like people and I've been told that I am natural networker. Through my international business, I took pleasure in meeting and cultivating a large international circle of friends, colleagues, and associates in the business, social and cultural environments; I was often asked to address the challenges of multicultural and intercultural living.

With the proverbial biological clock ticking, I made the decision to take a break from my business and curtail my traveling. Pregnancy, and the birth of my son, Cliff, followed in 1987.

As I always enjoyed civic activities and supporting good causes, I became involved in the American and international community. As this was before the Internet, Facebook, and Skype, such organizations were most helpful in staying connected with one's roots while dealing with the challenges of integrating into a new culture.

I served on the Executive Board of the American Women's Club for eight years in various capacities and was President from 1994 to 1996. In 2007, I was elected president of the American Club of Zurich and have the distinction of being the first woman president in the club's then fifty-two-year history.

The years passed quickly and I enjoyed my work/life balance and activities. Then, in 1996, I was approached by the U.S. Embassy to head the Zurich America Center/U.S. Consular Agency, a public and private enterprise providing consular and information services for Americans in Zurich. I was appointed by the U.S. Department of State to serve as Consular Agent (Honorary consul/Honorarkonsulin) and Director of the Zurich America Center, thereby representing the Ambassador in the greater Zurich area.

In that same year, I received a phone call from an American friend inviting me to tea, the purpose of which was to introduce me to a college friend who was visiting and whom she was sure I would enjoy meeting. That person was Nancy Falchuk, who at the time was president of Hadassah International. I recall it was a lovely autumn afternoon, the sun glimmering across the Lake of Zurich. We sat in the sunny dining room of Robin's charming home high over the Lake of Zurich. Nancy told me about Hadassah International, at that time a mere fifteen years old, and how they would like to establish an active unit in Switzerland.

Naturally, I was interested in this project. I felt that I could combine past and present experiences and put my skills to good use. Although I am a native New Yorker, I also have the privilege (and responsibilities!) of being Swiss. This is a commitment to the country I choose to live in and the community in which I live. Switzerland, a small, famously neutral country nestled in the middle of Europe, is very proud of being 720 years old, peacefully co-existing with its surrounding countries, with four distinct cultures and four different languages: German, French, Italian, and Romansh. Demographically, New York boasts the largest Jewish population in the U.S., whereas Switzerland has a mere 17,000 Jews, or 0.23% of its 7.5 million population. So, coming from New York, a city with the largest Jewish population outside of Israel, it was an interesting experience to learn about and integrate into Jewish life in the greater Zurich area.

So, why Hadassah? I saw Hadassah as an opportunity to cultivate and explore my Jewish roots in Zurich and it was a chance to connect three important aspects of my life: my hometown and city of my birth, New York; my Jewish heritage; and the city that I choose to make my home, Zurich. I am pleased that I have been able to nurture and build the Swiss unit in spite of (or perhaps because of) my American-accented German!

This has been a challenge and at the same time, a truly enriching experience. For me, a true synergy has been created through Hadassah, a thread that has been woven into the fabric of my life and my personal journey.

Flash forward to 2006. As president of Hadassah Switzerland and Hadassah International's liaison to Europe, I hosted another HI-er from New York, Melissa Kaplan, the newly-appointed director. Melissa is vivacious, intelligent, inquisitive, adventurous, and certainly open to new experiences. What a great asset for Hadassah!

At the end of her visit, my husband, Rolf, and I invited Melissa to join us for dinner. We thought that it might be more interesting and certainly more balanced if we were a foursome, so we invited a friend to join us, a young Zurich-based American lawyer, Marnin Michaels.

Well, you might say, the rest is history—certainly Hadassah history! Melissa and Marnin married in Jerusalem in 2010 and have settled in Zurich! Now, almost two generations after I first arrived and fifteen years after that first fateful meeting, Hadassah has opened an office in my new home town.

✦ ✦ ✦

✦ 59 ✦

A Life-Changing Gift
By Susan Metsch

Happy Birthday, Mom!

I t was September 1996, and I was in a quandary as to what my mother would like for her eightieth birthday. "Susan," she told me, "Please, no presents. Instead, I'd like you to become a member of Hadassah and do something for Israel." I did as she asked and joined Hadassah as a Life Member. I never expected to become an active member, but I soon caught the "Hadassah Bug."

As I learned more about the workings of Hadassah, I became more involved and committed to what Hadassah represents. I joined the study group, became organizational vice president, and then president of the Simcha Chapter. I attended regional events and National Conventions.

After a year of participating in the 2006 chapter's study group (Zionism), three members of the group (as well as two spouses, one mother, and a cousin), went on a personal Hadassah tour during the Intifada. Israel was very quiet then, and everywhere I went there were warm, welcoming greetings and thank yous for supporting and traveling to Israel. Visiting the Hadassah projects and the hospital were the highlights of the trip. During that trip, I was privileged to share in the observance of Israel's Memorial Day and to celebrate Israel's Independence Day. What an unforgettable experience.

Every step in my participation in Hadassah seemed natural to me. This was something that I wanted and needed to do. Although it was a gradual process, it allowed Hadassah to really become a part of me. I felt and still feel great pride and commitment for all that I can do to make the work of Hadassah successful. I am fortunate to be able to be a Keeper of the Gate and a Major Donor (given in memory of my dad). I believe in the survival and continuation of all the Hadassah projects. Seeing is believing, and I have done that several times during my visits to Israel. I feel like an ambassador for Hadassah!

How can I ever thank my mother for asking me to join Hadassah? Because of her wish, I have added another perspective to my life. I have continued to be an active supporter of Hadassah projects. Education is my passion.

Today, I am currently chairing the chapter's study group: *Hadassah, Zionism, and our Personal Connections to Israel*, and am on the Regional Board. The title and curriculum of the study group has evolved from all my personal experiences with Hadassah. Joining Hadassah was the best birthday gift I ever gave my mother, and it just keeps on getting better and better.

✦ ✦ ✦

60

The Miracles of Hadassah

By Jeanette Thorner

E ver since I was a young girl growing up in Queens, New York, I have been an ardent Zionist and very interested in the State of Israel. I was ready to pack my bags and go and live on a kibbutz in Israel, but my parents were not quite as enthused as I was.

About forty years ago, when I moved to Denver with my husband and two children, I joined many Jewish organizations to meet other Jewish women. At that time, the Jewish population of Denver was much less than it is now. Gradually, I dropped out of some of the organizations, as my time was limited with two small children and I felt that I was over extending myself. I became active in Hadassah and I held several board positions. In 1998, I became president of my now local chapter in Colorado Springs. I had been on the board in many capacities, but I never imagined that I would ever be president. I am a quiet person and although I was very passionate about Hadassah, I did not feel that I had the necessary leadership qualities required for this position. Judy Kaiser, the president of our chapter at the time, was relentless in urging me to be the next president of our chapter. She was certainly a difficult act to follow, as anyone who knows Judy can attest. Well, I did give in and I was president of our chapter from 1998 to 2000. I feel that whatever I contributed during that time, I received so much more in return.

The role of president taught me so much and enabled me to do what I never thought I was capable of accomplishing. I learned leadership and organizational skills and how to motivate the members and share my enthusiasm of Hadassah's work and goals. By far the greatest impact that being president had for me was the confidence that it gave me to speak in front of a large group and share my ideas. Up until that time, I dreaded speaking in public no matter what the subject matter. My voice would shake and I was extremely uncomfortable. Gradually, as it became more necessary for me to speak in public at Hadassah functions and I was so sure of the importance of what I had to say, I lost my fear and eventually found I actually enjoyed speaking in front of a group and even looked forward to being called on. This newly found confidence was a huge change for me and it also extended into my personal life, when I had the great honor of speaking at my children's weddings, expressing my profound joy. This may not seem like a big deal to some people, but to anyone who has experienced the fear of public speaking, it is very significant. It has changed my life and my enjoyment of my life.

It always impressed me that once a president completed her term, she continued to be active in her chapter, assuming many other positions and often being lovingly recycled. Where I witnessed the most evidence of Hadassah's work and global influence was at the many National Conventions that I attended, including one convention in Israel that I will never forget.

I was in awe of the officers of the National Board. Their knowledge, talent, and most of all their dedication and commitment to Hadassah was amazing. The many speakers at the conventions were unbelievable. We heard from doctors at the Hadassah hospital and learned about their outstanding work and cutting edge research, from terrorist victims treated at the hospital, and their miraculous recovery from their severe injuries, from students at our college and what their education there did for them, from government leaders from the United States and Israel, and so many more. Everyone attending these conventions went back to their chapters with new insights and energy.

We are a third-generation family of Hadassah Life Members and we look forward to continuing that tradition for many generations to come with our five grandchildren. We take much pride in being part of such an impressive organization that has been so instrumental in affecting so much change and progress in our country, Israel, and all over the world.

Thank you, Hadassah, for giving me a new lease on life with confidence and empowering me, and all of your members throughout the world. May you continue to grow and flourish from one generation to another. Happy 100th Birthday!

✦ ✦ ✦

61

The Grandson

By Gloria Gelman

It wasn't until the birth of my grandson, Dylan, that I understood what the word "life" in my Hadassah "Life" Membership really meant to me.

I have a love for Israel and for the Jewish people, and have been a member of Hadassah for more than twenty years. However, my feelings for Hadassah grew when Dylan was born and diagnosed with a rare genetic disease, Familial Dysautonomia, which is particular to those of Jewish descent. This is a terribly debilitating disease that affects the development of nerves throughout the body. Dylan takes no food or liquid by mouth, cannot speak, and walks with a swaggering gait. His laughter, however, can light up a room.

Hadassah Hospital is the only hospital in the world, other than New York University Medical Center, that does research on Familial Dysautonomia.

Although my past profession was as a speech pathologist/

audiologist, I was unable to help Dylan speak. Every day, I would try and use my knowledge to help him, but nothing worked. All I could do was love him. I decided that if I couldn't help him, I could help other children. I initiated a "Mitzvah Cap" project with the help of the many talented Hadassah women who belonged not only to the Philadelphia Chapter, but to other groups around the country. We started to knit and crochet hats for children who were losing their hair due to their chemotherapy. This project continued to grow at such a speed that we soon began to make colorful afghans as well. We all knew that few things make you feel better than being wrapped up in a cheery, warm afghan, where every stitch is made with love. Eventually, we added new children's books, and finally medical dolls.

What a project! Dylan was my inspiration and my fellow Hadassah women were there to help. As of this date, we have sent 8000 hats, 2000 blankets, 800 books, and 200 medical dolls, to twenty-three hospitals in eleven states. When our women travel to Israel, they take these items to Hadassah Hospital in Ein Kerem. During the Hadassah Centennial Convention in 2012, many Hadassah women will give these items personally to the children.

And what of Dylan, my inspiration for this project? He loves to watch television, do puzzles, and his interest in computers is growing. He is fourteen years old, and with the help of very special people and devices, he became a Bar Mitzvah in 2010.

Since Dylan cannot speak, in order to prepare for his bar mitzvah he learned to press buttons on a device that would "speak" specific prayers that signified his embrace of this experience. On the day of his simcha, there was not a dry eye in the synagogue.

While Dylan's inability to speak prevents him from expressing the impact that my Cap project has had on him, I do believe he experiences it. Since he and his eight-year-old brother and family live with us, he sees "Bubbie" packaging up all the crocheted items on a regular basis. His brother tells people that I send blankets and hats to kids in hospitals all over. We have traveled to Israel with three of my other grandchildren who were personally impacted by delivering the hats and blankets to the children's pavilion at Ein Kerem.

The combination of Dylan's special place in my life with the influence that Hadassah has made has been life changing, not just for my children, but for the children of so many other mothers I will never know. Because of Dylan, Hadassah has become a way of life for my family as well as for me. We can all see the impact of volunteerism.

Each year, I continue to write to our Jewish community to raise awareness of this Jewish genetic disease. The Hadassah forum has allowed our entire family to speak on this subject and to help others in need. My wish is that all Hadassah members will become Life Members and find their own path of personal involvement. By taking and exploring this path, you can truly experience for yourself what the "Life" in a Hadassah "Life Membership" can mean for you and for others.

✦ ✦ ✦

→ 62 →

Hadassah Saved her Life
By Jacqueline Silverberg

M y special thread began as a newspaper article in *The Jewish Chronicle* of London the summer of 1998. A young girl, Stacey Plax, was in intensive care at Hadassah Ein Kerem Hospital as a result of an accident while visiting Israel.

I placed a call to Norman Brodie, then Executive Director of Hadassah UK, who told me he was in touch with the Plax family. The girl was still in a coma and he gave me daily updates on her condition. Eventually, I would come to meet this family when Stacey's mother, Karen, would attend a Hadassah meeting a few months later. We met and there was instant affection.

A year later, when Stacey was all healed and strong again, she spoke at a breakfast for lawyers and accountants in London:

"When Jaci asked me to say a few words this morning, I wondered what a group of professional men and women would think seeing me in front of them. A young woman of seventeen, without a care in the world except my A-level exams, and who is going to be at Charlotte and Felicity's party next week, so what am I going to wear? Let me tell you what happened to me one sunny day in the Judean desert in the summer of 1998. Whilst on an Israel tour at the age of sixteen, I had the choice of either going on a jeep or going abseilling (what Americans call rapelling). I thought abseiling too dangerous and took the safer choice of the jeep. The jeep had no windows, no seatbelts, and a cloth roof. I don't know what I remember, but the jeep hit something, over-turned, and we went flying. I suffered a head injury, broke some bones in my face, and was knocked unconscious. A helicopter came to save us.

While aboard the helicopter, Professor Uriel Elchalal did an emergency tracheotomy, right there in the desert. We were then airlifted to Hadassah Ein Kerem. Professor Charles Sprung carried out surgery upon arrival. I was in a coma for about six days, remained in intensive care for twelve days, was then transferred to the neurological ward, and remained there for a couple of weeks until being taken to hospital in London."

Words cannot describe the miraculous work that the doctors and nurses carried out at Hadassah. They saved Stacey's life. Her parents, also on holiday in Israel at the time of the accident, were located by Jewish Agency workers. They were driven to Hadassah to be with Stacey. Even though they were tourists, they were treated by the doctors and nurses with immense care, love, and support. Stacey has always felt that she should dedicate her life to Hadassah and raise money for the extraordinary miracles that they carry out on a daily basis.

A year later, Stacey, her co-chair Vicky of Young Hadassah UK, who had also been involved in the accident, and I started The World-Wide Walk for Young Hadassah—a Bridge to Peace through Medicine over the Bridges of London.

Stacey and Vicky wrote letters for sponsorship money. They made phone calls and mustered the troops; all their friends were involved, their synagogue, their parents, and friends. Stacey's father, Julian, drove the car with my soon-to-be husband for the footage of what was to be the promotional video for the Walk. They were truly amazing in their tenacity.

Stacey went with me to Europe a year later, still having some residual damage from the accident—a gentle shyness—which she overcame whenever she spoke about how Hadassah had saved her life and how grateful she was. When I remarried, you can be sure Stacey and Vicky and their parents were guests at our wedding party. As the years have passed, my respect for Stacey has only increased.

After University and her master's degree, she worked at the Transatlantic Institute in Belgium for two years, which was inspired by her internship in Geneva with UN Watch. During this period, Stacey continued to volunteer and speak for Hadassah in many cities, including Vienna and Dusseldorf, and started a Young Hadassah group and a National Convention of Hadassah.

After working in Brussels, she returned to London and then decided to make aliyah to Israel. It was there that she met Ezra Gardner from Chicago, who also made aliyah. Today, she is engaged to be married into this larger Hadassah family. Ezra's uncle is Dan Krakow, the head of Young Judaea. Ezra's grandmother, Miriam Steuerman, was a devoted Hadassah member and treasurer of the

Kenosha Wisconsin Chapter of Hadassah. This thread of Hadassah was and is so interwoven within her life.

Our lives have been blessed by knowing Stacey and we think of her as another granddaughter. On April 2, 2012, we will return to Israel to dance at her wedding.

Thank you, Hadassah, for saving her life and to all the doctors, nurses, staff, and Professor Elchalal, who was there in the Judean desert (Stacey took Ezra to meet Professor Elchalal in July 2011.)

For me, Hadassah has been a part of my life for over four decades and I pride myself as being, many years ago, one of the youngest members of the National Board from Newport News, Virginia to hold a National Portfolio as Co-Chair of Young Leaders and Career Women, leading the current National President Marcie Natan on a Young Leaders Trip to Israel.

✦ ✦ ✦

The Momentum of Training Wheels (Al Galgalim)

By Lauren B. Lev

In 1996, my daughter arrived home from secular nursery school with a paper Seder plate that she had made in school that morning. It was carefully covered in paper Passover symbols: There was the egg, the greens, the salt water and, according to my four-year-old, the "dog food."

"Dog food?" I asked, since we didn't even have a pet.

"Yes," she said, pointing to the dog biscuit-shaped shank bone.

It was time for this unaffiliated family to seek out a little Jewish education. We found exactly what we needed at Hadassah and their Training Wheels program.

At first, since I was unable to get into the program offered in a neighboring Hadassah chapter, I was asked by the president of the Simcha Hadassah Chapter of East Meadow if I would enroll in the program's training lessons and bring the program home to our Long

Island community. It was my first taste of Hadassah as a new member and, although I was concerned, I was excited as well.

As part of the yearlong training program, a dozen families trooped down to my basement to share in the holiday cycle of Jewish celebrations. There, we all learned to sing, eat, and color along with this outline of the program, experimenting with the crafts that my husband beta-tested the night before to determine if he, like the four-year olds, could tackle them. My daughter and tag-along infant/toddler son learned the joys of Shabbat, the significance of Tu B'Shevat, and the inspiration of Shavout. It was a remarkable experience filled with glue, glitter, and laughter.

From there, while two other facilitators in the community took up the effort and ran their own series of Training Wheels sessions, I forged ahead with Wheeling On—bringing older, unaffiliated children, often of mixed marriages, their first taste of Judaism. Our regional president staged a grand graduation at the culmination of the year to recognize our efforts. But that was nothing compared to the life change that was yet to occur.

A young parent in our community brought her autistic young-ster to a series of Training Wheels sessions and recognized that the program needed adaptation for children with special needs. This Hadassah member's dedication and determination resulted in a unique friendship and partnership. I brought my knowledge and working experience on Al Galgalim, she explained the learning and educational realities of her son and others like him. Funding and support allowed for a version of this program to be developed, not just for Long Island, but nationwide.

The grant gave us the ability to expand the program from its original concept and to train other facilitators, not just locally, but at convention. It offered a tangible way to not leave any Jewish child behind, regardless of disability, when it came to Jewish learning. Our work and results were published in a handbook that would be used by other facilitators nationwide.

This was the first time I had ever worked with a philanthropic organization doing something creative that had the potential to touch so many lives. It was a profound moment when the final edition was printed and ready for distribution. It was an even greater moment when this version was put into active use in my own community.

I feel so fortunate to have been able to develop and complete a project that was bigger than me or my personal and professional goals. I was gratified that I was sustained and encouraged every step of the way by the women of Hadassah at the local, regional level in Nassau County, New York, as well as the New York-based national organization. I was amazed at how deep I had to dig in order to discover my tenacity when pressed to meet the varying expectations of many parents and children. How fortunate I was (and still am!) to be part of the possibilities that are Hadassah.

And my once four-year old? All grown up and a Life Member since she became a Bat Mitzvah. Today, she and her student-aide brother act as role models for youngsters preparing their studies and lives within the Jewish community. She has not only spread an understanding of Judaism among 150 local Girl Scouts by guiding/facilitating their efforts to earn Judaic badges, but today she is a religious school teacher at Temple B'nai Torah in Wantagh, NY.

And so it goes, from generation to generation.

✦ ✦ ✦

—✦ 64 ✦—

From Hadassah Member to Registered Nurse at Age 57

By Marian Kaplan

My dear husband of eighteen years, Marcus, was diagnosed with brain cancer when he was only fifty years old. At the time, our two sons, Jonathan and Joshua, were ten and seven years old. Until then, I had been a stay-at-home mom and was preparing to return to my previous career as an elementary school teacher.

Marcus had a rare form of cancer, and the physician who had more success than anyone else treating this kind of tumor was located in Portland, Oregon. For an entire year, we flew there every month from our home in Kansas, in an effort to save his life. With standard chemotherapy and radiation, our doctors had told us that Marcus would only survive fifteen months.

The tumor went into remission for more than three years before it reappeared on the other side of his brain. Again, we made monthly trips to Portland for treatment. Marcus had just finished the year of chemotherapy when I started working part time as office manager at the Greater Kansas City Chapter of Hadassah. As a new Hadassah member myself, not only did I learn about all the projects in both the United States and Israel, but I also got to know many of the wonderful Hadassah members in our community who were a tremendous source of support to my family and me.

During the eight-and-a-half years my husband survived after his initial diagnosis, we were blessed to celebrate our twenty-fifth anniversary and the Bar Mitzvahs of both our sons. When Joshua was still in elementary school, he had once asked me, "How can we thank all the people who helped us while Daddy was sick?" I had answered him by saying, "We can show our thanks by helping others, even if they are not the same people who helped us."

After Marcus passed away, I did a lot of soul-searching about what I wanted to do with the rest of my life. On one of my daily walks in the neighborhood, I thought about how much I would like to return to the excitement of learning on a college campus. I had recently experienced how wonderful it felt to be in such an environment when I took Jonathan, now a high school graduate, to orientation at our local university.

What would I like to study? I have always been interested in medicine, especially since high school when I volunteered and worked at Roswell Park Memorial Institute, a cancer research hospital in my hometown of Buffalo, New York. My pulse began to race as I looked through the college catalog and read about the requirements to receive a nursing degree.

Yes, that evening I decided that I wanted to give back to everyone who had supported us by becoming a registered nurse. But could I succeed in my fifties?

One day, while I was working at the Hadassah office, I happened to see a small article in *Hadassah Magazine* about Elsie Roth, a public health nurse from St. Louis. I read how Elsie conceived the idea of the Sarajevo project, and, with the support of Hadassah, personally helped deliver tons of pharmaceuticals, medical supplies, and clothing to war-torn Bosnia. Elsie started nursing school at age fifty-four, triple chai. I had been hesitating about enrolling in nursing school because of my age, but when I read about Elsie, I remember thinking, "If she can do it, so can I!"

So, at age fifty-four, I used my husband's life insurance benefit and started taking courses in anatomy and physiology at the local community college. I did well and was accepted into the Research College of Nursing in Kansas City, Missouri a short time later. The night before my first day of classes I was so excited that I got only two hours of sleep! In spite of my initial anxiety and rough patches along the way, I worked hard and was able to graduate with a bachelor of science in nursing with honors in three years.

Becoming a nurse at age fifty-seven was the biggest challenge I have ever had in my life. In gratitude to G-d for enabling me to reach my goal, I helped revive the Greater Kansas City Hadassah Nurses Council, a group of about twenty-five registered nurses in our community, and served as its president.

The summer after the official chartering of our Nurses Council, I attended my first Hadassah National Convention at a Disney resort in Orlando, Florida, and met nurses from across the United States with whom I am still friends today. Since that magical time, I have attended six National Conventions and participated in three fantastic Hadassah Nurses Missions to Israel. Currently, I am the advisor to our Nurses Council, serve on the National Hadassah Nurses Council Steering Committee, and am executive vice president of the Greater Kansas City Chapter of Hadassah. In June 2012, I will become the next president of our Chapter, which has close to 1200 members. I will be the first nurse to serve as its president in the ninety-nine years since Henrietta Szold came to Kansas City to start our Chapter.

How amazing it is that my life changed and became so much richer because I read a few, short paragraphs about a Hadassah nurse in our magazine! Elsie showed me that age need not be a barrier to following your dreams. Since my graduation more than ten years ago, in addition to being a volunteer for Hadassah, I have enjoyed using my nursing knowledge to coordinate a medical library and plan continuing medical education for physicians at a local community hospital.

Several years ago, I met Elsie and thanked her for inspiring me to become a nurse at midlife. Tears welled up in her eyes as we hugged each other during the Shabbat kiddush at a local synagogue when I told her my story. Since that special day in my life, we have become dear friends, tied together by our love of nursing, Israel, and Hadassah!

✦ ✦ ✦

65

Hadassah, My Son, and Me
By Jan Secunda

My first connection to Hadassah started when I was a small child in Brooklyn, New York. I always remember my grandmother collecting our old clothes for rummage to take to Hadassah. I didn't know what rummage was or what Hadassah was, but they went together.

I went to a few Hadassah meetings with my mother when I was in my twenties in Rio Rancho, New Mexico. I don't remember if I ever became a member, but I know I never got involved.

Fast forward twenty or so years to 1997. My son, Max, is getting ready for his Bar Mitzvah. I sent my sister a picture of him from my local Jewish newspaper with a caption about his Bar Mitzvah. There was an ad for CYJ Texas on the same page. She called to ask me if, as a Bar Mitzvah gift, he would like to go to camp that summer. He went to CYJ that summer and then to Tel Yehudah through high school. He went to Israel with machon and then spent a few summers as a counselor back at CYJ. He was also very active in the Desert-Mountain Region Young Judaea programs that were happening at that time. He went on every retreat. Some of the kids he became friends with through Young Judaea are still his closest friends today as a young adult. Then he went on Year Course. That sealed the deal. He would be indebted to Hadassah and devoted to Young Judaea for the rest of his life.

During this time, I became a member of Hadassah, but really didn't know any of the other members in the Albuquerque chapter or what they were doing.

One winter, there was a Young Judaea retreat in Albuquerque. I brought my son to the location to meet up with the others who had flown in from around the region. There I ran into the person who was the local Hadassah Youth Commissioner. She told me that they were looking for a new Youth Commissioner. Since my son was the only active Young Judaean in the Albuquerque area, she thought I would be perfect for the job. What could I say?

At first, I only went to a few board meetings a year. Most of them were during the day while I was working. Then I went to a few regional meetings of the Youth Commission. I met some mothers whose children were friends with my son. They were very involved. Little by little, I became more and more involved with our group, chapter, and region. While my son was on Year Course I went on a Hadassah Parents' Tour to visit him and the other Year Course students in Israel. We visited all of the Hadassah projects going on in Israel. What an incredible experience. I am now the president of Hadassah of Greater Albuquerque and have just made my soon-to-be daughter-in-law a Life Member. Young

Judaea and Hadassah have certainly been part of the driving force for Jewish continuity in my family. I'm hopeful that the legacy will continue.

✦ ✦ ✦

66

The Sun Shines at Night, Too!

By Helen F. Lodge

Following my conversion to Judaism, I was given a year's membership in Hadassah. I was engrossed in my profession as a healthcare food service administrator, and volunteering for non-profits, leaving little time for other activities or much thought to Hadassah.

Then, I lost my soul mate to death. Grief, I knew, is the price we pay for loving. I found solace in Judaism and the warm friendships within my synagogue and my community. I had taken a leave from my profession during his illness and, subsequently, accepted various avenues of volunteerism to "keep me busy."

I received a phone message from the local Hadassah Nominating Committee chairman, just leaving her name and phone number. I was out of town and could have waited until returning home a week later. No, she is a dear lady, I told myself. Call her. A thin thread was about to change my life. My beloved had said, "Some day they will ask you to be president of that organization," to which I laughed. I made the call, was stunned, and awed. With his prophecy coming to fruition, I asked a few questions about Hadassah and its mission. I was referred to the book, *It Takes a Dream*. It was a cold, rainy night, yet I found a bookstore and the book. Halfway through the night and the book, it was, "Yes, Yes! I want to be a part of this organization." I was aware that the sun was about to "come out" as a result of "that" night.

I was installed as the chairman of my professional licensing board, president of the Hadassah chapter, and president of the Symphony League within two days of each other.

I knew I could manage all three, but what I did not know was that my life would be changed forever by my involvement in Hadassah.

I attended the national convention in New York. I was sold on the mission and those who fulfilled it. The local Hadassah chapter held its first "Taste of Jewish Cuisine," a fundraiser bringing an awareness of Hadassah to the community. Marlene Post, Hadassah's president, came to speak at the University of Charleston. The event was attended by the Governor and First Lady of West Virginia and, again, created an awareness of the organization. Stepping out of the box, a project was launched jointly with West Virginia Tobacco Free. I was the editor of the newsletter and featured in "Jewish Women Who Make a Difference." Wow! There were so many stellar achievers.

In August 2001, I participated in the first Eishet Mitzvah in Israel. On the Haas Promenade, overlooking the gravesite of Henrietta Szold in the valley below, I experienced the warm sun and the wind kissing my face—or was it my departed soul mate? Whatever, the experience and the bonding with my Hadassah sisters solidified my commitment to Hadassah and Judaism.

Another thin thread—while there, a pizza parlor bombing took place. Hadassah was not deterred! We held the outdoor ceremony that evening, where our president, Bonnie Lipton, brought chills when she reported that upon her arrival at the Hadassah Hospital, she was told that "none of your people were injured." She replied, "These are all my people." What an impact! I visited the kibbutz where my beloved had practiced medicine for a year. I had visited the kibbutz with him, but, now alone, I felt a kindred spirit with the land and those he so loved.

During difficult times, I recall the early Hadassah days, the day of my Eishet Mitzvah, and the peace that both provide me. It sustains me and is often the wind beneath my wings as I continue with Hadassah and its mission. I am the chapter's co-president as we celebrate the 100 years of Hadassah, with significant events planned.

✦ ✦ ✦

My Elevator Story

By Fredi Brown

I t was July 2000, and I was attending my first-ever national
Hadassah convention in Los Angeles, California. I didn't know
many people attending, but I was excited to get my first taste of the
national level of Hadassah.

At some point during a break, I entered an elevator to go up
to my room. A woman in the elevator was wearing her badge that
read, "Linda Block," and I could see that she was from Houston,
Texas. As fate would have it, my son was in the process of moving
to Houston for a job with NASA.

"Oh, my son is moving to Houston this very week," I told her.

She took a look at my name badge and said, "You are from
Desert-Mountain Region. I take care of Rochelle Edelman's son
who lives in Houston [the same region], so I will also take care of
your son as well!" She gave me her name and phone number to pass
along to my son, Aaron.

Being a good Jewish mother, I called my son as soon as I returned home and told him of the encounter. I said to him, "Look, I don't know this woman from a hole in the wall, but she is a Hadassah lady, so I think you can certainly trust her and call her, if, G-d forbid, you need the name of a doctor or something."

Aaron moved to Texas and settled in Clear Lake, a suburb outside of Houston and the home of the Johnson Space Center, commonly known as "Mission Control." Linda, being Linda, invited Aaron over for various holiday occasions, and although it was a bit of a schlep, Aaron did drive to Houston once or twice in the course of his first year there, in order to be with Linda and her family.

About a year later, while getting her nails done, Linda sat next to a young woman named Lisa. Lisa was born and raised in Houston and lived there with her entire family. Naturally, Linda and Lisa began to chitchat, and in the course of the conversation, Lisa informed Linda that she is a speech therapist working in Galveston. The commute to Houston was too long and she was considering finding a condo in Clear Lake.

Linda, being the ever-vigilant Jewish mother, said to Lisa, "So, are you dating anyone?" to which Lisa replied, "No." Of course, Linda's next comment to Lisa was, "Well, I know the nicest young man who is living in Clear Lake. He is a rocket scientist at NASA, and he's Jewish."

Long story short: A few years later, Lisa and Aaron were married, and today are the proud parents of two beautiful daughters, Gabrielle and Alexis.

The moral of the story? Attend the Hadassah national conventions. You never know who you will meet in the elevator!

✦ ✦ ✦

68

An Affirmation of Faith

By Carol Charen

S ome might say that everything happens for a reason, and some may say that this is just not so. I say, I believe that there was a reason and a purpose as to why I had the pleasure of being selected to participate in a Hadassah mission. My story starts with my husband, Bob, being diagnosed with a rare liver disease. No cause, no cure, except for a liver transplant. Not quite fifty years old, his life and our lives depended on a very long donor list on which he could not seem to climb high enough to be selected for transplant.

I remember making the decision to rely on family and friends to care for him and our nine-year-old daughter, Hillary, while I was in Israel. My in-laws in Florida, and the recent death of my dear mother, made my decision difficult. But something that I didn't quite understand at the time made me take this journey. Initially, only the leaders of the mission knew about Bob's illness, just in case I needed to fly home during the trip. Accompanying me on my trip was a very special note written by our daughter. My instruction from her was that I was to place it in the Wall and pray to G-d that he listen to her.

That day will forever be a very special moment for me. As I waited in line to pray at the Wall with all of my Hadassah buddies and our leaders, Judy Saxe and Iris Altschuler, I took out the very large piece of construction paper my daughter had given me. With a reassuring smile, Judy said that the paper was a bit too big to fit in the thin crevices of the Wall. Determined to fulfill my daughter's request, she and Iris helped me tear the paper away, only leaving her message visible. "Dear G-d," it read, "please bring my Daddy a new liver. Thank you." It was then my turn and I placed her note into the wall, repeating to G-d what Hillary had written.

Although it took another three years, with doctors telling me that he would probably die waiting, we never lost hope and finally we got our call that there was a liver for Bob. No one will ever convince me that the reason I was chosen for this mission was anything other than about my Bob.

When my Mom passed away, I had one hundred Hadassah moms taking care of me. When my Bob needed a new liver, I had the support and love of all of my Hadassah buddies and my mission to Israel to save my husband's life.

Every time we hear that someone has gone to Israel, they always say the same thing: "It was life changing." My story is a true affirmation of that and the faith that both my family and I have in Hadassah, the power of prayer, and our beloved Israel.

It has been eight years since that very spiritual morning in Israel and we all continue to be forever grateful!

✦ ✦ ✦

69

The Other Side of the Bus

By Susie Kahn Enteen

Growing up, Hadassah was always a part of my life. My mom was involved in her local chapter and on the regional level. I couldn't wait until I was old enough to be a part of Young Judaea and to eventually go to camp in North Carolina. Who knew that I would be the one to take it all the way—from the local groups, to the regional board, to Camp Judaea, Camp Tel Yehudah, Year Course, and Hamagshimim in college. And yes, eventually, to becoming a third-generation Hadassah Life Member, president, and more. Being a part of Hadassah and Young Judaea played such a huge role of my life. I would even go so far as to say that my experiences in Hadassah and its youth programs truly helped to shape my feelings towards Israel and being Jewish.

In 2000, I was part of a delegation chosen to represent Hadassah on the Young Women's Mission trip to Israel. Filled with excitement, we arrived in Israel and went straight from the airport to our tour bus. This was my fourth trip to Israel, and although I was thrilled to have the opportunity to return with this group of fabulous women, something just didn't feel right. It was as if I wasn't meant to see Israel from the inside of a bus—I longed to be on the other side, to be part of the scenery. As we drove across the country, the other women chatted and excitedly recapped the different experiences that we were having. I found myself staring out the window at the houses, the schools, the shopping centers— at the life that was on the other side of the glass. I wanted to be the lady pushing the stroller across the street on the way to the grocery store, or the one picking up her mail outside of her apartment building. I didn't want to be walking around with a camera in my pocket and a map in my bag. "Tourist" was not a label that fit.

Towards the end of our trip, when I was asked where I saw myself in five years, I felt a rock in the pit of my stomach. The intention was to get us to think of what we were going to be contributing to the organization upon returning from our mission. The trouble was, I didn't see myself growing and moving ahead in Hadassah. Instead, I felt as if my future held something different, something more. The desire to live in Israel was stirring inside me. Little did I know that feeling would eventually become a reality.

Five years later, my husband, Coby, asked the question, "Why not aliyah?" and I just didn't have an answer. All of my thoughts kept pointing in the direction of us getting back to Israel, of going home.

In 2006, Coby and I, with two young boys in tow, made aliyah. We longed to raise our family in a place where our neighbors weren't trying to convince us to hang Christmas lights every December. We knew there was something special here, a different taste to living. We currently live in Modiin, a town in the center of Israel, halfway between Jerusalem and Tel Aviv. Our weekend getaways vary between the Dead Sea and bed and breakfast places on Kibbutzim around the country. Our kids speak Hebrew with their friends and English at home. We have regular picnics in the Jerusalem forest and in other beautiful parks near our home. Most exciting, we expanded our family in 2009 when our daughter was born (fittingly!) at Hadassah Hospital.

To this day, my heart often melts as she, now three, jumps up and down excitedly when she sees a passing bus, one similar to the tour bus that I rode twelve years ago. I now know how it feels to be on the other side of the bus, on the right side of it for me. I'm finally part of the scenery, living my life, raising my children, and being stared at by some other tourists as they ride past and wonder what my life is like, at home, here in Israel.

✦ ✦ ✦

70

Full Circle at Hadassah

By Adam Jenshil

It was Summer 2000. I was responsible for Young Judaea's summer high school Israel Program, Machon, a five-week leadership program that is supported by Hadassah and scholarship funds to Young Judaea. The granddaughter of the wonderful family who had donated the neonatal unit at Hadassah Mt. Scopus was a participant on the program, and during her time traveling around Israel, it was decided that she should tour the unit. She was given the VIP treatment, and I recall that she was a little embarrassed by the attention given to her as she met doctors and nurses and saw the amazing work that was carried out within the unit to help the tiny babies there.

I accompanied her on this visit, and while it was interesting, it was a bit unsettling as well. At that time, my wife was pregnant with twins. Knowing that twins are often born early, I hoped I would not need the emergency services of the neonatal unit.

Two and a half months before her due date, my wife Dganit, began having contractions. In an effort to prolong the pregnancy for the health of the twins, she was admitted to Hadassah Har HaTzofim, where they managed to hold off labor for a month. I remember visiting Dganit in the hospital every day, watching two heartbeats on two monitors, nervous every time one heartbeat would slow, even the slightest bit.

One day while I was visiting, we laughed over the irony of my recent visit to the neonatal unit with the Young Judaea group participant. While we still hoped we wouldn't have need of it, there was something comforting knowing it was there, just in case.

At thirty-four weeks, we were already feeling better. The twins had time for their little lungs to get stronger, and they were much closer to full term. We were still hoping for another month, but when one of the monitors showed a dangerously low heartbeat, they rushed Dganit off for an emergency C-section. I was not allowed to accompany her into the operating theatre. I remember pacing around the waiting room like a father from the 1950s, praying that everything would be fine, that the twins and Dganit would all be OK.

After what seemed like an eternity, the doctors brought out two incubators, each holding one of our tiny, premature twins. I only got to see them for a few seconds, tears of relief in my eyes, before I went in to see Dganit in recovery. I remember a surreal feeling as I gazed down at these tiny beings who had finally entered our world. I split my time between visiting with my wife in recovery, and visiting with my gorgeous twins. Our son, Lee, weighing 3.7 pounds, was hosted by the very neonatal unit I had seen on my tour. It had gone from a place I hoped I'd never see, to a place for which I was deeply grateful. Lee spent about a week or so there, before moving to the nursery. Our daughter, later to be named Maya, weighed four pounds. She spent a few days in the neonatal unit and then was moved to the nursery.

Today our children are happy, healthy, eleven-year-olds with no knowledge whatsoever of their early start to the world.

A few years after the visit with the Young Judaea student, and after my own experience with my twins, I was able to meet the family of that same high school student, the ones who had donated the funds to create the neonatal unit, when they came to Israel, and accompanied them on the tour of the unit that they had made possible.

I wonder how many people have the opportunity to stand in the spot where their own children received emergency, life-saving, medical care and to thank the family that donated the money to make that care possible?

A year and half ago, our son Ari was born, but this time at Hadassah Ein Kerem, as we now live in Tzur Hadassah, which is closer to Hadassah Ein Kerem. He was also born after an emergency C-section, when his heart rate decreased to a dangerous rate, but this time I was allowed to be there and talked to Dganit through-out the operation. Ari was larger than his older brother and sister, so he only spent a few days in the newborn unit and then enjoyed another few in the Hotel before we went home!

Having met my wife while we were Young Judaea Year Course counselors at the former Hadassah Youth Center at Mt Scopus, and now being the director of that same program of which I was also a participant in the late 80s, it is clear that professionally and personally, I owe so much to Hadassah. When we have medical issues on our Young Judaea Israel programs, we want them to be treated in Hadassah hospitals. Every time I go to the hospitals, I think of my own personal, successful experiences there and how grateful I am to Hadassah for providing such top quality medical care to my family and to our Young Judaea participants in Israel.

✦ ✦ ✦

+ *71* +

Hadassah and Advocacy

By Rebecca Krasnegor

T here was no surprise that I would be involved in Hadassah. It might just as well have been genetic. After all, I had grown up in a strong Zionist atmosphere with my mother, president of her Hadassah chapter, and my father, active in early American Zionist organizations. I counted pennies and nickels when Aunt Kate opened the JNF Blue Boxes and watched as she inscribed Jewish National Fund certificates with her beautiful handwriting for the many donors. I sat quietly as my mother conducted chapter meetings in our living room. I attended a Zionist camp where visiting day was a fundraiser for Youth Aliyah. I was active in Young Judaea, and had experienced Israel with the Machon Katit-Summer Institute. I was primed to be active in Hadassah.

I was a founding member of our Ben Gurion Group of the Northern Virginia Chapter and held many portfolios. Later, when we formed the Potomac Chapter, I was there in many capacities.

It was not until I attended an event with Hadassah, A Day on the Hill, that I experienced a different side of Hadassah. I had earned a master's degree in political sociology, but this was the event that merged my interests and background. It afforded me the opportunity to make Hadassah's positions, such as stem cell research and the genetic non-discrimination legislation, relevant to my representatives.

One such meeting with Hadassah Leadership Academy women and Senator Kennedy's health assistant lasted for over an hour, with the women voicing personal stories relating to genetic testing and how it would affect their lives. Within a month, the legislation on Genetic Non-Discrimination was passed by Congress. These Hadassah women had a direct impact on our legislative process.

What pride I experienced when former Senator Elizabeth Dole noticed my red folder and expressed her admiration for our organization. Volunteering at the Washington Action Office gave me the opportunity to teach our women how to advocate. It was gratifying to lead groups of women to experience the same feelings of empowerment in Hadassah's name.

Hadassah and advocacy filled my life and gave me confidence leading to greater expressions of leadership.

✦ ✦ ✦

✦ 72 ✦

My Second Journey

By Diane Hunt

I n 1980, I converted to Judaism. For my entire life, Jewish people have been very special to me. I had met a wonderful man and wanted to know what background this person came from. He was Jewish. We did not stay together, but I had a friend where I worked who was converting to Judaism so she could marry. During our conversations, she told me about the lessons she was taking at the Union for Reform Judaism in New York City. I looked into the classes and was told I had to have a sponsoring rabbi.

I chose a congregation in the city and my journey began. I attended two different rabbis' classes on different nights, and when the courses were over, I made my decision to convert. It was not a popular decision in my family, which at this time included my nineteen-year-old son, but in my heart this is what I wanted. I had a private ceremony in the Village Temple in N.Y.C.. Dear Rabbi Dennis N. Math presided. I had little mementos to give each invited guest, had my conversion papers framed, and began my journey as a Jew.

I went to services every week and participated in the rituals associated with Pesach, Sukkot, Yom Kippur, and all of the other holy days. I remember my first trip to Borough Park for my Lulav and Etrog; it was so exciting! I was just thrilled to be mong my people. I would go to the Lower East Side for pickles and bialys; I frequented Judaica stores and began to build my Jewish Library that Rabbi Math had recommended.

My life as a Jew increased with every passing day. The only time I ever fretted was after September 11, 2001. I live in Bay Ridge where there is a large Arab population. That fear didn't last long as I bought a larger Star of David and replaced the one around my neck with the larger one.

As my knees are bad, reading became my major way to connect and learn about other Jews. I wanted to be involved, but I'm not too imaginative and I couldn't figure out how I could do anything. Then one day, there was a notice in the local paper about a meeting of a group called Hadassah. Aha! Here was my chance to get involved in more Judaism! I just couldn't wait for the meeting that, conveniently, was less than a block away from where I lived.

Roni Schwartz of Hadassah was the force behind this effort, and she had found Shelley Wine, who was to be the first president of the newly revitalized Bay Ridge Chapter of Hadassah. It took a while, but gradually, the chapter started to grow. We needed officers and I became membership chair. I did that for a couple of years, and was then asked to join the board of the Brooklyn Region as recording secretary, which I am still on. I am also the Jewish National Fund Chair for Brooklyn Region.

The Bay Ridge Chapter had no place to hold meetings, and I loved going to meetings, so one day I went to a meeting of another chapter. I loved it and transferred in. Medinah needed a treasurer so, here I am ladies! I also perform other little tasks for Medinah as needed. I am an adopted member of Bay Ridge and Park Slope Chapters, where I also perform small tasks for them as needed.

Two years ago, there was a huge fire in my apartment building. Even though my side of the building didn't burn, water damage escalated to mold and mildew. I lost almost everything, except what survived when the firefighters threw things out the bedroom window. Emotionally, I could not go back in to search after the building was deemed safe to do so, but I was able to tell some friends what I wanted and the location. One of the things I wanted was my conversion papers. I walked out of the burning building with a dress, two pieces of underwear (it was 11:45 p.m.), and my pocketbook. I didn't even take my cane. I was in a fog.

The city put me up in a shelter room. I had a bed, a four-drawer chest, and a small fridge. Well, can you guess who came to my rescue? My Hadassah sisters, that's who. These wonderful women took up a collection for me that allowed me to buy the everyday things I needed. The supplies to do laundry, keep my body clean, my breath fresh, summer clothes, a winter coat, shoes—you get the picture—all had to be purchased. Thank G-d for these women.

I am a valued member of this huge Hadassah organization, where I've never felt swallowed up, where I love what we do as an organization, and the women that make it happen. As I try to think how many years I've been a member, I really can't remember. It hasn't been all that long, but it feels like I've had a home with my dear Hadassah sisters forever!

My journey continues every day.

✦ ✦ ✦

73

Hadassah Made A Difference

By Rita Fuchs

My story started years ago, when I was living in New York with my family. We were blessed with best friends, Mario and Sylvia Kravietz. Mario's family had run away from Poland just before World War II. Sylvia was very active in Hadassah and became a Woman of Valor She loved Hadassah, and I loved her.

Some 14 years ago when they decided to move to Florida, we soon followed suit.

Unfortunately Sylvia and Mario both died in a horrific traffic accident. After our shock of losing them both, I realized there was a Hadassah chapter in our development. I immediately joined in tribute to my dear friend, Sylvia. But something was still missing in my life and I didn't know what it was.

One day, as I was looking at our Hadassah bulletin, I saw an ad for a class on learning to read Hebrew. I jumped at the chance. I spoke to Goldie Bernstein and asked to be part of the class she was forming. I pestered her to make sure she wouldn't forget me. What a blessing that class turned out to be. I met four women who would turn out to be lifelong friends. We learned to read Hebrew, and became Bat Mitzvah (Eshet Mitzvah). We began to study the Torah, reading the Five Books of Moses, reading the Siddur. After that, we began to read about our history. How could we understand that every time we dove into our history it would lead to the thirst for more knowledge? Prior to meeting with this group, I knew nothing of my Jewish faith or of our history.

So here we are, years later, a firm friendship in place. We still meet once a week to study and share our lives with one another. We lost Goldie years ago but we know she would be so proud of what we have accomplished. For us, Hadassah was the key. I became co-vice president of membership four years ago, registering close to 300 new members during our centennial year. We work to build Hadassah as a state-of-the-art living institution so that we can be part of connecting our Jewish history to the Jewish future.

My dear mother always told me to look for the open doors in my life. Hadassah was that open door. Thank you, Hadassah.

✦ ✦ ✦

74

The Missing Link

By Lonye Debra Rasch

I t was many summers ago—about 1992.

I was a young leader in Hadassah, attending the pre-convention Hadassah Shabbat morning services, led by two Hadassah pros, Barbara Goldstein and Barbara Spack. They offered me the opportunity to have an Aliyah to the Torah at the service, which I graciously accepted.

I had never had an Aliyah before. As a child, I went to Yeshiva and, at that time, there were no Bat Mitzvahs for Yeshiva girls. I don't remember thinking much about it at all. This was just the way it was—something the boys did.

My parents belonged to an Orthodox temple, so there was never a time when women were called to the Bima during Shabbat services. As a young adult, I didn't belong to a synagogue; so, here, again, no opportunity to have an Aliyah.

That morning at the Hadassah convention, I walked up to the

Torah, a little nervous, but not too concerned because I was fluent in Hebrew and knew I'd have no trouble reciting the blessings over the Torah. But what I wasn't prepared for was the feelings I experienced after the Aliyah. I remember saying to myself, "Wow! This was really special! I can't believe I've been denied this spiritual experience all these years!"

I once heard former Hadassah President June Walker speak to a group of Hadassah women and inspire us with the words, "Hadassah is the address to fulfill yourself as an American Jewish woman." When we do things we didn't know we could do, or didn't even know we wanted to do, we add a dimension to ourselves as Americans, as Jews, or as women. We discover a new side of ourselves—and, sometimes, as in my case, new spiritual experiences. Being part of Hadassah gave me an opportunity I had never considered—to have an Aliyah—which, ultimately, led me to learn to read Torah.

In time, I joined an egalitarian Conservative synagogue, where our wonderful cantor taught a class in Torah trope. It was difficult for me, but I loved it and practiced until I could get it right. I read Torah about every six weeks in my synagogue. As I continued to chant the Torah, it brought me into a very close bond with my Judaism and my heritage—culminating in my reading the Ten Commandments one Shabbat morning. I recall the moment that hundreds of congregants stood up as I read those pivotal words of the Torah. That was a "heady" experience, which brought home to me so vividly the meaning of *D'or L'Dor*, of Jewish continuity.

And I have Hadassah to thank for lighting the spark that led me on this journey.

✦ ✦ ✦

75

My Jerusalem, My Hadassah

By Barbara Sofer

I live in Jerusalem. I vote in Jerusalem. And I work in this remarkable city of Jerusalem. My office is in the center of Jerusalem, Hadassah's Office in Israel, on Rav Kook Street.

I was at my office on January 27, 2002, a winter day with especially clear blue skies. My cousins Mark and Rena were in town visiting from New York. Theirs wasn't just a tour. It was a sort of pilgrimage of thanksgiving.

Four months earlier, on September 11, Mark was at work early, in his law office, in the Twin Towers. When the first plane struck, he started walking down 38 flights of stairs. He was in the stairwell so he didn't hear the announcement that everything was under control, he could go back to his desk.

And he was already in the lobby of the building when the second plane struck. He left his car, and took the last subway out. By the time Rena called in a panic, Mark was safely out of the building.

They were grateful, and they wanted to express their thanks to G-d here in Jerusalem. They brought their daughters Lauren, fifteen, and Jamie, twelve, newly Bat Mitzvah'd, with them.

On the last day of the visit, the girls wanted to buy Israeli sandals downtown near my office. We made a plan to meet after the teenagers had finished their shoe shopping. Anyone who has shopped with teenagers understands why.

Mark phoned me from Freiman and Bein, a shoe store on Jaffa Road, near King George Street, less than two minutes from my office. I grabbed my phone in one hand and in the other a manuscript I was editing to return to Mark's stepmother in New York. It was the story of her rescue in the Holocaust in Berlin by a woman named Maria.

I remember looking up at the blue sky and thinking what a magnificent day it was. I felt ebullient and started skipping towards my cousins. Suddenly, a blast rocked me backwards. A black cloud rose above the area of the shoe store. I was still far enough away so that I wasn't hurt. The street was instantly closed and pedestrians held back. I begged the police to no avail to let me through so I could find my cousins.

When my mind cleared, I made my way to a small hospital downtown. There I first found Mark. Rena and Lauren had been taken to another hospital. Jamie, the twelve-year-old, was supposedly in the next room in the same hospital as Mark, but I didn't recognize her at first. Her face was distorted; her eye was bulging.

The downtown hospital doesn't have an eye department. Jamie needed the internationally recognized experts at Hadassah

Hospital. Soon Jamie and I were riding together in an ambulance, sirens screaming. I kept promising her that everything would be all right. At last, we arrived at Hadassah Hospital. Jamie was hurriedly carried into the emergency room.

Until that moment, I'd been the calm one. But once on the terra firma of Hadassah Hospital, I started to lose it. I demanded immediate care for Jamie. Where in the world was the ophthalmologist, I wanted to know? A young woman tapped me on the shoulder. "Hello," she said. "I'm here." I looked at her name tag and I understood. My cousin Jamie had been blown up by a young Palestinian woman, a medic who entered Jerusalem on an ambulance. She strapped a pack of explosives on her back, killed an old man, and injured 100 others, Jews and Arabs. She also killed herself. Her head rolled nearby where my cousins stood, on Jaffa Road. At Hadassah Hospital, the ophthalmologist was also a young Palestinian woman. She would repair Jamie's sight.

There we have it. On one hand, the wantonness and the waste. On the other, the hope and the healing.

We have to choose.

Which will it be? Choose life, urges G-d in the Bible. Choose the blessing, not the curse. We will, with the help of G-d, the true Builder of Jerusalem, as we say in Psalm 147, the One who must ultimately bind up our sorrows.

✦ ✦ ✦

Kaddish

By Sharon Cadoff

My story is not unique, but just one in a multitude of what a yahrzeit at Hadassah can mean to a family, or a group of people.

In October, 1999, the diagnosis was confirmed—metastatic prostate cancer. We dried our tears and turned to the necessities—medical research and our personal papers. Joel and I had written into our wills "before distribution of any assets, after my demise, I direct that my trustee establish a yahrzeit on my behalf at Hadassah Hospital, Ein Karem, Israel."

Yes, we belonged to a synagogue, yes our children would say kaddish for us, but we wanted prayers to be said in the Abbell Chapel, a place we visited on our first trip to Israel, which was, ironically, Hadassah's Winter in Netanya program held during Operation Desert Shield. We were awed and inspired by the beauty and serenity of the chapel. The decision for our yahrzeit to be remembered here was a promise we made to ourselves.

Joel succumbed after a valiant battle in November 2003. In May 2004, I was installed as the president of the Lower New York State Region.

Little did we know then that I would not be with my family on Joel's first yahrzeit. I would be on a Hadassah President's Mission, with people I barely knew and who barely knew me.

Upon my arrival in Israel, I checked the agenda and saw that we would be at Ein Kerem on the afternoon preceding Joel's yahrzeit. On my request, Marlene Post arranged for me to see the yahrzeit book and I asked if it would be possible to chant kaddish in the chapel. Most of my colleagues were unaware at this point that we would gather after lunch in order to recite kaddish. They were shopping in the hospital gift shop when Marlene gathered them and told them of my desire, my need, to say kaddish and the need for a minyan in order to say the prayer. They dropped their gifts, and came to share my prayers and pain. As I chanted those ancient words, *Yiskadol, Vyiskadash,* I was no longer alone. In that special place, on that special day, their tears flowed with mine, they became not only my colleagues, but my family.

Your story may be different, but as I looked up at the sunlight streaming through those famous windows, I knew it was a double mitzvah: I was in Eretz Yisroel at that moment, and in future years, Joel would be remembered there.

✦ ✦ ✦

— 77 —

"It's A Hadassah Kidney!"

By Katie Edelstein & Belle Simon

Think back to the day when you received your first driver's license and you were asked whether or not you wanted to become an organ donor. When Katie was just a teen, she did sign, but she never would have predicted that one day she would donate a kidney while she was alive.

Katie recalls, "During the months leading up to the transplant, many people asked me why I was doing this at the age of 55. Why would I put my own health in jeopardy—and possibly the health of my children in the rare instance that one of them might need a kidney transplant? Why would I do this for someone I barely knew?"

For Katie, the answer was simple. Her years of involvement in Hadassah had taught her so much about Tzedakah and Tikkun Olam, and the importance of helping those less fortunate. "How many times in life do we have the opportunity to make such a profound difference in someone else's life? Someone was in dire need of something that I had to give, and I was the only one available right then to help. I could give something precious to another human being and change her life completely. Why wouldn't I do it?"

Belle's story began in the spring of 2001 when her internist informed her that he had been watching her creatinine level rise, an indicator of reduced kidney function. Belle learned that she had a progressive disease that would ultimately result in kidney failure. Dialysis and a possible kidney transplant were in her future. She learned that she would not be eligible to register for a kidney transplant until she was actually on dialysis, and she also learned that her brother was not a match.

In May 2003, at age sixty-five, Belle began dialysis and the process to be listed for a transplant at Mount Sinai Hospital in New York, where the wait for a kidney was then five to six years. As a winter resident of Florida, she also began the process to become listed at Jackson Memorial Hospital in Miami, since the wait for a cadaver kidney there was only eighteen months.

Although dialysis kept Belle healthy, there were restrictions placed on her life. She spent three hours, three days a week, tethered to a dialysis machine. Her diet was restricted, and she was unable to travel freely.

Meanwhile, Katie had gone to the Hadassah Midwinter National Board Meeting in January, 2004. It was there that then National President June Walker announced that Belle, a long time Hadassah member, required a kidney transplant. Katie leaned over to her friend and said that she was interested in donating her kidney. Her friend's response was, "What, are you crazy? Save it for your kids!" But that response was not enough to deter Katie from quietly approaching Belle and indicating that she would like to be her organ donor, a response that Belle had clearly not anticipated. When Katie was asked if she wanted to go home and first discuss it with her husband, she said no—not because she didn't value her husband's input, but because she knew he would support her in any decision she made.

Of course, the first step was to ascertain if, indeed, Katie was a match. Miraculously, it turned out that she was, and the women learned in mid-March that the transplant surgery would take place on May 11, 2004, almost one year from the date that Belle's dialysis had begun.

"I actually looked forward with great anticipation to May 11," Katie recalls. "I remember the special people who were by my side, before and after the transplant. I remember the thoughts that were spinning around in my head. I remember the feeling I had when I awoke after the operation, and the joy and relief I felt when I heard the doctors exclaim that the kidney was working. 'Of course it's working,' I responded. 'What do you expect . . . it's a Hadassah kidney!'"

Since that time, both Katie and Belle have appeared at countless Hadassah and non-Hadassah events to talk about the benefits of organ donation, the imperative to sign an organ donor card and to talk to family members about becoming an organ donor. Both have spoken to many people who seek advice and moral support from those who have gone through the process.

Two weeks after the organ transplant, Belle and Katie were united to celebrate before Katie returned home to Bellingham,

Washington. At that celebration, Belle's granddaughter Rachel, then ten years of age, gave Katie an illustrated poem that she had written especially for her. Still sitting proudly on Katie's desk, it reads:

Dear Katie,

To make a sunflower grow older and stronger, you must take care of it. For my grandma to grow older is one thing, but growing stronger is another thing to worry about. You know to start to feel strong, we need our organs. You planted a seed in our hearts, as well as lending an organ to my grandma. You made a sprout appear. You made the Simon garden grow by donating just one seed.

Rachel's words made Katie realize that what she had done was not for Belle alone, but also for all those who loved and cared about Belle and would have been lost without her.

Katie and Belle are forever linked through Hadassah and by the courageous and generous act of the kidney donation, and they celebrate each anniversary of the transplant with love and excitement. It is the actualization of the principle of Pikuah Nefesh, the Jewish value of saving life.

This is a Hadassah story!

✦ ✦ ✦

78

Tears of Sorrow, Tears of Joy

By Adrienne Fishman

S everal months before our Hadassah mission to Israel in 2005, I read the book, *If A Place Can Make You Cry*, by Rabbi Daniel Gordis, his account of making aliyah with his family and living through the Intifada. Throughout the entire mission, I was haunted by this title.

Israel made me (and often, my stoic husband) cry from profound sadness as well as ecstatic happiness. Fifteen minutes after we checked into our Tel Aviv hotel the first day, the sirens went off to mark Yom HaShoah, the day to remember the Holocaust victims. We stood on our balcony overlooking the street, the Tayellet, and the Mediterranean Sea, and watched as everything came to a halt. Drivers got out of their cars, pedestrians stood still, and the siren reminded us never to forget.

A few days later, we came to Yom Hazikaron, Memorial Day for the soldiers who died and for those killed in terror attacks.

The War of Independence, the Sinai War, the Six-Day War, the Yom Kippur War, the Lebanon War, the Intifada—so many wars in fifty-seven years. No wonder this place can make you cry. Our group assembled at a seaside ceremony at Hadassah Neurim Youth Village to mark this solemn occasion, and at 8 p.m. the siren again sounded. Everyone stood with heads bowed. Torches were lit, poems were read, songs of hope were sung. On a big screen, photos were continuously projected of the fifty-five former students of Neurim, so young, who lost their lives fighting for Israel, and of a former student and a teacher who were killed in terrorist attacks. Everyone recited Kaddish, and El Maleh Rachamim was chanted. The sadness was palpable and there wasn't a dry eye in the place, but the evening ended with the singing of Hatikvah, "The Hope."

Yom Hazikoron came to a close with a spectacular national ceremony on Mount Herzl, ushering in Yom Ha'atzmaut (Independence Day). We watched the ceremony from the new Menachim Begin Center in Jerusalem on a giant screen, with simultaneous translation on headsets. We felt like ambassadors! Twelve speakers lit torches, a fabulous choir sang, and a young dance troupe performed. When they got into formation for the number fifty-seven, Israel's new age, the tears of joy were flowing! Fireworks went off and it was time to celebrate!

Our group went to a Moroccan restaurant in Jerusalem. Tables were laden with stuffed grape leaves, borekas, olives, humus, pita, roasted peppers, marinated mushrooms, and other Mid-East specialties. There was music and joyous dancing that lasted for hours. In between, we were served a four-course dinner, with the main course carried around the dining room in huge kettles with sparklers ablaze!

We didn't want the party to end, but when it did, many of us went to Safra Square to witness Jerusalemites of all ages dancing in the public square until the wee hours.

Another opportunity for tears of joy was during our visit to Hadassah Hospital. At Ein Kerem, we kvelled as we heard about the work of our doctors, nurses, and social workers. These gifted healers work not only with the body, but also with the spirit and emotions of the patients and their families. We heard Marlene Post, past National President, remind us that all Jews are one family, and all Hadassah is one family. We met a terror victim, Steve Auerbach, a big, strapping *oleh* from New Jersey. Steve, who worked in the security field, spotted a terrorist getting onto his bus and tried to shoot him, but got shot first and was rendered a quadraplegic. He lauds Hadassah Hospital for the care he received, and says if he had to do it all over, he would do the same thing.

We were at Yad Vashem, the Holocaust memorial, on our last day. If one place can make you cry, this was it. The new museum, which opened in March, grips you by the heart and the throat so that you can hardly breathe and cannot speak at all by the time you've walked along the maze of exhibits designed to herd the visitor, just as the victims were herded.

The last night of the trip was very emotional for me; the culmination of a very moving week combined with the sadness of knowing the mission would be over the next day. We were at Hadassah College of Technology in Jerusalem, which now trains over 1,500 optometrists, speech and hearing professionals, photographic technicians, and chefs each year.

We were treated to a sumptuous buffet prepared by our

Culinary Department students. Dressed in their chefs' attire, they handled the affair with great poise and skill. During the dinner, we were asked if anyone from the group wanted to come to the microphone to share his or her feelings about the tour. Many people came forward, including my husband, to express how moved they were by what they had experienced during the week, and to thank Hadassah for such a high quality tour. One of the men became a Hadassah Associate right then, and one of the women made her granddaughter a Life Member and her not-yet-born grandson, whom she had just learned about two days before, a Hadassah Associate. My husband made me a Keeper of the Gate!

We felt that our Hadassah mission was the trip of a lifetime, from the welcoming *Baruchim ha'ba'im* (blessed are those who come), to the parting greeting *Tseischem le'sholom* (go in peace). Only in Israel!

✦ ✦ ✦

— 79 —

All Together Now
By Lois Mirsky

"My feeling is that the desire to learn and educate oneself is inherent in the Jewish culture." —BARBARA G.

N o one in our Machon study group knew anything about "thin threads" in 2005, but six years later, our thin thread has matured into a strong, thick thread that binds us together, through our passion for Judaism, for Israel, for Hadassah, and for opportunities to study and debate.

"Now that we know about the power of a thin thread, we agree that this thread, which grows stronger each year, is what keeps us together as Jewish women and as friends. Our connection is remarkable." —MYRA G.

It all began around my kitchen table on a hot summer day in 2005, where six members of the Plymouth Massachusetts Chapter of Hadassah gathered to talk about forming a Machon Hadassah Leadership Academy study group. Susan M. had been inspired after hearing a regional Hadassah leader speak emotionally about how great a study group would be for our chapter.

We were excited about having an opportunity for study through Hadassah. As we sipped ice tea and talked for a few hours, the six of us agreed that we were ready to adopt the Machon curriculum.

"I never imagined when we started that it would become so much a part of my life," says Susan. "I love the mix of ages, backgrounds, and walks of life."

We invited others to join us through "Connections," our monthly e-newsletter. Fifteen Hadassah members indicated they were interested.

During the first year, we weathered the ups and downs of growth along with personality clashes, power issues, and individual needs and wants—much like any group goes through in the process of growing.

After a year, our group dwindled to twelve participants. By the next year, there were eight dedicated study group members, all of whom continue to meet monthly as we begin 2012.

What's wonderful about this group is not just our basic curriculum, but our acknowledgment as Jewish women about how differently we grew up.

Growing up Jewish has been at the core of many of our conversations. "I love being Jewish," says Ronnie H. "I am proud of our history and feel a sense of belonging, even though I was not immersed in Judaism when I was growing up. I am now and I have a strong commitment to Machon."

What fun we have at our monthly meetings. We eat, of course. We share our experiences as Jewish women, and we venture into subjects that require thought and open-mindedness. We have studied Hadassah curriculums with titles ranging from, "Torah Study: So You Think Your Family Has Problems," "Israel and Zionism, " "They Lit the Way," and "Extraordinary Women Leading Extraordinary Lives," to mention just a few.

We have been challenged and we have learned. "When I walk into one of our Machon meetings," writes Ronnie L., "there is a feeling of total relaxation. There is always food, which surely feeds the Jewish soul. My mind is always stimulated. The hugs and kisses are genuine. We all know that we are a family of unique women."

Gloria says she has a strong connection to Hadassah because her mother made her a Life Member. "Machon is the thin thread in my life. I appreciate the strong connection with my Judaism that I really don't experience as clearly in any other place and I like being in a group with all Jewish women."

Barbara's feelings sum up what our Machon group is all about: "I joined Hadassah to meet Jewish women who had similar interests in education, health issues, and supporting the State of Israel. Machon has answered all of these needs, and in the process I met a group of very diverse women who have turned into a cohesive group of friends."

Dotty goes one step further. "My Machon experience has motivated me to read more about Jewish history, to listen to the ideas of others, and to continually think about what being Jewish has contributed to who I am today."

The Machon name has been retired and has been replaced

by "Go Forth and Study." The eight women in the Plymouth Massachusetts Chapter of Hadassah will do just that within the context of their passion for Judaism, Israel, and Hadassah.

✦ ✦ ✦

80

All in the Family
By Ellin Yassky

As a young child, the name "Hadassah" was synonymous with "Mom's going to a meeting," or "Mom's going to work at the Hadassah thrift store." All I knew about Hadassah at that point was that it was central to my mother's life and that the women shared great recipes. As I grew older, I began to understand a little more about Hadassah. When I asked, "what *is* Hadassah?" I would get explanations such as, "It's an organization that supports medical care and research in Israel" or "It's a Zionist organization." Given that the State of Israel is only eight years older than I am, it would take me a while to really understand the context of her devotion.

As time went on, I began to have a better understanding of what Hadassah meant to my mother, to our Jewish community, and to women who were connected by this one, driving commitment throughout our country and beyond. At age thirteen, my Bat Mitzvah gift was a Life Membership to Hadassah. I got my pin and felt really special, but still didn't quite understand why my mother (and father) was so devoted to this organization.

It was around then that my parents began to tell me about our family's connection to Dr. Chaim Yassky. He was an ophthalmologist who initiated programs to eradicate trachoma, and was one of the driving spirits behind the establishment of the Rothschild-Hadassah University Hospital on Mt. Scopus. In 1931, he became the Director General of Hadassah and in 1948 was killed in an Arab attack while en route to the Mt. Scopus Hospital. Seventy-nine people were murdered that day: a convoy filled with doctors, nurses, their guards, and medical supplies, ambushed at Sheik Jarrah, the narrow road leading up to the hospital. I was to learn that Dr. Yassky was the son of my father's great uncle. And while my father was never to meet Chaim, my parents did host his wife, Fanny, several times when she visited here in the United States.

Through the years, I grew to learn and respect the "Hadassah Ladies." They were driven, they were dedicated, they could be proud of the fruit of their labors, nourished by a sense of pride and Zionism by American Jewish women across the country. At a time when few women held full-time jobs, the "Hadassah Ladies" put in more time, sweat, and dedication than anyone who labored at a nine-to-five job. Everything was a fund-raising opportunity, whether a birth, a Bat Mitzvah, an acceptance to college, or a wedding. And today, I still use the dishes in my home that I bought at the Hadassah Thrift Store in Fair Lawn, New Jersey.

But connections are important only if they are respected and tended. And while my mother's dedication to her Hadassah chapter grew, it took me until I was a mother myself to fully understand what Hadassah was all about. Even though I became engaged with my own town's Hadassah chapter and participated in meetings, events, and support, it wasn't until my first visit to Hadassah with my children to feel and hear that "*click*" that we all hope for.

In 2005, my brother and his son accompanied my two children and me to Israel, as a way to celebrate my son's Bar Mitzvah. After visiting the monument at Sheik Jarrah commemorating the place where Chaim Yassky's convoy was ambushed and visiting their graves at the Sanhendria, we made our way to Mt. Scopus. The buildings. The facilities. The nurses. The mothers. The children. The doctors. The activity and life. All built by dedicated men and women, one heartbeat at a time. And the click? Was it when we saw the building that used to be Chaim and Fanny's home, now the Hospice? Was it the recognition of the many names chiseled on dedications? Was it this thin thread of connection? Was it even the moment, later the next day when my ten-year-old daughter received her own Life Member pin, standing under Chagall's stained glass gems at Ein Kerem?

No. It was just a serendipitous moment while walking with my children down a long hallway in Mt. Scopus. It was when something made me turn and look back at one of the walls bearing the names of those who loved Hadassah and who found a way to support it, even when times were tight. There it was, along with those of many other loving donors—the names of my parents, Rhoda and Ben Yassky. It was the moment when, in one form or another, my entire family stood together on Mt. Scopus: my parents (long since passed on), my children, my brother, and one of his sons. It was at that precise moment that we all felt the force behind our parents' dedication to Hadassah, and the directive that we must carry it forward, instilling its importance in our children, who stood there, in disbelief, watching my brother and me cry, at a loss for words to explain the complexity and beauty of being together at that precise place and moment in time.

✦ ✦ ✦

81

The Unseen Heroes of the 2006 War

By Suzanne Dunklin

"Hadassah: For such a time as this. What time is this?" These words were first uttered at a time when a plot for the destruction of the Jewish people had been hatched and was in the process of being carried out. These words, and hence Hadassah, are still applicable today. There are still individuals, groups, and nations that are plotting and attempting to carry out our destruction today. The thing is, we are not going anywhere. I know this because I have seen what the women of Hadassah do and what they make possible for the future. Because of what I have seen over these last thirty years, I know that, just as Esther did once, long ago, we do the same now—we continue to make it possible for Israel and the Jewish people to not only survive, but to thrive.

I witnessed this when I was staying at Hadassah Neurim. I witnessed it when I saw youths from broken backgrounds coming and going to school there as a part of Youth Aliyah. These students don't merely get an adequate education, they receive a superior education, and are given all kinds of opportunities to work in different areas to find their skills and special niche in life. One young man that I worked with has Asperger's syndrome; he has grown tremendously since being there, because he has been given the opportunity to work with horses. He has blossomed incredibly over the short time that I knew him.

During the summer, camps are held at Neurim to help offset the cost of running such an excellent program. These camps raise on average a quarter of a million dollars. However, the summer of 2006 was different. There was a war. The camps meant to bring in funds were canceled, and children were brought down from the North away from the bombings, their families to a place of safe harbor. I would hear on the news about the Lebanese refugees but never about the Israeli refugees. It was as if they didn't exist. Mind you, I was surrounded by hundreds of refugee children.

One day, I was helping to set out food, because the families were coming for a day of fun. It was then that it hit me: Israel doesn't have refugee camps. Israel has Hadassah. These children that I had been surrounded by for weeks were at camp—not a refugee camp, but a summer camp. It was an impromptu, well-organized summer camp. The children came with only the clothes on their backs and their prayer books. House mothers went to get clothes, swimsuits, and toys. The camps that were to raise money were cancelled without even a second thought, because the people at Neurim, and Israel in general, knew that we would always be there to meet any financial needs that would arise.

When the children arrived, volleyball nets went up and soccer balls were set free. The younger children each received a water machine gun to help them deal with the heat as well as what they had seen on a daily basis. Some of these children had only recently arrived from Ethiopia and they did not know how or why to use a knife and fork. At this special summer camp, that skill was taught during meals. At one point, I went around picking up litter. It was everywhere, despite all the available trash cans, which were empty. The children watched me, and then a few joined in, running and bringing the trash back to the bag that I was carrying. It seems that they did not know what to do with disposable plastic cups and candy wrappings, because they had never seen them before. Once the children saw what to do, the litter on the ground greatly decreased and those empty trashcans quickly filled.

It is not that the war was gone from the minds of anyone there; in fact, the planes and the helicopters flying overhead made it very clear that the war was continuing.

One night, I stepped outside with my dog and saw my first cruise missile go by. On the first day of the war, before it had been announced, I noticed what looked like wakes in the water where submarines had gone under. It was only upon verifying this that I realized we were at war. At night I would lie in bed and hear the planes, heavy with bombs, fly north over where I was, and then hear the emptied planes fly back south. It was about twenty minutes between hearing a plane go one way and then hearing it come back. Road blocks became a daily part of life, normally manned by policemen. I, like the children, was without TV, radio, or computer, so I was isolated from the news; however, I quickly learned how to tell which way things were going by how carefully each person was screened as we went into the mall or got on the bus.

The scariest day for me was the day that police were not manning the checkpoint. Instead, soldiers were. A man decided to walk toward the soldier off of the sidewalk; one of the soldiers started yelling at him. I looked at this kid—meaning the soldier— and I saw fear in his eyes, as he kept telling the man to step back onto the sidewalk, but the man just kept coming. The soldier grew more terrified and raised his gun, yelling/pleading with the man to step back, and finally he did. Watching everything that took place in front of me, what hit me was that the soldier wasn't afraid of the man, he was afraid that he would have to shoot the man.

However, I found that in Israel life goes on. This was clearly demonstrated when the parents came to the camp that day, and Hadassah had turned a field into a huge playground with giant slides, rides, cotton candy, snacks, and drinks, followed by a picnic lunch and a special program. I looked around and wondered what the press would make of this—children playing and laughing, a group in a distant land using their resources in time of war to insure that children were kept safe, and at the same time not deprived of their childhood. That is truly amazing.

Just as in Esther's time, the world would still have us gone. This was drilled home even further after I returned to the United States. Upon hearing that I was an Israeli, a person that I had always thought of as a friend looked at me with such hate that I thought, here in front of me is my neighbor who would turn me in if she had the chance. Just as so many did not so long ago in Europe.

Israel has an answer to the world that hates it, and that answer is Hadassah. When Hezbollah decided to bomb Israel and take captive soldiers, there was no question as to whether or not we would be there. They knew that we would and are there. I wish every one of you could have been at Hadassah Neurim that day to see the marvelous work that you do, not just in health, education, and building the land, but in maintaining a sacred promise—the promise that it shall never happen again. Never again will our children be denied the right to have a childhood. Never again will we let our lives be run by terror, but by love, joy, and family. Even when that family is across the sea, we remain one. Baruch HaShem!

✦ ✦ ✦

→ 82 ←

My Family Thread

By Fanchon Weiss Auman

Hadassah had always been a part of my life. Both my grandmothers were active Hadassah members, one even serving as president of two different chapters in Chicago, Illinois. My mother, Rachel, made sure her three children, Matt, Jenni and I, plus her eight grandchildren, all had Life Memberships. My sister Jenni served as president of her chapter in Highland Park, Illinois.

It was during a moment of great personal challenges for my sister Jenni and our family that my passion for Hadassah was ignited. It was July 2008, and Jenni was fighting a medulloblastoma, a brain tumor, which had metastasized to her spine and bones. Sitting in her room in Highland Park Hospital, my sister and I, surrounded by our daughters and other family members, discussed the details of her hospice care. I needed a way to move forward, a way to keep going in my life without her. I needed something that would always be our connection. It came to me. I announced my decision to become active in my St. Louis Hadassah Chapter and to become part of the Walk on Sunshine.

The Walk on Sunshine was the idea of community activist and friend, Suzy Esstman, who was then living with an inoperable brain tumor and wanted to help raise awareness and research funds for the disease through Hadassah. Though Esstman passed away in 2007, new protocols and diagnostic tools have since been developed with help from the funds generated from these walks.

What is the thin thread between Hadassah and my sister? Through my need to keep connected to Jenni, I became passionate about Hadassah's Walk on Sunshine program. Two years after my sister passed in 2010, I was asked to speak at a regional meeting in St. Louis, where I was moved to tears when women in the chapter knew, and spoke about, my sister with love. Hadassah was a living, continuing, connection with Jenni.

Last year, I accompanied twenty-seven teens to the JCC Maccabi Games in Israel. We had an extra day on our itinerary, so we took the group to Hadassah Hospital, Ein Kerem. When we arrived in the chapel, the home of the beautiful stained-glass windows designed by Marc Chagall, someone asked me to speak about my connection to Hadassah. It was a surreal moment of connection in my life with my family, Hadassah, my sister Suzy, and the future, as I was able to explain to the group, many of whom were friends of Suzy Esstman's children, why the Walk on Sunshine event they were participating in was so important. There, I made my husband, Harry, a lifetime Associate. I let them know that the money they raise goes to the incredible research being done at that very Hadassah medical facility. I made the connection, and I knew my sister was smiling down on me.

My granddaughter Rebecca Jane was born on January 17, 2011. On that day, she became a Life Member of Hadassah—fifth generation, with the promise of continuing my thread.

✦ ✦ ✦

✦ *83* ✦

Hadassah from the Inside Out . . . Again

By Anne Rothenberg

N aomi Michal Rothenberg was the newest member of our family and our first granddaughter after three delicious grandsons. My husband, Jeff, and I had planned to be in Israel for her birth, but Naomi arrived two and a half weeks earlier than expected. She was very tiny, weighing a little over two kilos (about five lbs.), so the staff at Hadassah Ein Kerem kept her an extra day until they were sure that she was eating well and gaining weight.

We left the United States with an entourage, including Naomi's great grandmother, Miriam Biskin, her aunt, Elishe Binder, and Amiad, Elishe's six-month-old son. Although I am sure that our luggage was overweight, the El Al personnel were so excited that four generations were traveling together, they overlooked that minor detail.

We landed at Ben Gurion Airport on time, and our first stop on our way to Jerusalem was at our son and daughter-in-law's home in

Modiin. Famous as the home of the Maccabees, this bedroom community is situated between Jerusalem and Tel Aviv and is the fastest growing city in the country. Aaron, Chava, and their sons, Binyamin and Yonatan, live on Petida (Topaz) Street with several other young, growing families.

I will never forget the vision of my mother and daughter on the sofa holding the beautiful Naomi, named for my father who recently passed away. Unlike the boys in the family who were all bald, she was born with brown hair. Her head was the size of an orange and her body, delicate and tiny.

Aaron and Chava had hoped to have a "Simchat Bat," a celebration in honor of their daughter during the two weeks that Aaron's grandmother and sister were in the country, but seriously doubted they could make the arrangements that quickly. Instead, they asked us to host a party in our apartment and invite our friends to attend. We were delighted to celebrate her birth and began inviting people within a few days.

The celebration was delightful and Chava gave a wonderful speech welcoming her daughter into this world, and explaining how they had chosen her name. My father, Irving Michael Biskin, had always taken pride in the fact that "Irving" means "beautiful" in Gaelic. Naomi means "beautiful" or "pleasant" in Hebrew. Michael and Michal are the same name. Chava blessed her daughter with the same characteristics as my father—long life, good looks, friendly ways, and generous spirit.

A few days later, our world was shaken. For those of us who haven't had babies in many years, we learned that the protocol for their care has changed. Parents are now told by their pediatricians to take infants younger than three months, running a fever of 100.4 degrees, to the Emergency Room. Naomi was not nursing well this particular day; she was moaning in her sleep and felt warm to Chava's touch. She took Naomi's temperature and it was higher than 100.4. After consulting the doctor, Chava was told to take her to the ER. She called me at 11 p.m. to tell me that she was on her way to Shaarei Tzedek Hospital. I strongly suggested that she go to Hadassah Ein Kerem where Naomi was born a few weeks earlier, but Chava reminded me that Hadassah's ER had been very overcrowded when Aaron had brought their first born there five years earlier.

"That was before we opened the new Center for Emergency Medicine, which has an entrance and waiting room for sick children, separate from the one for adults," I informed her. In addition, a friend from the Hadassah Office in Israel was able to check the condition of the ER. Fortunately, it was not busy at all and Naomi was seen right away.

In the early morning, I learned that Naomi had been admitted. She had been subjected to a spinal tap and several blood tests and would be observed for several days before being discharged. Unfortunately, that meant that the baby would be at Hadassah Ein Kerem over Shabbat.

During the last Lebanon War, I emailed then National Hadassah president, June Walker, of blessed memory, after reading an online article about the numbers of people in the north who had been left homeless, and was wondering what Hadassah was doing to help. She replied that Hadassah had opened every facility we owned as shelters—from the youth villages, Neurim and Meir Shefaya, to the hotel at Hadassah Ein Kerem. I never thought that our family would make use of this facility as well.

Construction was going on everywhere at Hadassah Hospital at Ein Kerem. For anyone who has never been to the Abbell Synagogue at Hadassah Hospital, which houses the Chagall windows, the Mother and Child Center (where Naomi had been born and was now being treated) and the Judith and Sydney Swartz Center for Emergency Medicine, are within yards of each other. In addition, a shopping mall and a hotel had been built. Each hotel room is equipped with emergency buttons, enabling the inhabitant to reach a nurse, if needed. Often, new mothers check out of the hospital and into this hotel for a few more days of care before returning home.

The four-star hotel provided us with kosher, Shabbat meals so that we could eat with our son and his boys, and could walk to the Mother and Child Center to visit Chava and Naomi. Our presence on the Ein Kerem campus also enabled us to take Binyamin and Yonatan to Shabbat services in the Abbell Synagogue under the gleaming colors of the Chagall windows. The boys were awed by gorgeous creations named for the Twelve Tribes of Israel, and Binyamin was especially impressed that one of the windows was named after him.

That year, with the passing of my father, Jeff and I secured a Perpetual Yahrzeit in his memory through Hadassah. My father's name is inscribed in a book kept at the Abbell Synagogue and kaddish will be recited in perpetuity on his yahrzeit. Our Shabbat at Hadassah enabled me to say kaddish for my father myself in this magnificent setting.

We spent much of the afternoon visiting Naomi. Out her window, we were able to see the beginnings of Hadassah's latest project, the new inpatient tower. Named for Sarah Wetsman Davidson, the fourteen-story structure includes 500 beds, twenty state-of-the-art operating rooms, and fifty intensive care beds. The tower will provide a huge boost to Hadassah's capabilities in a wide range of fields, such as cardiology, telemedicine, and laparoscopic surgery, and will facilitate the use of advanced robotics and computers. In turn, these will enrich the research and teaching conducted at Hadassah.

The ending to this story is a good one. Naomi was released on the fourth day and the tests were negative. She is now a thriving and beautiful young lady of four, who has no recollection of that traumatic weekend.

During my term as president of Hadassah Capital District, I never could have imagined that I would get such an up close and personal look at all of our projects in Israel. I never dreamt that Hadassah, for which I have devoted countless hours as a volunteer, would play such an amazing role in the life of my own family.

✦ ✦ ✦

✦ 84 ✦

My Jerusalem Heritage

By Leah Bassan Silver

The Arabs were saying Jews were only in Palestine due to their arrival after the Holocaust to colonize the country. European countries, themselves colonizers, have labeled Jews "colonizers" rather than legitimate citizens of a state of their own.

I knew this wasn't true because my parents had been born in Palestine at the beginning of the 20th century.

My father had told me about an ancestor who had made a steel door with a trick lock to protect Rachel's Tomb, and another one who had made Jerusalem habitable outside of the walled part of the city by clearing Jerusalem of wild animals, first trapping them and then sending them to European zoos, or setting them free outside of the city.

When my father retired, my parents returned to live in the land where they were born. After Israel had regained the whole city of Jerusalem, I visited my parents there. My father took me to the ruins of the Hurva synagogue and told me about an ancestor who had worked high up on its interior. That the synagogue has been refurbished and is now in use is especially gratifying to me as a fulfillment of my ancestor's wishes.

My father's uncle was a commercial photographer at the beginning of the twentieth century, and documented Jerusalem's Jewish charities; the negatives of these incredible photographs were made of the fragile glass plates used before the invention of film. A number of years ago my nephew sent me a clipping from the *Jerusalem Post* in which there were copies of several of those pictures taken by my great uncle.

One of those photographs had been taken before World War I. It showed Jewish men sitting on benches, praying at the Western Wall. When the British took over Palestine, General Allenby entered Jerusalem and announced that he would be making no changes there. The Arabs rioted and claimed that the Jews had no right to pray at the Western Wall, that while they might have stood around and uttered a prayer, they had no authorized right to do so. But my great uncle had produced the photo that proved that Jews had prayed there on benches and thus secured the Jewish right to pray there during the time of the British Mandate. I am so proud that someone from my family had enabled our people to carry on this tradition, uninterrupted in time!

Many of my great uncle's photographs had been willed to the Jewish Agency Archives, and I was privileged to see some of them there myself. The archivist had even made me a strip with the negatives of some of the images. I made a little booklet with copies for my two daughters, enlarging a photograph of

HaRav Kook teaching in a yeshiva, as a gift for my son-in-law.

But though my immediate family and I know about our historic family heritage, the rest of the Jewish world, even the children of Jerusalem, might believe what they hear and doubt the existence of their Jewish Jerusalem heritage. What could I do to stop the blotting out of the memory of my Jewish ancestors and the long-time residence of Jews in Jerusalem?

The *Jerusalem Post* clipping said that the photographs would be in a book about photographers in Palestine in the early twentieth century that was being researched and prepared for publication. I helped to get the book published in a large, coffee-table format. The children of Jerusalem could never afford to learn their roots from such an expensive book.

I concluded that we must get pictures of Jewish Jerusalem before the Holocaust on a website for all to see. With Hadassah College's expertise in photography and computer science, I thought it might be a good project for them, so I asked them to do it and promised to cover the cost.

I was so excited when Nava ben Zvi (the Hadassah College president) told me the College would create the web site! But then we learned that the Archives would not release their pictures. Our wonderful Nava would not give up. She gathered content for the website from photographs in private collections that had been taken by my great uncle and other Jerusalem photographers at that time. This site is now located on a Hadassah educational website, www.snunit.k12.il/jerusalem-photo.

So now our Jerusalem children can see pictures of Jewish Jerusalem from a century ago, and I can see the Jerusalem of my ancestors. One of my favorites is the Shaarei Tzedek Hospital's barn with the cows that provided fresh milk for the babies at that time, so long ago when there was no refrigeration. We can all see that and many more pictures of Jewish Jerusalem before the Holocaust any time we want, thanks to Hadassah!

✦ ✦ ✦

85

Bonding, Ballasting, and the BRCA Gene

By Carol M. Towbin Greenberg

"What a dope I am," is what I thought to myself as my brain tried to access what I had learned from Hadassah about BRCA gene cancers as the result of many years of magazine reading and organizing health programs.

"Great!" is what I excitedly blurted out. Not exactly the reaction the oncologist was expecting when he told me I had stage- three ovarian cancer several years ago.

"Great?" He queried.

"Yeah. Now I can join a sister study," I responded, already planning the advertisement for an educational project in my head. My mind was working overtime on the internal conversation and was less focused, as it should have been in retrospect, on the one that was occurring in the doctor's office.

"Sister study?" he repeated haltingly.

"Yes, I have three sisters. How do we sign up for a study or

BRCA gene testing?"

"There . . .th . . .there is no sister study for ovarian. Do you understand what I am saying to you?" he almost shouted as if I did not hear him or at the very least that I was not taking him at his word.

"But I thought I read about a breast study that included ovarian."

"You are very sick and could die," he almost protested.

Yes I understood, but I was neither surprised, given my family history, my own survey of symptoms that did not show up on standard exams and ultrasounds for the previous two years, or the humorless gaze in my husband's eyes that told me that he knew this dark secret, way before I was privy to this official information.

"I know," I responded with a lot less animation, "but I only thought if I have to go through this maybe it is for a reason."

It wasn't until the following Tuesday, just a day after my surgery, that I realized that I should be more careful when I think out loud. "We were worried about you," started my internist hesitantly when she visited me in the hospital.

"No, not to worry," I assured her, "I was told the surgery went fine." I responded through a lifting morphine haze.

"I know that," she said. "But I read the oncologist's notes, and he wrote that your behavior was inappropriate."

"Oy," I remember thinking. "Here I go again."

So, again I found myself explaining that I did not mean it was great that I had cancer, but now that I was finally diagnosed, it could be treated and I could maybe use the experience to help create a meaningful project.

I am a Hadassah woman. I do not follow orders and I do not cower in the face of adversity. I adapt, I plan, I strategize, and when all else fails, I know I have the strength and wisdom of over 300,000 other women, most of whom I have never met, to support me, give me advice, make vital connections for me, and to help outline issues of importance.

Yet, back to my original thought, "What a dope I was." I was president of my chapter when I first read, and then reported to other Hadassah women, this breakthrough at Hadassah hospital in BRCA gene identification. I was on the regional board when I booked Hadassah speakers to provide informative talks on cancer and genetic links, and yet even now, when the "C word" (as my mother, of blessed memory, used to call her stomach complaints in wistful whispers) applied to me, I was not remembering that BRCA had anything to do with other cancers except breast.

Was I thinking? Why did I not pay better attention to my own Hadassah materials? Knowledge is power. Hadassah has empowered me to keep positive because the work they have done in gene therapy has had an impact on my family. My mother and mother-in-law both died very young, and in an age when they were not even told with what they were afflicted. A plaque to their memory graces the Moshe Sharett Institute, but more than an excuse to visit Israel to see this wall decoration, I know the funds somehow have changed my options as a cancer survivor. I now know that though I am BRCA positive, my children will be spared. There is comfort in that knowledge.

Knowledge provides optimism. Recently, I found a note written in the height of my chemo daze, thanking a Hadassah regional board member for help locating health resources and advocacy materials that I could use for local BRCA projects we were calling the Teal Ribbon Project (TRiP, because cancer is a trip you do not want to take alone).

Hadassah materials, regional resource personnel, and speakers were important to the success of TRiP. Our health events attracted several hundred people and gained the support of both area hospitals and the American Cancer Society. Though an HPV and not a BRCA cancer, cervical cancer was included in the TRiP goals because, at that time, Hadassah was promoting "What Women Need to Know," and ever an educator, I thought it was a good fit for our youth health initiatives.

Sometimes at Hadassah events, I was listed by my name and the portfolio I held in our organization. Not so much who I was, but, appropriately, how I served the organization. In some ways, over the last few years, cancer has sidelined my participation in my own passions. So on that first programming day of this past Hadassah season, when we went around the room to introduce ourselves to each other, I started slowly, "I am Carol," I said. "A Life Member of Hadassah."

"Aaaannnd?" someone in the room prodded me to continue.

"... and a cancer survivor who is living proof of the Miracle of Hadassah."

✦ ✦ ✦

86

Converting To Hadassah

By Dan Ornstein

Though my parents taught me to support and love Israel from an early age, I truly became a Zionist the summer that I was seventeen. That was when my father quietly prevailed upon my mother to let me work on a secular kibbutz with a friend who had family there; quite an unconventional "Israel Teen Summer Adventure" for a religious kid from Queens. That summer, I learned to love the land, its people, and the meaning of Zionism. I also began to comprehend the mitzvah of loving every member of the Jewish people, no matter where they come from politically, religiously, ethnically, or geographically. Yet, for all of my immersion in Zionism, Israel, and Judaism from childhood until very recently, Hadassah never played a part in my thinking. I had friends in college who had spent time on Young Judaea Year Course (some of whom made aliyah), but their experiences had little impact on me.

My Jewish and Zionist backgrounds are preludes to a confession and the story of how I became a devoted supporter of Hadassah.

A few years ago, during a conversation with a colleague about Jewish communal life, I offered a not-too-kind and un-informed opinion about the antiquated nature of Hadassah and "Hadassah ladies." Mildly stunned and amused by my simplistic stereotyping, this friend, a long-time supporter of Hadassah, remarked, "You know, those Hadassah ladies built the State of Israel." Realizing I had put my foot in mouth, I apologized, backed off, and stored her polite reprimand in the back of my mind.

Only in February 2008, did I understand what she meant when I (finally after all these years) toured the Ein Kerem campus of Hadassah Hospital in Jerusalem with members of my congregation. At the hospital, I was transformed. Stuart, a member of our tour, whose mother of blessed memory had been a prominent and passionate leader of Hadassah in Florida, approached me about going to the Ein Kerem campus to see the plaque erected in his mother's honor some years before. For him and his wife, Anne, this would be an important part of their pilgrimage to Israel and the homage paid to his mother who had died less than a year before. I had a little fear that going to Hadassah would result in one more fundraising schpiel that we would have to endure.

Nonetheless, I knew that it was the right thing to do: it would comfort my congregants and honor the memory of their beloved mother and mother-in-law. Besides, we would see the Chagall Windows, always a feast for the eyes and the soul.

The real feast took place well before we saw the windows. In fact, by the time we got to the hospital synagogue where they are housed, they felt almost anticlimactic to me. Another member of our congregation, Anne, who is also an active leader in Hadassah in our area, lives a good part of the year in Jerusalem with her husband, Jeff. (Their children made aliyah several years ago.) Ever the gracious hostess to groups from our area of New York when they visit Jerusalem, she gladly accompanied us on the tour. There, a volunteer from the development department gently guided us and patiently answered our questions. With love for the great miracle that Henrietta Szold had planted in the rich soil of American and Israeli Zionism, she did more than show us around; she taught us. All without hard sells, fundraising pitches, or appeals to "pocket-book conscience."

Our soft-spoken guide almost did not need to speak on behalf of Hadassah's vitality and vital work. She could have left me alone in the middle of the pediatric emergency ward of the Mother and Child Center, and the hospital would have done all the talking for her. I do not exaggerate when I say that I witnessed Hadassah's Jewish mission of compassion and humanity at work merely by standing inside their walls. The patients, families, and staff who moved busily around their corridors and lobbies probably represented every shade of politics, religion, and ethnicity to be found in Israel, and perhaps around the world. Anywhere else, their differences might divide or even destroy them. At Hadassah, they were united by the universally human and specifically Jewish quest to heal the sick.

A seemingly random encounter as I passed through the emergency ward connected me to Hadassah indelibly. As a congregational rabbi, I constantly visit patients in local hospitals. For me it is very holy work, but it is only one small piece of what is usually a very busy day. I often find myself needing to rush out before I can fully process how the people I visit and help have also helped me spiritually. As we toured the ward, I suddenly noticed two very traditional families, one Palestinian and the other Haredi (Jewish ultra-Orthodox), sitting side by side with their sick children, waiting for care. Here were two families silently bridging both sides of a generally impassable gap of culture, history, politics, and religion with one of the most basic, shared dimensions of human existence—love for our children. To this day, I cannot shake that image from my mind.

Stuart and Anne found his mother's plaque, and quite by accident, Ellen, another member of our tour, found the plaque honoring her uncle of blessed memory. I learned once again that those plaques are much more than good fundraising tools. In the best sense of the word, they are *matzevot*, monuments bearing testimony to a person's great qualities that live on through his or her good work in the places touched by his or her life. Though my congregants remembered the loss of their loved ones with sadness, we all felt genuine joy that they live on through the great mission of Hadassah on behalf of the Jewish people and the world.

That day at Ein Kerem, I "converted" to Hadassah. Since then, I have begun working with members of our region to bring the inspiring message of this great Jewish organization to the entire community. I have purchased a Life Membership for my wife, and we have made our older daughter a youth Life Member. (A Life Membership for our younger daughter is on its way.) The money is obviously important, for without it Hadassah cannot continue doing the mitzvot that it does, especially now. Yet the money is only a means to Hadassah's greater end—being G-d's partner in healing the world through education, outreach, medicine, and research. I am proud to be a part of this partnership.

✦ ✦ ✦

87

A Fork in the Road
By Wendy Salkin

I have been a Hadassah chapter co-president for almost six years and I have also been living with metastatic breast cancer for three years.

When I was first diagnosed, I was surprised that people were quick to assume that I would step down from my Hadassah position. That was something I had not even contemplated, because doing that would be relinquishing something that was so much a part of my life. I think people were not saying that I wouldn't be capable of continuing, but that I would probably want to spend my time doing other things rather than continue with my Hadassah responsibilities. By thinking that, they showed that they did not know me very well.

I had joined Hadassah thirty-four years ago as a young bride. When I moved to my present home in northern New Jersey two years later, I chose to join the chapter that had been established in my community in 1961. This was an historic chapter that had its first board meeting on the very day that patients were being moved into the new facility at Ein Kerem. It was also a chapter of multi-generations of grandmothers, mothers, and daughters. Therefore, it was a chapter that was very welcoming to new members of all ages and one in which I felt I could grow to fill an important capacity. I was impressed by how supportive the women were of each other. If something went wrong with a project, no one placed blame and the women worked very cooperatively towards their common goal—the fulfillment of Hadassah's mission. The members were bound by their love of the State of Israel, which was still relatively new at that time. The chapter operated almost like a family, and the chapter functions had a distinctive warm and friendly atmosphere.

After serving for many years as chapter treasurer, one of the two co-presidents felt she could no longer continue in her position. Several of the longtime members of the executive board invited me out to lunch to discuss the possibility of my assuming the vacant co-president position. I really did not hesitate to accept, as it had long been a secret dream of mine. My husband was most encouraging as he felt I would be very capable. My two children, a son and a daughter, were also grown and no longer needed as much of my attention. I was very excited as my co-president began to give me advice about the best way to conduct meetings. She was and still is a wonderful role model and source of inspiration.

Advancing through the ranks of the executive board to the position of co-president has helped me grow in so many ways. I started out feeling very shy and hesitant to take on a leadership role. However, once I took the plunge in my beginning positions,

I learned many skills. I now have confidence to develop a meeting agenda, solicit reports from various chair people, and run the meeting in such a way that we adhere to time guidelines as well as give everyone who wants to participate an opportunity to be heard. I am careful in this respect to continue our chapter's tradition of warm hospitality. My experience has been most rewarding. I agree with what my co-president has always said: people who are involved with Hadassah personally gain much more than they give.

Prior to being diagnosed in 2008, my life, as anyone's, had had some ups and downs. In good times and bad, Hadassah was always my anchor, giving me something positive to focus on and a sense of accomplishment. When I faced the challenge of cancer treatment, I had to look deep inside myself and make the decision that as difficult as it was, I was not going to just give up and let the disease define my whole life. I remember being so weak and sick that when I accompanied my husband to make photocopies of things I needed for the chapter bulletin, I had to sit on the floor next to the machine waiting for him to finish. However, going home that day, I had the great feeling of knowing that I had completed the task. Maybe it was very small in the grand scheme of things, but it meant a lot to me.

In the fall, when I began my first intensive chemotherapy treatments, I was so touched and gratified when the women of my chapter rallied to help make sure the chapter continued to function smoothly. Some of the women faced personal challenges of their own, but it was clear that they had an overriding commitment to the well being of our chapter. They were all longtime members of Hadassah and it was this shared history that carried them through.

After an absence of several weeks, I was very pleased to be able to attend my first function—a wonderful Chanukah party that a member had come forward and volunteered to have in her home. I remember that very special afternoon as a turning point in my being able to resume my Hadassah responsibilities.

Since then, I have continued to have some very difficult times. However, I feel that for now I have done the right thing for my chapter and for myself by persisting in my efforts to do my very best for Hadassah. My chapter has won many awards on the regional level. However, more than that, in my continuing to be there for my chapter, I have helped ensure that the chapter has continued to be there for the members who appreciate its special and unique qualities. We all work together to further the wonderful work of Hadassah and we work hard on every meeting and event to make members feel happy that they came.

In addition to becoming a Life Member many years ago, along the way I have added more Life Members and Associates, so that now I am a member of a five-generation Life Member family. My family members continue to be my biggest cheerleaders. It has been a great privilege to be able to participate in Hadassah's extraordinary work that benefits so many people in Israel, America, and around the world. It has given me a chance to be involved in something very worthwhile, something larger than myself or my illness. I hope that by sharing my story, I will be of help to other Hadassah members who are facing their own challenging times.

+ + +

→ 88 →

Ten Pieces of a Hadassah Life
By Iris Shur

About four years ago, my mother was moving to an assisted living facility. We were going through all her papers and one manila envelope turned up that held all the papers that my grandmother, Susan Feller, had left behind when she died.

I remember feeling so very sad that Grandma Sue's life had been reduced to maybe ten pieces of paper, especially since my life is composed of thousands of pieces of paper! How on earth was she able to condense everything, I wondered? What did she consider important enough to save for her children and her grandchildren? But I put the envelope aside to be looked at another day since there was a lot of packing to do for my mom.

A few weeks later, a fellow Collier County Hadassah board member, Lanny Rashbaum, proudly handed me the newsletter, *What's New What's Hot*, from National Hadassah. She wanted me to read an article about her mother, Bess Katz, who at one point had become Hadassah's National Treasurer. I took it home and read it.

Several days later I noticed the manila envelope containing my grandmother's papers on my desk. I had a few minutes, so I decided to see what she had deemed worthy of saving that would signify the important things in her life.

What was in the envelope? There were several newspaper articles about my mom detailing awards she had won. There was a gorgeous picture of Grandma in her twenties. Then there was a piece of thin cardboard from Kmart nylons. On the back my grandmother had written in black marker, "Sorry children, to leave this mess." That gives you a good idea of my grandmother and certainly made me cry. Ten pieces of paper and she was sorry for the mess! Wait until my kids see my closet!!

There was a note from Grandma Sue which said, "I served two years in each of the following chapters: president of Henrietta Szold Chapter of Hadassah, organizer and president of Forte Towers Chapter, organizer and president of Herzl Chapter of AJ Congress, and president Louise Wise Chapter of American Jewish Congress." Then she wrote, "above information is not for publishing." (Sorry Grandma. Just thought your children would like to know.)

A Hadassah Service Award to Susan York (my grandmother had remarried) for "Your selfless devotion to the high ideals of Hadassah, etc." from the Maison Grande Chapter 1979–1980 was also in the envelope.

Grandma also saved her end-of-the-year Hadassah speech from the Henrietta Szold Group of Hadassah. It was typed all in faded caps and in it she thanked everyone for everything, person by person. For example, "Thank you Malke Shklair, who as always gave of her time, day or night, snow, sleet, rain or hurricane, to bring in $580.91 for her pet project, JNF." Or, "TaDa (Thank you) Miriam Press, who wore many hats, as she went about her business of raising Life Membership figures by ten, selling Israel Bonds, wills, and bequests and in short our girl Fri on any day of the week."

Another cherished certificate certified that my grandmother, Mrs. Susan Feller, was a Life Member of Hadassah. It was signed by Charlotte Jacobson in March 1965.

The final piece of paper in the envelope was a letter from Hadassah. It was dated March 16, 1965. This is what it said:

Dear Mrs. Feller:

May I extend to you congratulations upon your election to the President of the Forte Towers Group in the Miami Beach Chapter of Hadassah. As a leader of this Group, you face a challenge which I feel confident you will meet. I know you will derive great personal satisfaction from this opportunity to be of service to Israel through Hadassah and I am sure the Forte Towers Groups will grow and flourish under your leadership. My very best wishes for a successful administration.

Sincerely yours,

Bess S. Katz, (Mrs. Saul Katz),
National Organization Chairman

There were carbon copies to Mrs. Nat Barth and Mrs. Gerald P. Soltz, perhaps someone reading this has a connection to those women.

So, the letter was signed Bess Katz, National Organization chairman. Hmm, I thought the name sounded familiar. Then I remembered the article I had read about Lanny's mother. What was her name? I dug around for it. Unbelievably, it was Lanny's mom who had signed the congratulatory letter for my grandmother. Lanny's mom was Bess Katz. I got goose bumps, so did Lanny when I told her.

We always say "small world," but this was "tiny world," wouldn't you say? But most remarkable of all was that my grandmother saved only ten pieces of paper from her life and Hadassah was most of them. Now I am a past-president of Collier County Hadassah in Naples, Florida. Did my Grandma Sue leave a legacy, or what?

✦ ✦ ✦

89

A Scleral Miracle from Hadassah College of Optometry

By Sharyn Miller Spitzer

I want to share my miracle with you. I am home now and my sons and I are about to light the first candle for Hannukah. Amazingly, I can see without any contact lens in my left eye. I can read the note my older son had scrawled for my brother: "Aaron—We are off to the hospital. The doctor called and said it's time. . . Mom is getting her new eye. Don't worry. It will all be history by the time I call you. Josh."

That was eleven years ago in Montreal when I experienced my personal Hannukah miracle. So many times I had said, "I can't see it. Come and give me a hand." Now my vision was restored thanks to a donated cornea, the greatest gift of my life. How can I explain the terror I had previously faced when my world became a blurry sea of color?

Driving was so scary, especially entering the highway and merging traffic. The nights were a terror with oncoming traffic shining their lights from the other side of the highway. Bright sunlight was also blinding for me. I came to the point where I had to admit to myself that I could not drive any more. I was a single mom of two teenagers and I could not drive. I just could not see. I had to learn to get around by foot and on public transportation. I had to admit that I could not see the little street signs and I also could not see the big overhead green signs on the highway. In the supermarket, everything was just a sea of color. Even with my contact lenses I could not negotiate alone anymore. My sixteen-year old son became the family driver even though he did not yet have his driver's license. The law said that he needed a licensed driver in the front seat so he could drive with his learner's permit. I was the licensed driver. He was my chauffeur.

The morning after my first new eye was implanted, the doctor took off the bandage and I was able to see the words on the milk container. No glasses. No lenses. The letters were there. My friend, Ana, took me out to lunch on the way home. The daylight was shocking and I hid behind dark glasses. And in the evening, I lit the Hannukah licht. I said the Shecheheyanu prayer of thanksgiving. A great miracle had happened to me! I could see without contact lenses and eyeglasses on top of them. Absolutely miraculous!

Many years have passed and I always remember on Hannukah to share my story with people in my community. Some gracious, unknown person had the foresight to sign his driver's license and be an organ donor. And I was the fortunate recipient. It is so important to think ahead. The gift of renewed sight gave me a new quality of life. I would have gone on living, but my life was dark and dim. Now it was full of bright colors and an appreciation of the details of life, like the pattern of the floor, the different shades of green on the leaves in the garden and the words on a printed page.

In 1997, when I made aliyah, my move was not a planned one. Before I left for a summer stint as a volunteer teacher in the North of Israel, my doctor in Montreal asked me to be in contact with Drs. Landau and Frucht at Hadassah Ein Kerem at the Eye Disease Clinic. He told me that he respected their fine work with people who, like me, had keratoconus, a rare disease of the eye, where a cone grows on the cornea. Dr. Joel Rosen of the Montreal Jewish Hospital explained that just in case I had a rejection problem or lost a lens, I should be in contact with them.

When I decided to remain in Jerusalem, I phoned and made an appointment to see Dr. Frucht at the Eye Clinic at what is called "little Hadassah" on Strauss Street. After five minutes he told me to come see him or Dr. Landau at Hadassah Ein Kerem on Monday morning. He explained that only there did he have the machinery to look into my problem. I became a constant visitor, sometimes being checked every second week, for years. I had what Dr. Landau called dry eye syndrome. The wonderful hard contact lenses which I was wearing were rocking back and forth on my corneal grafts, like a carrot rubs on a grater. Ouch! He prescribed every eye drop on the market to make artificial tears. Jerusalem has a desert climate and is often hot and dry, so the climate only aggravated my condition. As the years went by, eye treatments and eye technology advanced. I continued to suffer great discomfort. Some days were good some were not so good. And the sunlight was absolutely blinding. I arrived one morning without an appointment to the over-crowded clinic in sheer desperation. Dr. Landau mentioned that there was something brand-new, not yet on the market, called a scleral lens which might be my salvation.

I was having Shabbat lunch with some neighbors and one man kept looking at me strangely. He watched me remove and reinsert my lenses several times during the afternoon and use lots of drops. Finally he admitted that he was an optometrist and asked if I was acquainted with Philip Fine at Hadassah College of Optometry. A few days later, the neighbor sent me to see Philip Fine.

On the day that I went to meet Philip, I was absolutely miserable. He took one look at me and said, "I can help you. You have kerataconus." Philip asked his masters students to work me up and take pictures and maps of my left eye. He said, "We'll do one eye at a time. Be patient. This will be a long project." After almost twenty hours of measurements and trial and error, Philip and his students agreed that the only solution for me was a scleral lens. My eyes rejected the first round of lenses after six months.

I came in crying and begging for eye glasses. Fine, they'd give me eye glasses with the proviso that I would sign that I would not try to go out of my house with them. In other words, they insisted that "They won't work for you and we won't be responsible." Life was dark and I was tripping and falling. I could not go out alone. My husband became my eyes for me. There had to be a better solution.

On what proved to be the first day of the rest of my life, Philip tried something new from Soflex, an Israeli start-up company in Acco, whose lenses were just appearing on the market. The scleral lens actually fit. It did not rock or grate or scratch. Philip gave me a sample trial lens to try for a week. It was not good, but good enough. These scleral lenses must be precise. They are huge, the size of an American quarter, and they need to be filled with a saline solution before they are inserted. Ultimately, the company made me hand-made lenses.

In ecstasy and praise I shouted to Philip and his students, "Welcome to the new world. I can see!" My eyes don't hurt. They aren't itchy and scratchy. The lenses don't rub."

I became the full-time volunteer for the masters students at Hadassah College of Optometry. I was the "live model." Philip Fine took me to conferences and workshops and all his optometry colleagues and the top people from Soflex examined me. Everyone learned to fit the lenses with me as the live model. No more theoretical dummies to practice on.

Simultaneously, as all this saga was going on, my twelve-year-old grandson was aware that I was writing a family memoir. He needed to add his opinion and wanted to help me since he is the oldest grandson. He understood that these lenses cost more than $10,000 a pair in the States. He told me that Philip Fine, a man from his shul in Karnei Shomron (in Israel), worked at Hadassah College. My grandson was amazed to learn that I had already been going to Mr. Fine's clinic every week for months and that he had found a solution for me. So my grandson said that we need to pay for the lenses and they cost a lot of money. Even if Mr. Fine could get them for me for free or almost free, we'd need to get the money. My grandson's idea was for me to go to America and talk to the Hadassah ladies and tell my story. He figured that they would all buy my book and we could donate the money to Mr. Fine to buy a piece of equipment for the students to use in the clinic. That way, we could say thank you for my scleral miracle, which enabled me to paint and sculpt again, work in my kitchen, read a book, and watch my grandson play tennis.

When I told my elderly parents in Florida about my miracle from Hadassah College, my ninety-year-old father was the first to contribute money to subsidize my lenses. Excitedly I told him, "Daddy, I can see and it doesn't hurt anymore." Over the transatlantic telephone line, we both cried. But this time, they were tears of joy.

✦ ✦ ✦

—◆ 90 ◆—

My Miracle of Miracles

By Bonnie Juran Ullner

Hadassah. What did it mean to me prior to June 2009? It was one of the many Jewish organizations that I received mail from periodically and which, in theory, I supported. I knew my maternal grandmother, for whom I am named, was a volunteer for Hadassah, and that her cousin, Charlotte Jacobson, had been a National President. That was about the extent of my knowledge.

This was before my then sixteen year old daughter Jessa went on a Cincinnati Jewish Federation trip to Israel and fell gravely ill after about a week. She was taken to a hospital in the north and, at the insistence of my brother who lives in Jerusalem, was transported by ambulance to Hadassah Ein Karem. There she immediately took a turn for the worse. In addition to the apparent liver failure, there was now also kidney failure, plummeting blood pressure, and the need for her to be put on a ventilator as she could not breathe on her own.

Luckily, when my daughter's asymptomatic genetic disorder, Wilson's Disease, decided to manifest itself on July 13, 2009, she wasn't in Poland visiting the concentration camps or even back-packing in some remote area in the United States. She was in Israel and was in driving distance of a state-of-the-art hospital called Hadassah which, among other things, is a major liver center. The doctors were unbelievably able to quickly diagnose her with this rare disorder, stabilize her, cleanse her blood to keep her alive, and make contact with a hospital in New York that put her at the top of the U.S. regional liver donor list. Additionally, two doctors and one nurse flew with her (after sixteen seats were taken out of an El Al jet in order to set up a mini-ICU in the middle of the plane) to Columbia-Presbyterian Hospital in New York. Columbia-Presbyterian meanwhile had located a possible donor liver in Tennessee, and flew down to harvest it soon after the Israeli team delivered Jessa to their ICU. Within twenty-four hours of her arrival in New York, her was undergoing the ten-hour liver transplanta-tion surgery that would save her life. Miracle after miracle occurred during those few days, and G-d was watching over Jessa, our family, and the staff at Hadassah Hospital. What had started as a nightmare and a dire situation with a bleak prognosis turned into a miraculous, heroic, round-the-clock, beyond anyone's imagination, life-saving series of divine acts that resulted in her being alive today.

So what does Hadassah mean to me today? Hadassah is a central part of my life, in that I am eternally grateful and indebted to them for saving Jessa's life and it is a priority for me to spend a significant amount of my time doing all I can to help support Hadassah in every way and let the world know about this amazing organization. I have become a Life Member as well as made my mother and both of my daughters Life Members. I speak to Hadassah chapters when asked and I tell them that I am a Jewish mother, just like many of them, who sent her teenager on a trip to Israel to connect with our Holy Land and learn more about her people. And, unbeknownst to me when I sent her, Hadassah, their Hadassah, my Hadassah, would save this precious Jewish child's life and treat her as if she were a member of their own family. I tell the Hadassah members sitting in front of me, most of whom are volunteers, that Jessa's very existence is the fruit of their labors . . . the countless hours they have volunteered and dollars they have raised over the almost 100 years of Hadassah's existence, all played a part in those crucial minutes and hours and days that gave the hospital staff the tools and knowledge and resources to save Jessa's life. It was nothing short of a miracle and a spiritual event that my Jewish teenager's life was saved in Jerusalem in Hadassah Hospital, 6000 miles away from me but in the best place on earth she could have possibly been. Hopefully, Jessa's story will inspire others to get involved with and give to Hadassah, and thus from something so terrible will come something good, as more lives are saved through the miraculous work of Hadassah Hospital.

✦ ✦ ✦

91

My Best Audience

By Elynne Chaplik-Aleskow

W hen I received the call from the president of Hadassah Chai Chapter inviting me to perform my stories, I was delighted. I had performed for other Jewish organizations but had not had the honor of performing for Hadassah.

From the moment I arrived at the meeting, I felt a warmth from the ladies that can only be described as a feeling of being home among one's own Jewish sisters. I mingled and enjoyed the high tea served with finger sandwiches, delicate sweets, and lovely serving pieces.

When I was introduced to read my stories, I walked up to the lectern and looked at my audience. It was a wonderful turnout of about seventy women and one man, my beloved husband, who never missed any of my performances.

My mother, sister Linda, dear friend Sandy, and some special cousins were in attendance. But my guest of honor was my girl-friend Arlene who had flown in from Florida to Chicago to see my program. Every time I looked at my audience while performing a story, I would see my beloved childhood friend's face smiling at me.

I remember that afternoon for many reasons. As audience members, the Hadassah ladies and I fit like a hand and glove. They were with me through every emotion my words conveyed. As an author performing her own stories, nothing could be more thrilling than to feel the audience moving with you in sync.

My Hadassah audience was generous, supportive, responsive, and filled with Jewish connection. The experience for me was unforgettable. Looking at the faces of the ladies I had just met sitting among my family and dearest friends gave me an exquisite feeling of gratitude.

After my program, my family, Arlene, and I browsed some of the charming gift shops in a nearby suburb. In one of the shops, Arlene fell in love with a red friendship treasure box that I secretly bought and surprised her with. This box became a treasure to her. We referred to it often when speaking.

Recently, I went to see Arlene's daughter, Bari, and her family who were in town for the weekend. Bari handed me this beloved box and I cried. When I opened the box, I saw that Arlene had saved many of my notes and quotes along with clippings she found about friendship that spoke of us. I looked at this box and wondered why fate dictated that I now have it back. It was a confirmation that my friend had died several months earlier.

I have now put my notes from Arlene into the red friendship box with her notes from me and have placed the red box in a special place of honor in my home. When I look at the box, I feel I can touch my friend.

That Hadassah event that Arlene had traveled to was the last time I saw my friend. That afternoon was a blessing for me on so many levels. The Chai Chapter of Hadassah invitation and event added a glow to my life that will continue forever in my mind and heart.

✦ ✦ ✦

─+ 92 +─

Past Dept. Commander, JWV

By E.G. "Jerry" Farris

After leaving the U.S Air Force in 1965, I went to school to become a nurse. I worked for over thirty years before retiring due to disability. I joined Hadassah and Jewish War Veterans at the same time and worked my way through the ranks in JWV to become the Commander of the Dept. of PA in 2010. Through JWV, I met someone who asked if I would speak to school children about nursing for Hadassah.

For three years I went to area middle schools talking about nursing and my experiences. Watching the students as they began to connect and ask questions was great. There were some who smirked when they learned Hadassah was a "Jewish" organization. But I think one of the greatest feelings of accomplishment was when a young eighth-grade Muslim girl jumped up and begged to be the one to escort me to the school entrance. As we got to the staircase, she turned and firmly embraced me, declaring, "I finally know exactly what I want to do when I get out of school!" She had been undecided about becoming a physician, and her parents were pushing toward that goal. She said she wanted to be a pediatric nurse, because then she could have a more intimate relationship with both the infants and the children.

My years as a nurse prepared me with the knowledge of what nursing was about; but my tenure as Department Commander gave me the ability to stand before others and speak with both authority and confidence.

I will be forever grateful to Hadassah for the opportunity to share my life of nursing with others, and to JWV for both the recognition of my service to my country and instilling in me the confidence to do my job well.

✦ ✦ ✦

93

Transformation & Commitment—My Zionism

By Luisa Narins

I was born and raised in Lima, Peru to a Catholic family, though I personally never identified with that religion and kept searching for something that I could hold and truly believe in. When I moved to the United States, I married a Jewish boy and learned more about Judaism. The marriage ended, but my connection to Judaism was cemented. I had found the faith I could hold and call my own. I officially converted and later once again married in a traditional Jewish wedding; he was my B'shert.

When my new husband moved to Salt Lake City, Utah to complete his training in general surgery, I followed, of course. There Hadassah found me. When my dear friend, Laura Green, heard I was not a Hadassah member, she quickly signed me up; I became a Life Member, my husband became an Associate, and immediately I took a board position in the local chapter. After my husband completed his training, we moved back east to New York City and I continued to be active in Hadassah. Because I believed in the message and the work this organization stands for, it was very easy to become engrossed. I split my time between two chapters and my local region. I currently hold eight different portfolios as well as serving as a region vice president. My husband created a new word for my volunteer work; he will often ask me if I'm "Hadassahing." The usual answer is "of course." The truth is that we are both deeply committed to Hadassah; as a transplant surgeon he has presented the Pikuah Nefesh program in several different states around the country, we are both Keepers of the Gate, and hope to become Centennial Founders in a few months.

Last year, I was fortunate enough to be part of the Face2Face Young Women's Mission to Israel. At first, I was a little apprehensive to join this program. I had promised my husband that my first time in Israel would be with him, but we both realized this was a magnificent opportunity and he encouraged me to join the mission. The program was a whirlwind tour; we hit the ground running and never stopped. We visited the Hadassah projects, we toured north and south, and we enjoyed every minute of every day, making real and lasting friendships. I keep in touch with my mission friends and I know I can count on them to be there for me when I need them.

My "Thin Thread" moment came during this mission to Israel on a Friday afternoon as we were preparing for Shabbat and I was walking through the Mechaneh Yehudah Market. I noticed people around me wishing each other "Shabbat Shalom." How comforting it was to hear those words uttered so frequently and freely.

This is the moment I realized why Israel is so important to us as Jews. We need a Jewish State, a land where being Jewish is the norm, not the oddity. When I lived in the Upper West Side of New York City, I knew 90 percent of the people around me were Jewish, but never did we walk around the streets saying "Shabbat Shalom" to each other. Israel allowed me to experience this freedom, and that is the moment I became a Zionist.

This Peruvian born, naturalized American, Jew by choice, will stand with Israel and advocate every opportunity I have. I will be there in 2012 to celebrate 100 years of Hadassah. I will rejoice during the Shabbaton following Convention, as I take part in my Adult B'nai Mitzvah. Eretz Yisrael is my home because home is where the heart is and my heart is with Israel.

+ + +

94

History Shaping the Future

By Benita G. Ross

Like so many, I was familiar with the vast collection of literature, film, and commemorations in Israel and elsewhere that were focused on the Holocaust. I felt steeped in the history and saturated by the connections commonly made to the Shoah and the reality of the State of Israel.

Despite extensive European travel, I had avoided actually traveling to the horrific sites of Jewish destruction. However, in the last several years, I had a growing sense that I, too, needed to personally bear witness.

Three years ago, I learned about the Youth Aliyah Poland Heritage Mission. I decided that this represented a very different opportunity. Through this program, Hadassah funds one hundred students from our Youth Aliyah Villages who otherwise would not have the experience to personally confront the issues of the Shoah as most other Israeli high school students do. While this is certainly part of the national Israeli culture, I realized that for many of these students with non-European backgrounds, this is not their familial history. To be accepted in the program, they must complete a study course with skilled staff and Israeli-trained guides.

In March 2011, I was able to accompany these remarkable students and extra-ordinary staff for the eight-day mission.

Through films, music, drama, poetry, and personal interactions, we walked the streets of Warsaw, Lublin, Krakow, through Madjanek, Treblinka, Auschwitz, Birkenau, and Plaszow. We saw the remnants of the Warsaw Ghetto's wall, Mila Street, and the deportation sites. We visited the Tykocin shtetl, which could have been lifted straight out of a Sholom Aleichem story. We danced by the grave of the great Hassidic Rabbi Elimelech. The students walked through memorials carrying Israeli flags. On chilly mornings, they were actually wrapped in the flags for warmth. Kaddish was recited followed by the blowing of the shofar, and the singing of HaTikvah.

Often, I was overwhelmed with tears and a student or staff member would come to me and ask, "Ma shlomech?" (How are you?). My answer was always, "I am fine because YOU are here."

For these students, the experience confirms their precious value to Israel's present and future. Never in my years of Hadassah leadership have I felt so absolute and direct an impact on Jewish continuity. More times than I can count, publicly and individually, they thanked Hadassah for making this possible.

For me, this moving and transformative event validated my passion, involvement, and appreciation for what Hadassah has allowed me, and 300,0000 others, to accomplish.

✦ ✦ ✦

— 95 —

Giving Back
By Anonymous

First-time wife at 41.
First-time mother at 42.
Second-time mother at 44.
Breast cancer survivor at 46.

My husband and I were leading our crazy, blissfully happy lives when I was diagnosed with Stage 1 breast cancer in October 2010. Only now, a year later, am I even able to write this.

I sit here now on the other side of a lumpectomy, sentinel node biopsy, chemotherapy, and radiation. I kept up my fulltime job through it all. I never felt sorry for myself. I never looked back. It was a process that needed to be gotten through, and thank G-d for my husband, I/we did get through it with flying colors.

I do not make the above statements glibly. These statements are simply truthful. I did not then, and do not now, worry too much about the emotional impact this all has on me. I didn't think I would ever feel completely innocent or carefree again, but sometimes I think that I really do.

So life, at least the parts that are most important, is basically back to normal. Lots of checkups, some anxiety, some physical remnants, some inconveniences. But basically, we are really OK, and able to revel in the miracles that is our love for each other and our small children. I even managed to get a promotion at my job during this time.

Since I was so lucky that I found the lump when I did and so fortunate that I was able to be treated by the very best and that every doctor I consulted (and being the information-junkie that I am, I consulted a LOT), told me I would be just fine, what I DID worry about was how I was ever going to figure out a way to GIVE BACK for my good fortune. I am not public about my situation for various personal reasons, so giving back to the breast cancer community, other than donations, was not my best option.

When I was a teenager, my mother made me a Life Member of Hadassah. A running thought during the past few difficult years centered around becoming involved in the organization, although I never acted on it. In August/September 2010, prior to my diagnosis, I reached out to the region where I now live and was then contacted by one of the membership vice presidents of my local chapter. The vice president and I communicated a few times, I was diagnosed, and then, clearly, with other things on my mind, I dropped the ball.

But she didn't. Unbeknownst to her as to *why* I had stopped responding, she reached out to me again in February 2011. Her thoroughness, persistence, and warmth came through every word of her email and included an invitation to a new member soiree taking place that month. I was midway through chemotherapy at that point and STILL hadn't figured out how I was going to give back to the world, or some portion of it, for G-d's good grace to me and my family.

I went to that new member soiree. And I never again had to wonder how to give back. There it was. My answer. Almost as if I didn't make the decision, but it was made for me. I would give back to and through Hadassah, this wonderful organization and the wonderful women I have begun to know through it.

That night at the soiree, they joked that they would never see me again. I am somewhat younger than most of the chapter members, and I also look younger than my years. Those attending that evening didn't know that because of the rite of passage I had gone through in the past year, I was probably now something of an old soul. But more importantly, their legendary warmth and welcoming arms were, and still are, the perfect answer to the question I couldn't stop asking. What better environment than Hadassah to help me find an answer to my year-long quest?

✦ ✦ ✦

✦ 96 ✦

Group Therapy
By Faye Sidder

We began as a Hadassah study group.

Sixty-three years later, we still meet regularly. We study, we discuss, and sometimes the study group becomes group therapy. On August 26, 2011, we celebrated the ninetieth birthdays of five of our thirteen members. One of our women was absent because she was in the hospital. The mood was festive in the private room of a fine restaurant. (These were women who prided themselves on their hospitality and culinary skills.)

Our study group lunches featured homemade delicacies prized by our facilitators and speakers, and once a year we invited our husbands to a feast of special dishes we each brought. As we gathered, we put our walkers aside and there were hugs and kisses all around. There were flowers on the table and printed menus and gifts wrapped for the honorees. After the drinks were poured, we lifted our glasses for a toast. First, we remembered by name each of those who had passed away. Then a toast to our absent member with a prayer for her recovery and a happy toast to each of the ninetieth birthdays.

As lunch was served the memories began to flow. Some of us began our Hadassah experiences as teenagers in Little Women of Hadassah. We remembered a Sunday meeting on December 7,1941 when we were interrupted with the frightful news of the bombing of Pearl Harbor by the Japanese. The realization hit that we were at war and our lives were about to change. We were about to grow up, fast. Most of the boys we knew went off to war. There were war-time weddings, and college, and jobs for us. When the war ended and the men came home, there were many more weddings followed by many babies—the baby boomers.

The revelations of the horrors of the Holocaust, followed by the formation of the State of Israel, the Promised Land, inspired us to enlist in The Cause. Detroit had a vibrant, productive chapter of Hadassah. We served on committees, on boards, as officers, as group presidents, and one of our members was president of the Metropolitan Detroit Chapter of Hadassah. We developed our skills: enlisting new members, raising funds, supporting Youth Aliyah, fostering education. We formed a new study group. It was named Aliyah. Who knew that a number of our children would indeed make Aliyah to Israel in the future?

Through the years, we studied a wide variety of subjects: Torah, medical ethics, Jewish women writers, and much more. Our teachers were outstanding rabbis and professors. We also built close, strong friendships and shared our family joys and sorrows—our prides and our losses.

The passing years have slowed us. Today, we revel in warm, loving feelings as we realize that after all the years of meetings, we are still celebrating our unique group. Hadassah brought us together and we have lived to appreciate the meaning and purpose it added to our lives. When the cake was carried in, lemon chiffon, with "Happy 90th Birthdays" written in icing, five friends blew out the candles. Cheers and hugs all around.

✦ ✦ ✦

✦ 97 ✦

A Father's Story of Healing at Hadassah
By Teddy Weinberger

A Letter to Marcie Natan, Hadassah National President,
August 1, 2011.

Dear Ms. Natan,

In December of 2010, our son, Ezra (then 18) was diagnosed at
Hadassah Ein Karem with nasopharyngeal carcinoma. This cancer,
which attacks the juncture of the nasal passages, auditory tubes,
and upper respiratory tract, is relatively common in Southeast Asia,
but rare in Israel. That fact is of little comfort, however, when it is
your child who is ill.

If your son is diagnosed with cancer at a relatively early stage,
you are put in the horrible position of agreeing to make him very
sick at a time when he seems okay. Ezra's oncologist, Dr. Amichay
Meirovitz, did an excellent job in preparing us for the side effects
of Ezra's treatment: He scared us silly. Because of Ezra's youth
and large build, Dr. Meirovitz was being as aggressive as possible
in order to knock the cancer to kingdom come. The protocol for

Ezra's treatment was that he would receive an initial strong dose of chemotherapy (requiring an in-patient stay of several days), followed by weekly chemotherapy and thirty-two exceptionally high-powered radiation treatments. Nurse Michelle Peleg, who treated Ezra in the day-patient chemo ward, said that she had never seen such a massive course of treatment.

And so began our intense relationship with Hadassah. For six and a half weeks, Sunday through Thursday, we would travel to Hadassah Ein Karem. We usually took the scenic route from the Mevasseret Tziyon area, cutting through the Jerusalem hills and the winding picturesque roads to the hospital. Is there another world-class hospital situated in such a pastoral setting? I doubt it.

Upon reaching the hospital's main gate, which opened automatically for our pre-approved license plate, we would head for the exclusive, small parking lot of the Sharett Institute of Oncology (your hospital parking rights are in direct proportion to the severity of your situation). Ezra would then hustle in to put his name down on the day's radiation list. Rules are that you must sign-in in person; however, you are then free to take care of other business and your spot will be held for you.

Often, Ezra did have other business. One of the truly exceptional things about Hadassah is that it offers world-class care across the board. Dr. Meirovitz insisted right from the start that Ezra see dental specialists Drs. Motti Sela and Anat Sharon in order to make sure that Ezra's teeth and mouth would come through all that radiation. Another side trip Ezra would make would be to Naama Hirschberger, the psychologist attached to oncology. I'm proud of Ezra for taking advantage of Naama's help and for unburdening himself to her. With us, Ezra was very careful not to worry us. Even when he could not eat due to severe pain in swallowing food and a loss of appetite and had to have a feeding tube inserted into his stomach, Ezra never said he was hurting—although sometimes I would tell him, for G-d's sake Ezra, it's okay to complain.

While Ezra went about his business, I would go about mine. (I should note at this point that when my wife took Ezra, her strategy was different than mine: She would just sit and wait.) I would go back to the car, get my jogging gear, change in one of the always-clean bathrooms (hourly cleanings are posted and supervised), and get out on to the Hadassah Trail. Hadassah grooms a beautiful hiking trail surrounding the hospital. Running at a moderate pace, I could make a loop around the entire trail in about thirty-five minutes. I would then return, change back, and if the time was right (1:30 p.m.), head off for mincha, to what has to be not simply the most aesthetic hospital chapel ever built, but one of the most beautiful synagogues in the world—the chapel with Marc Chagall's magnificent windows.

I loved staring at those windows as I davened. The colors put the whole experience on an otherworldly plane. At the conclusion of the afternoon prayer service, I could eat the lunch provided to patients' families by Lottie's Kitchen (e.g., hamburger, pasta, and mixed vegetables). Yes, it's true: With the complimentary parking, the beautiful run, the spiritual uplift, and the free food, I could almost forget that my son had cancer. And Ezra preferred it this way. He didn't particularly like to sit next to me even when I did wait with him for his radiation turn.

When Ezra's treatment came to an end we met with Dr.

Meirovitz. We asked him if Ezra could plan on attending a family wedding in Chicago in August. We thought he would say, "Let's wait until the results of Ezra's PET/CT scan in July." To our surprise, Dr. Meirovitz said, "Go." After the meeting I asked Sarah, "Did I hear what I just heard?" We had basically been told that, as far as Dr. Meirovitz was concerned, the PET/CT was simply a confirmation to what he, as a man of science, already knew: Ezra's cancer had been wiped out. No one was celebrating just yet, though. Ezra was at his lowest point physically. He had lost a lot of weight, his whole nasopharyngeal area was sore, and he had no appetite, no active taste buds, and when he forced himself to eat or drink something, swallowing caused him great pain.

Somehow, Ezra managed to get through the next few months. At first, the side effects of the treatment continued in all their power, but gradually their severity lessened. On July 7, Ezra had his PET/CT scan. We learned the results on July 21—normal metabolic activity in the nasopharyngeal area—no trace of cancer.

There are dozens and dozens of names on the walls leading to the entrance of Hadassah's Sharett Institute. And there are hundreds of thousands of Hadassah members, including my wife, a Life Member thanks to her grandmother, Mrs. Sylvia Ross (of blessed memory). If we could, we would personally thank every single Hadassah supporter. As Haddasah's Centenary President, please be so gracious as to accept our thanks on behalf of the entire Hadassah community.

In 1948, the mighty Babe Ruth succumbed to nasopharyngeal carcinoma. Sixty-three years later mighty Hadassah was there for our son. Thank you.

◆ ◆ ◆

✦ 98 ✦

"101"

By Phyllis Stern

I am Phyllis Stern of Norwich, Connecticut. I am one year older than Hadassah! In February 2012, I will be 101 years old. It's hard to believe that I was a year old when Henrietta Szold held the meeting at Temple Emanu-El, which established Hadassah.

My life was transformed in 1945 when my husband and I moved to Norwich, Connecticut. I had been active in the Council of Jewish Women, but a new friendship inspired me to join Hadassah, and that inspiration has enriched my life.

I lived through the emotions of the terrors of World War II and the Holocaust and the struggle for a Jewish state in Palestine. Being a member of Hadassah during the years leading up to the establishment of the State of Israel was thrilling. To know that my organization was participating in the growth and development of our new homeland was fantastic and made me so proud. It is heartbreaking that Henrietta Szold died before the State of

Israel was born—but my generation lived it through her and for her.

For the last twenty years or so, I have been deeply moved by my chapter giving me the honor of saying the Hamotzi at each special chapter event. And I always comment that I am so proud to be a life member of a Jewish women's organization that has thrived and grown through all my years to be almost as old as I am!

✦ ✦ ✦

99

Passing The Torch

By Stephanie Goodman

In June 2012, Megan Goodman was called as a Bat Mitzvah at Congregation Ner Tamid and asked to share the genesis and inspiration behind her mitzvah project and her understanding of her Torah portion. The following excerpt is a portion of what this mature thirteen-year-old told the congregation, inclusive of both her grandmothers. What she did not share that morning, was that her request that she receive no personal gifts, and only donations to Hadassah, yielded over $10,000.

When I visited Jerusalem two years ago, I had the opportunity to visit Hadassah Hospital. At the hospital, there is a beautiful chapel with stained glass windows, designed by Marc Chagall, inspired by the same twelve tribes in the Torah portion. Hadassah is a Jewish women's organization founded to promote unity, healthcare, education, land development, and youth programs. It parallels my Torah portion, as Hadassah is very much the modern day gift in thanks for freedom and is critical to the future of Israel. At the time this Torah portion was written, each family, or household, was represented by his tribe's leader. A household, over 2,500 years ago, consisted of a man and all that was his: his wife, his children, and his possessions. Imagine what they would think now about a women's volunteer organization dedicated to improving the lives of so many all over the world! This is the reason I have chosen Hadassah as my mitzvah project.

Hadassah is dedicated to innovative and creative funding for women and girls in the United States and Israel. Its mission is to improve the status, health, and well being of women and girls, and encourage and facilitate their active participation in decision-making and leadership in all spheres of life.

Hadassah represents the strength and leadership that I hope to exhibit as I take my place in the world. I follow three generations of former Hadassah presidents. My great, great grandmother Molly Wise, my grandmother Adele Morse Platt, and my grammy Margie Richards all spent many years of their lives dedicated to fundraising for Hadassah and supporting their many causes. My great grandmother Mildred Satz, Nana Dottie Goodman, my mother, and I are all Lifetime Members of Hadassah. It is my honor, even at the age of thirteen, to take my place as a woman in the Hadassah organization.

In lieu of gifts in honor of my Bat Mitzvah, I have requested that all invited to my Bat Mitzvah celebration make a donation to Hadassah. Furthermore, for all here in our sanctuary this morning, I hope you will learn more about all the programs Hadassah offers. This is my gift in thanks for my freedom and with dedication to my future—as the People of Israel in the Land of Israel. Shabbat Shalom!"

Megan chose to direct her donation to the new hospital building with the addition of her name, and to use a message on a large brick of the Centennial Path to inspire others to do the same.

Two years ago, Megan visited the hospital and spent hours finding the numerous inscriptions of the names of her grandmother and great grandmother honored throughout walls and pillars of the campus. She looks forward to returning soon to find her name alongside the many people she admires for their commitment to Hadassah. She also aspires to have an impact on women's issues globally in her future career choices.

✦ ✦ ✦

100

Enough Is Enough

By Paige Sass

I t was almost to the very moment when I was to ascend to the position of Southern Region of Hadassah President, after so many, many years of working my way up the ladder, that I was hit with a dual diagnosis of breast and lung cancers.

OK, I have arrived at some sort of peace with the cancer treatments, the loss of independence, the hair loss, and the vomiting attached to the cancer; I have even reconciled myself to the fact that the volunteer job I have devoted eight years of my life to achieving was not going to happen now.

But on May 14, 2012, when I turned on the television and saw some of my friends lined up outside in the courtyard of the *Today Show* holding signs reading "Hadassah—100!" —that was like a dream morning for me!

"Enough is enough!" I said loudly to no one in particular. But that is how I felt at that magic moment. Enough dwelling on the things tying me to cancer. Enough. Today I tie my journey to that of my Hadassah sisters and to what they are fighting for. On that morning, unlike any day in recent memory, my spark was re-kindled by a simple few moments watching a television show. I am again excited about everything Hadassah: giving of my time, my talent, and treasure to this organization is my great pleasure.

Later, I was so proud to say to my husband, Neil, and Lynn, my sister, "Look, there's Mindy and I think that's Ronnie, all promoting Hadassah's Centennial and saying 'Hi' to the world from the Today Show plaza!"

Good work, I thought to myself. Good for you, girls. I just wish I were there with you all. For right now, along with my support-ive husband and friends, I am tackling the cancers with the same energy I'd planned to access in taking on the presidency.

But next time. Next time, I'm going to be there holding a Hadassah sign right next to you all.

✦ ✦ ✦

The Hadassah Leadership Academy Transformed My Life

By Ruth Gursky

I'm proud to have been chosen as a member of the third Hadassah Leadership Academy (HLA) class (2003–05). The HLA is a unique, two-year program of Jewish study and leadership skills for Jewish women of all ages from around the country that trained us to become future leaders in Hadassah and our local Jewish communities. Participating in the HLA made me who I am today—a Hadassah leader and donor, eager to roll up my sleeves and help propel our 100-year old Women's Zionist Organization into its second century.

On my HLA Mission to Israel, three buses carrying 120 HLA participants visited sites of importance to Jewish history and Hadassah.

In Israel, witnessing our projects first-hand, I felt the indescribable thrill of being a part of a cause that embodies the important

Jewish values that I hold dear: *tikkun olam* (repairing the world), *pekuah nefesh* (saving lives, one person at a time), *klal Yisrael* (embracing that we are one) and *l'dor v'dor* (passing our wisdom, values and love of Israel to the next generation).

All that we saw and did provided me with an understanding and admiration for Hadassah's mission and the life-saving work, the work we do that transforms caring into action on a daily basis (or "practical Zionism" as we like to call our mission in Israel and the United States).

Over the course of our whirlwind journey, we were also privileged to hear from a variety of people who shared their views on leadership with us. These are a few of the things I learned:

Major Tamir, a slightly built Ethiopian born Jew, is the commander at the Erez Crossing between Israel and the Gaza Strip. In his brief talk, he shared details on two recent incidents at this border crossing: one, which turned out well (thanks to a sharp-eyed officer who apprehended a terrorist with a detonation device in his underwear when he tried to use an expired ID card at the checkpoint), and another, which resulted in tragedy (a disabled Palestinian woman took advantage of the compassion shown by Israeli soldiers and detonated herself, killing or wounding several officers). While Major Tamir was talking to us and telling us these stories that I really didn't want to hear but was riveted by nonetheless, I looked across to the border crossing—only a few hundred yards away from us—and wondered, what if one of the people crossing into Israel at that very moment decided to detonate himself or herself . . . and I'm sure I wasn't the only HLA'er thinking these nervous thoughts. And while Major Tamir's relaxed tone and cheery countenance made me feel safe, I was just as happy when we alighted our buses for safer terrain. Lesson learned: Leadership means balancing the taking of risks with the showing of compassion.

Lt. Gal Hirsch, a hunk right out of Central Casting, is in charge of training new Army recruits. He explained that a leader should develop a dual vision of the present and the future. It's the leader's job, he believes, to move those under his command from the "here and now" to the "what could be" through education. "Follow me!" is his leadership mantra. As it turned out, we passed several groups of new Army recruits during our journey, when we visited the Western Wall, at Ben Gurion's burial site and again at the Church of the Holy Sepulchre, which we visited on a Shabbat walking tour of the Old City. Interested in learning why our soldiers were visiting a site of such importance to a quartet of Christian sects, our guide explained that new recruits are taken there to learn about the other major religions that share a claim to Jerusalem. Through education, he explained, it is hoped that they will gain respect for diversity. Lesson learned: Leadership means having a vision and sharing it with others.

Marlene Post, a former Hadassah National President, and the woman primarily responsible for creating the HLA program during her tenure, spoke to us during dinner at the Hadassah College Jerusalem, a meal cooked and served by college students. She shared that one should not be afraid to announce to the world that you "want to be a leader." In fact, she encouraged us to say it out loud at our respective tables. I did, quietly, to those seated at the table near me and my friend Lillian, seated to my right, said: "You already are, Ruth!" Lesson learned: Leadership requires chutzpah.

At our closing dinner, Jackie Cohen, the personable and knowledgeable National HLA Chair, tweaked Lt. Hirsch's leadership mantra and promoted a warmer, gentler approach. Instead of "Follow me," Jackie's philosophy is: "Take my hand and come with me." As one who watched her lead by example during my two years in the HLA and beyond, I'd say she's right on! Lesson learned: Leadership is a partnership.

All that I studied in the HLA on Jewish peoplehood, the land of Israel, leadership skills, and Jewish values crystallized for me on this journey to Israel. This was a special week, a week of learning, a unique opportunity to deepen my relationship with Hadassah and Israel.

I thank Hadassah for creating the HLA and giving me and so many other program participants the opportunity to grow in personal strength, Jewish knowledge, leadership abilities, appreciation of Hadassah's work, dedication to Zionism and love of Israel. As individual members and as an organization, may we continue to go from strength to strength, always keeping our eyes on the future!

Happy 100th Anniversary, Hadassah!

✦ ✦ ✦

Contributor Biographies

Fanchon Weiss Auman grew up in Chicago's Hyde Park neighborhood and currently resides in St. Louis, Missouri, with her husband, Harry. They have four children and four grandchildren. She earned a bachelor's degree from the University of Illinois and a master's from the University of Michigan, both in physical education. She has worked at the St. Louis JCC since 1993 and is currently the director of Sports Recreation & Aquatics. She is actively involved with Hadassah; vice president for Health and co-chair of the Walk on Sunshine. She also enjoys playing tennis and spending time with her family.

Edith Barr has always been active in Hadassah wherever she has lived. She has been education vice president, program vice president, group and chapter president, region education vice president, region program vice president, region special services vice president, and region area vice president. She is a trained Ivrit L'Hadassah teacher, Training Wheels leader, and leadership-training instructor. She was a Young Judaea leader for eighteen years. She has worked as a systems programmer and director of recreation in assisted living. She and her husband, Mort, have three daughters and ten grandchildren.

Tamara Greenspan Bennett, feels that Hadassah has been an important part of her life, from chapter president to region president to the first chair of Hadassah Southern California, San Diego. Previously, she has served on the National Board, HSC Cabinet, and Executive Committee, and is currently PPAC, on both the national and local level. Tamara is currently on the HSC, San Diego Leadership committee. She is a Life Member and Keeper of the Gate. She was a lay volunteer of the Institutional Review Board of Children's Hospital and now volunteers at Sharp Coronado Hospital. Tamara is married, has three children, five grandchildren, and is a five-generation Hadassah family.

Leona Brauser has been an active member of Hadassah since 1954, serving as president in three different cities. In 1997, she was the founding chair of Hadassah's annual gift giving program, Keepers of The Gate. Forty million dollars have been raised through this program to support Hadassah's life saving work. Leona has been a member of the National Board for fifteen years and presently serves as the Golden Keepers National chair. She is proud that all the members of her family are Life Members.

Fredi Brown became a Life Member of Hadassah in Peoria, Illinois, in the 1970s. After moving to Scottsdale, Arizona in 1997, Fredi joined the Chai Group of Hadassah and worked her way up the ladder to president of the Hadassah Valley of the Sun Chapter in 2003, and president of the Desert-Mountain Region in 2010. She has a long history with volunteerism; Fredi currently serves on the Board of Trustees of Copland House, which enhances awareness and appreciation of the heritage of American music through the legacy of Aaron Copland. Her family is part of the Hadassah family. She and her husband, Howard Treshansky, are Keepers of the Gate and belong to the Circle of Founders.

Sharon Cadoff, widowed after forty-three years, is part of a four-generation Hadassah family of Life Members and Associates. She was elected president of the Lower New York State Region after retiring from a career in education. Mom of three times two, bubbe of five, her community activities include president of the PTA, service on her temple's Board of Directors, and publicity chair for the local League of Women Voters and the 50+ Singles group of the JCCGW.

Carol Charen has been a member of Hadassah for almost twenty years. After attending a young women's membership tea, she was hooked! Over the years, she has held many portfolios including co-president of the Raquela Group, Camden County chapter president, area vice president, and organizational vice president for the Southern New Jersey Region. Presently, she is the Region Services vice president. Carol says that Hadassah is a part of who she is and truly one of the best gifts she has ever given herself. She is married to Bob for twenty-two years and is mom to Hillary, now twenty-one and a college student. She states that "the sisterhood and passion to our mission continues."

Elynne Chaplik-Aleskow is a Pushcart Prize nominated author and award-winning educator and broadcaster. She is the founding general manager of WYCC-TV/PBS and distinguished professor emeritus of Wright College in Chicago. Elynne's performances of her stories have been broadcast on

NPR and WGN radio. She has performed in New York City at the Museum of Motherhood and throughout Chicago. Her work was featured in the production *Dear Mother* in Los Angeles at The Lyric Theater. Her stories and essays have been published in numerous anthologies and magazines. Visit http://LookAroundMe.blogspot.com.

Lynn Ross Davidson, a member since 1981, is a past president of the Massapequa-Aviva Chapter. Since 1991, she has held various portfolios on the Nassau Region executive board. Lynn had previously been a member of the Friends of Sprout Lake and the board of Camp Tel Yehudah. Lynn is part of a three-generation Life Member family that includes her daughters, Amy and Lauren. Her husband, Michael, and son-in-law, Daniel Hoffman, are Associates. Lynn and Michael have made several wonderful trips to Israel with Hadassah. Lynn is looking forward to celebrating Hadassah's centennial in Jerusalem in October.

Lindy Davis (née Knight) is based in Auckland, New Zealand. She's married with three adult children, all Life Members of Hadassah, thanks to their grandmother, Valda Knight, who was an inspiration to all the family. Lindy is a journalist and has worked on several lifestyle magazines. Her first junior fiction novel, *The Golden Scarab* was published in 2007 and she has recently completed the second in the series.

Suzanne Dunklin was born in Detroit, Michigan and was raised in Southfield, Michigan. She is a graduate of Oral Roberts University and Norfolk State University, with a bachelor's degree in social work in 1995 and a master of social work degree in 1997. Suzanne converted to Judaism in 2005, at which time she became a Life Member of Hadassah. She went on the Poland/Israel Mission in 2005, which she credits as having changed her life.

Katie Edelstein of Bellingham, Washington is an elected member of the National Board of Hadassah and the Hadassah Foundation Board. As a past National vice president, National membership division coordinator, and president of the Pacific Northwest Region of Hadassah, Katie continues to find inspiration and connection to the land and people of Israel as well as identifying opportunities to play a part in tikun olam, exemplified by her kidney donation to her fellow National Board colleague in 2004. Katie is supportive of Hadassah's projects through her Society of Major Donors' gifts.

Peg Elefant, formerly of Corvallis, Oregon, and now residing in Seattle, Washington, is a thirty-four year Life Member of Hadassah. She has served in multiple Hadassah leadership roles in the Corvallis chapter, the Pacific Northwest Region Board, and the national workforce. Her most current Hadassah position is National Online Training Chair. Steve Elefant, her husband of thirty-three years, is a proud Hadassah Associate, as is her son, Dan. Sharon, her daughter, is a twenty-seven year Life Member and has enthusiastically welcomed Hadassah contributions to honor her simchas!

Susie Kahn Enteen is a young Hadassah woman who grew up in New Orleans, and later made Aliyah from South Florida in 2006. She is currently living happily with her husband, Coby, and their three children: Aviv, eleven; Ilan, eight; and Sivan, three, in Modiin, a town in the center of Israel. She teaches English at a local elementary school.

E.G. "Jerry" Farris, from Whitehall, Pennsylvania, served two years in the USAF. A Life Member of Hadassah, she gave presentations in local middle schools for three years for Hadassah and the Johnson & Johnson's program "The Future of Nursing." A veteran devoted to the betterment of our veteran community, she works hard to obtain that end. The mother of twins, she has three grandchildren and always has time for family.

Diana Feld grew up in Brighton Beach, Brooklyn with her parents, Edith and Aaron Bregman (who met and married in Palestine). She was a member of Habonim, IZFA, YZOA, and studied in Israel in 1949. She pursued Yiddish and Hebrew music at Brandeis Hebrew Art Institute in California in 1950 and still entertains and lectures on Jewish themes. Her fondest memory is singing for Yitzhak Rabin. The National Yiddish Book Center's website featured Diana's oral interview about her mother's Yiddish poetry, which she published. She and husband, Stanley, divide their year between Florida and the Berkshires. She proudly wears a three-generation pin!

Adrienne Fishman resides in Fairfield, Connecticut, where she has been active in Hadassah for thirty-two years. She has been bulletin editor, fund-raising vice president, programming vice president, presidium member, and chapter president. In 2005, she went back to Israel after thirty-seven years, this time with her husband, Neal, a Hadassah Associate. Their Hadassah Yom Ha'atzmaut Mission to Israel inspired her essay for *Thin Threads*.

Alana Fodeman served as president of the Fairfield Connecticut Hadassah Chapter for thirteen years between 1993 and 2011. During that time, her chapter raised over $1 million dollars for Hadassah's projects. In addition to serving as president of the local chapter, Alana has served on the Connecticut Region of Hadassah Board and on the National Board of Women's Division of Israel Bonds. After four grandsons, Alana recently became the grandmother of her first granddaughter, Harper (Hadassah) Fodeman, adding a new member to her four-generation Hadassah family.

Ellen Frick-Delman was born and raised in New York. She relocated to Switzerland in 1984. She is director of the Zurich America Center and U.S. Consular Agent (Honorary Consul). Her various volunteer positions include president of the American Women's Club (1996) and she has the distinction of being elected the first woman president of the American Club of Zurich (2007–9) in the Club's fifty-two year history. She is co-chair of the Swiss American Charity Golf Championship and is a member of the Corps Consulaire de Zurich. Ellen is a founding member and current president of Hadassah Switzerland and Hadassah International's European Liaison. She is married and has one son.

Rita Fuchs was born some seventy-five years ago in New York City, and says, "How lucky I am. My husband and I just celebrated our fifty-fifth year of marriage. We have been blessed with two sons who are married to two wonderful girls and have four grandchildren. Some very special people have found their way into my heart. Joining Rabin Hadassah, co-chairing membership and meeting the women of Hadassah have all been life fulfilling. Hadassah has truly become an open door in my life."

Esther Gastwirth was born Esther Dykman in 1923 in Vilna, Poland. She was the only member of her family to survive the concentration camps. After marrying another Holocaust survivor, she emigrated to the United States and is blessed with a family, which includes great-grandchildren. She became an active member of Hadassah in 1957, and is now a Life Member in the Judith Epstein Chapter of West Palm Beach, Florida. She also speaks about the Holocaust in schools, and writes fictional short stories loosely based on her experiences.

Gloria Gelman, a Life Member of Hadassah, a Daughter of Sarah, and the recipient of the Myrtle Wreath award, is married and has three daughters, one son, and nine grandchildren. She has a dual MBA degree in speech pathology and audiology from Temple University and New Jersey University. Gloria has held many portfolios in Hadassah, and is currently vice president of Grass Roots fund-raising for the Greater Philadelphia Chapter of Hadassah. Gloria advocates and enjoys working on projects that make life better for children.

Ida Gnieslaw was born in December 1929 in Brussels, Belgium. She speaks Yiddish, French, Hebrew, English, and Flemish. She was one of the early members of Kibbutz Nirim. The kibbutz was established in 1946 and Ida came down with about twenty more young people from Ein Ha Oresh in 1948. They came as reinforcements to protect the kibbutz. As Nirim is directly opposite the Gaza strip, during the war in 1948 she defended the kibbutz from the Egyptian army. She tells me that she was in charge of "first aid". (Submitted with approval by Kathleen Hyman.)

Linda S. Goldstein, CPA, holds a master's degree in research and statistics and serves as treasurer and chair of Planned Giving and Estates on the Greater Miami Region's Executive Board. Linda is a Keeper of the Gate and member of the Society of Major Donors, a proud recipient of Simcha Chapter's Woman of the Year Award, Hadassah's prestigious National Leadership Award, as well as her Synagogue's Woman of Valor Award. Linda's family consists of four generations of Life Members and Associates.

Stephanie Goodman is the proud mother of Megan, and honored to be the descendent of three generations of former Hadassah presidents. The spirit and mission of Hadassah inspire her as she looks for ways to teach her daughter the important values in life. She is truly honored that her story has been selected to inspire others.

Helen Gordon, a native of Elmira, New York, first visited Israel in 1950. She participated in the Second Israel Summer Institute, resulting in her lifelong support of Hadassah and its work. She has visited Israel a number of times since then with her husband, children, and grandchildren. She now lives in Rochester, New York.

Carol M. Towbin Greenberg, a lifelong educator, attended public schools and put herself through college: UF (BA '76 highest honors), UCL (full scholarship), and Duke (MALS '86). Settling in Savannah with her high school sweetheart and their two wonderful children, Carol was a teacher, principal, and commissioner before founding the Jewish arts agency, MorningStar, in 1989. She created and donated over 419 cultural programs, earning many civic awards and honors. She proudly has served Hadassah for over twenty-five years.

Janice Greenwald, a past National Vice President of Hadassah, currently serves in the Development Department, the Jewish Education Department, and is on the Ethics Committee. Janice is on the Board of Governors for State of Israel Bonds, and is chair of its Women's Division. She is a member of the Executive and Ritual Committees of Temple B'Nai Israel and will serve as president this year. Janice and her husband, Louis, are the parents of three children and have five grandchildren.

Ruth Gursky, New York Region president, is a three-generation Hadassah Life Member, Hadassah Leadership Academy graduate, Founding Chair of the HLA Alumnae Association, and past president of the Shatil Chapter. An attorney, fundraising consultant, personal trainer, and running coach, Ruth has logged hundreds of volunteer hours across a spectrum of organizations and has been honored many times for her leadership and community activism, including receiving the HLA Distinguished Alumna Award for her commitment to Hadassah.

Muriel Haber's first experience with Hadassah was as a child in Brooklyn, New York. When her husband and their four daughters settled in New Jersey in the 1960s, Hadassah invited her to a tea, and their relationship resumed. She was able to hold many offices, make their daughters Life Members and make her husband, Stan, an Associate Member. On July 14, 1997, she celebrated her Bat Mitzvah at Hadassah National Convention in Chicago. She is grateful to all her Hadassah sisters for enriching her life. She says, "May we all go from strength to strength."

Sarah Harris was born on July 3, 1910, to Russian immigrant parents. She was the cherished only daughter, with two older and two younger brothers. At the age of sixteen, Sarah graduated from Western High School and entered Goucher College, from which she graduated in 1929. In 1938 she married LeRoy F. Kappelman and raised three daughters while continuing her organizational work, eventually becoming president of Hadassah, HIAS, and the Federation of Woman's Organizations of MD. Following the death of her first husband,

Sarah remarried at the age of seventy to S. Herbert Harris in 1980, who passed away in 2008. In July, Sarah will be 102 years young!

Ellen Hershkin of Dix Hills, New York is a member of the National Board and Executive Committee of Hadassah, currently serving as National Secretary. She is a former National vice president and has served Hadassah in many significant portfolios. A past president of both the Dix Hills Chapter and Suffolk Region, Ellen, part of a four-generation Life Member family, joined Hadassah in 1973. The Hershkins are founders in the Mother and Child Center at Hadassah University Hospital, Ein Kerem.

Barbara Strauss Heyman was born in Norristown, Pennsylvania and moved to Monaca, Pennsylvania when she was eight years old. She is the second oldest in a family of eight children. She married in 1965 and moved to Conway, Pennsylvania. She has been a single parent since her children were five and eight. Barbara has two grandsons, Etan and Tamir. She currently serves on the Freedom Area and the Career & Technology Center School Boards. Hadassah has been her real passion.

Sheila Horvitz was born in New York City in 1944 and presently resides in Colchester, Connecticut with her husband, Dr. Victor Horvitz. They have two daughters and five grandchildren. After over thirty years as an attorney/mediator, she now focuses on her family foundations, devoted to Alzheimer's research and domestic violence prevention. A Life Member of Hadassah, she has served as president of her chapter and is a Hand of Healing award recipient. She is thrilled to chair her chapter's Centennial Celebration Committee.

Diane Hunt was born in Bay Ridge, Brooklyn, New York in 1945. She has spent most of her life there. She loves helping people out, and everyone knows how much there is to do for Hadassah. She has been blessed in her adult life to be able to volunteer with babies who are addicted to drugs, to caring for people in Hospice, helping at her Senior Center and at the USO. She is a happy woman. She loves her life, her Medinah Chapter, and the ladies of Hadassah.

Adam Jenshil is the director of Young Judaea's Year Course in Israel. Adam was a participant on Year Course twenty-three years ago. He was raised in London, England and been involved with FZY. He was a counselor on Year Course, where he met his wife, also a counselor. He moved to Israel in 1995, trained as a tour guide and completed his army service. For many years, Adam worked on Young Judaea's short-term programs from summer to Birthright. He spent three years as YJ's shaliach (emissary) in New York and New Jersey, and now runs the successful Year Course program. Adam is married to Dganit and they live in Tzur Hadassah with their three children and a dog.

Marian Kaplan was born in London, England, and grew up in Buffalo, New York. A graduate of Goucher College, she received her master's in education at Stanford University. After teaching elementary school for ten years and then staying home to raise her sons, Marian became a registered nurse. Currently, she lives and works in Overland Park, Kansas and is executive vice president (president-elect) of the Greater Kansas City Chapter of Hadassah. Her hobbies include reading and traveling.

Carol Goodman Kaufman of Worcester, Massachusetts has volunteered with Hadassah since her first week of married life. She currently serves as National Chair of the Programming Department. She is also active in her synagogue, the Jewish Federation, and chairs the Jewish Community Relations Council. Professionally, she is a psychologist and writer, having published one book and several hundred articles, including a monthly travel and food column. She is now attempting fiction, with a murder mystery set in the pastoral Berkshires.

Barbara S. Keil is a Delaware native. She was a columnist for the *Philadelphia Sunday Bulletin*, and freelance writer for *Delaware Today* magazine and *Mid-Atlantic Country* magazine. Barbara is a past president of the Wilmington Chapter of Hadassah and has chaired the Jewish Voice Editorial Committee, served on the board of Jewish Federation, JCC, Delaware State College. She is married to Judge Charles K. Keil. They have two children, Dr. Lea Keil Garson and Dr. Mark Keil, and four grandchildren.

Rebecca Krasnegor is the current President of the Northern Seaboard Region of Hadassah and a five-generation Life Member. She has been a volunteer with Hadassah's Washington Task Force for many years. After graduate work in sociology at Columbia University, she worked in survey research at a private non-profit organization evaluating government programs. Rebecca is the owner of Redmont Associates, an appraisal and dealership with specialty in contemporary art and jewelry from Israel.

Lydia Krieg is a graphic artist and business owner. During the 1987 Intifada, she worked in Israel with the Israel Defense Forces in the Volunteer for Israel program. Lydia is also a strong supporter of the March of the Living Program in Israel. She is a proactive member of the Florida Atlantic Region Executive Board in Delray Beach, Florida and she served as the program vice president from 2009 to 2012. Lydia subscribes to the following: She is privileged and proud to be a part of the continuing story of an organization that is about people, about making the world a better place—Tikun Olam.

Selma Kron and her husband, Norman, were proud owners of a skilled nursing facility in suburban Philadelphia for a quarter of a century. One year, *Good Housekeeping* listed the facility as one of the top in the nation. However, when her husband developed cancer she decided to close that chapter of her life. They gifted their business to the Jewish Federation of Philadelphia in 1994 and established a Charitable Remainder Trust. They were instrumental in building the Gene Therapy Center at the new Mother and Child Pavilion at Hadassah Medical Center. Selma's oldest daughter, Andi, who lives in Los Alamos, New Mexico, is now volunteering at Hadassah Neurim near Netanya, tutoring students in English.

Cissy Lacks is a writer, photographer, and teacher. She is a recipient of the PEN/Newman's Own Award, which is given each year to one person in the United States who has defended First Amendment rights at a personal risk. She has had several one-woman photography shows in her portfolio and publications in both the creative and non-fiction areas. She has a Ph.D. in American Studies and a master's in broadcasting. She can be reached at: cissylacks@gmail.com

Dorothy Lasensky believes that when you have a passion for something, it marks your life forever. She has been a nurse for the past forty-eight years. Her journey through the profession has taken her into the fields of pediatrics, obstetrics, medical-legal consulting, operating room and school/camp nursing. She has practiced in five states and Canada. As a long time humanitarian, she has volunteered in Mexico, South America, and Israel. World travel, grandchildren, community work, and enrichment courses occupy her days now.

Deborah Rabinowitz Layman is a native New Yorker who married a boy from Birmingham and has lived in Alabama for over thirty years. She and her husband, Hank, are the parents of three sons and the grandparents of one long-awaited little girl. Deborah is a writer, producer, and marketing consultant. Like many Jewish mothers, she has a reputation for being opinionated and bossy—but it's for your own good. Read her blog at www.deborahlayman. blogspot.com.

Nancy R. Leavitt's story tells of the memories she has had during her fifty-two-year connection with Hadassah that began with her mother's devotion to the organization. It obviously made a strong enough impression on her to last until today. The proof of that is her four-generation Hadassah pin that she wears with great pride. She credits her Quicken computer program with keeping her records as Chapter Treasurer accurate.

Carolyn Gray LeMaster is a fifty-five year plus Life Member of the Little Rock, Arkansas Chapter of Hadassah. She is the author of the award-winning book, *A Corner of the Tapestry: A History of the Jewish Experience in Arkansas, 1820s - 1990s*. A Little Rock native and a Bible scholar, she has spent the past thirty years researching, writing extensively, and lecturing on Arkansas Jewish history. The Little Rock native is the mother of four children (one deceased) and ten grandchildren.

Lauren B. Lev, resident of East Meadow, New York, is a Hadassah Life Member and proud recipient of the Nassau Region of Hadassah's Woman of the Year Award. Besides being wife to Howard and mom to Amanda and Lathan, she is an advertising executive and an adjunct assistant professor teaching courses in advertising and marketing communications at SUNY, Fashion Institute of Technology. She is also a marketing instructor at Long Island University, C.W. Post.

Sybil-Frances Kimbrig Levin was born in 1928 in Carmel, California. She studied at Cornell University, the Pratt Institute, and New York University earning a master's in nutrition. She has worked as a home demonstration agent, consultant home economist, English language instructor, and a community college nutrition instructor. She has resided and worked in a number of places including New York, North Dakota, D.C., Cameroon, Tunisia, Spain, and France. She is married to Norman Balfour Levin, Ph.D., a Hadassah Associate. They have a daughter, Gnarity, who is a fourth-generation Hadassah Life Member.

Patricia Levinson was born in South Africa. In 1966, she moved to Israel and engaged in biochemical research at the Weizmann Institute in Rehovot. The Levinson family moved to Schenectady, New York in 1970. Patricia has been an active Hadassah volunteer for forty years, including twenty-two years on the National Board. She created the Hadassah Women's Health Education program, and currently runs the four-language Hadassah International website. Patricia is actively fundraising for Hadassah in her new home in St. Petersburg, Florida.

Suzanne Libenson grew up in Erie, Pennsylvania, and earned a bachelor's degree at the University of Michigan, Ann Arbor, where she met her husband, Eli. In 1984, they made Aliyah to Israel with their three children. She worked at the Association of Americans and Canadians in Israel (AACI), and as senior editor in the Department of Resource Development at the Weizmann Institute of Science. Since her retirement in December 2010, she has been doing freelance editing and proofreading.

Linda Ettinger Lieberman is a third-generation Hadassah Life Member, Founder, and Keeper. A resident of White Plains, New York, she has been a member of Elana Chapter for almost thirty-five years. Linda is the recipient of Hadassah awards including Henrietta Szold Award in 1983; Hand of the Healers Award in 1990 and 2003; and National Hadassah Leadership Award in 2006 in recognition of her many years on the Elana Board advising the Scarsdale Chapter, and for service on the Westchester Region Board.

Marion Lipsitz became President of the St. Louis Chapter of Hadassah in 1956 at age thirty-five while she was pregnant with her fifth child. Having recruited hundreds of new members, a Founder, Keeper of the Gate, and Myrtle Wreath Award recipient, she is currently a Board member at ninety-two years young. She worked at the JCC for forty-three years as membership director, during which she graduated Washington University and traveled to Israel once a decade. After seventy years of involvement, Hadassah remains her passion.

Bonnie Lipton, Hadassah National President from 1999–2003, currently serves as building chair of the Sarah Wetsman Davidson Hospital Tower, Ein Kerem Campus of the Hadassah Medical Organization. During her years of service in the National Major Gifts Department, Bonnie served as building and development chair, followed by National Chair of the Hadassah Medical Organization. An Honorary Fellow of the World Zionist Organization and former member of the Executive Committee of the Zionist General Council, she was a member of the Board of Governors of the Jewish Agency for Israel.

Western New England Hadassah, UJA Young Women's Cabinet, Israel Bonds, AIPAC, Hillel, and more have experienced her leadership.

Helen F. Lodge enjoys an equally successful professional and volunteer career, serving in leadership roles on local, state, and national boards and commissions. She spent twenty-eight years in healthcare food service management and has received numerous awards including: Heart Association "Heart of Gold"; YWCA Women of Achievement; Governor's Lifetime Achievement; WV Symphony Distinguished Service; WVUIT Alumnus of the Year and the Academy of Nutrition and Dietetics Medallion Award. She is a past-president of Hadassah in Charleston, West Virginia, and current co-president.

Anne Lowe has been a chapter president in Princeton, New Jersey, Milwaukee, Wisconsin., and twice in Tucson, Arizona. She has also been president of the Great Lakes Region of Hadassah and on the National Board for four years. Anne has been on the Camp Young Judaea-Midwest committee for nigh on thirty years, and all three of her children were Young Judaeans. Married to David Lowe, they have eight grandchildren, four of whom attend CYJ-Midwest. She is an artist, writer, and full-time employee of the Jewish Federation of Southern Arizona.

Ruth M. de Sola Mendes is from Mt. Vernon, New York. As a Young Judaean, she became the leader of Westchester Region Israeli Dance Group. She attended Camp Tel Yehudah from 1952 to 1954 and participated in the 1955 Summer-in-Israel program. She later got involved in Hadassah with her mother, Margarete Wasser. In 1978, her mother, husband Richard, and four-year-old daughter were the only three-generation Life Member family at the first Hadassah Convention in Israel. Rica attended Sprout Lake, Tel Yehudah, Summer-in-Israel, Year Course. Her grandchildren attend Sprout Lake. Her passions are Jewish education and history and Jewish cooking (Ashkenazi and Sephardi).

Susan Metsch, born June 23, 1943, grew up in the Bronx and Laurelton, Queens, New York. In January 1966, she graduated from Queens College of the City University of New York and married Lawrence R. Metsch. Thereafter, she lived in New Haven, Connecticut, Glasgow Air Force Base, Montana, Myrtle Beach Air Force Base, South Carolina, Lajes Field, Azores, Portugal, Jacksonville, Florida, and, in 1972, settled in Miami, Florida. In 1976, she received a master's in learning disabilities from Florida International

University. Susan has two married sons and five grandchildren. She has been a teacher, tutor, and a member of several community boards. Susan is the past president of the Simcha Hadassah Aventura Chapter.

Shirley Krick Michalove from Atlanta, Georgia is a past president of the Southeastern Region of Hadassah. A Life Member of Hadassah since 1968 and part of a four-generation Life Membership family, Shirley has been involved with Young Judaea and Camp Judaea for over fifty years. Since her retirement from managing medical practices, she has served as a docent at the William Breman Jewish Heritage and Holocaust Museum of Atlanta. Shirley has two grown children and two granddaughters.

Lois Mirsky is a Life Member of Hadassah and is affiliated with the Plymouth, Massachusetts Chapter. She graduated from Wheelock College in Boston with a bachelor of science degree in education. Her professional career included teaching and working for a variety of non-profit organizations as a writer and development officer. In addition to her volunteer work with Hadassah, she is a literacy tutor, takes courses in lifelong learning programs, and writes stories for her memoir collection.

Luisa Narins hails from Lima, Peru. She has degrees from Harvard University and the Fletcher School and has lived in Boston, Philadelphia, Salt Lake City, New York City, and Harrisburg, Pennsylvania. Luisa is a professional actor; you can find her playing the role of a doctor in *Law & Order*, body double for Kim Cattrall in the *Sex & the City* movie, as the laughing woman in *30 Rock*, or as Gramma Letty with the traveling theatre group *Winceyco*.

Marcie Natan is Hadassah's National President. Since joining the organization more than forty years ago, she has served as president of the Eastern Pennsylvania Region, National Secretary, National Treasurer and national Vice President. Among other positions, she has served as chair of Hadassah's Planned Giving and Major Gifts programs and of Hadassah College. A resident of New York City and Lancaster, Pennsylvania, Marcie is part of a four-generation Hadassah Life-Member family. She has traveled to Israel more than fifty times.

Florence Kaplan Nathanson was born in Brooklyn in 1926. Upon graduating from nursing school in 1947, she went to work for the Jewish Hospital of Brooklyn. There, upon learning of Hadassah's desperate need for nurses to work in a transit camp for new immigrants established at Rosh Ha'Ayin in Israel, she left in January, 1950 to work there as a volunteer for nine months. She was married in 1953 and has two sons. Florence is a Life Member of Hadassah.

Dan Ornstein is Rabbi of Congregation Ohav Shalom and a writer, living in Albany, New York with his family. He is currently completing a children's book, *Four Bright Lights: A Hanukkah Tale Of The Underground Railroad,* with the illustrator Jacqueline Freedman Kahane. He is also currently writing a book on poetry and prayer.

Diane Paige is the mother of four daughters, twelve grandchildren and four great grandchildren. She has enjoyed several careers. Diane is a retired R.N. and interior designer. When she retired, she became involved in charitable organizations. For the past three years, she has been president of Turnberry Chapter of Hadassah, in South Florida. Her hobbies have been painting and writing. At the age of eighty she had a poem book published called, *Feelings.* She claims this book to be her family legacy. Says her daughter, "She is an inspiration to her family and friends."

Lee (Emily) Pinchuk served as a past president of the Suffolk Region, as well as fourteen years as president of Smithtown Chapter. She is a three-generation Life Member and a Centennial Founder and Keeper of the Gate. Her husband, Norman, and children are part of the Hadassah family. Part of her volunteer work includes spending a week each summer at Camp Adventure for children who have cancer, as well as participating throughout the year in many different activities. In her other life, she was in the world of fashion and beauty. Hadassah is one of the greatest loves of her life.

Lonye Debra Rasch, member of the National Board of Hadassah for over a decade, has been a Zionist for as far back as she can remember and credits the Young Judaea youth movement for leading her to fall in love with Israel. Lonye spent her junior year abroad at the Hebrew University in Jerusalem, where she met her husband, Stephen. A freelance writer and editor, she is also the mother of two daughters, Faye and Rebecca.

Bilha Ron is a life-long teacher. Born in Israel, she graduated from Levinsky College of Education in Tel Aviv and served in Israel's War of Independence. She taught in Israeli public schools and language academies (Ulpan). After moving to the United States, she earned a bachelor's degree in English from Walsh University. She was education director of the Temple Israel Religious School in Canton, Ohio, and served as Jewish education specialist for the Canton Jewish Community Federation. In 1999, she moved to Delray Beach, Florida, and continues to lecture extensively on Hebrew literature, biblical studies, the Holocaust, and politics of the Middle East. Bilha is married to Samuel Ron and they have three children and four grandchildren.

Benita G. Ross of Canton, Massachusetts, is a National vice president and serves on the Executive Committee. She is the National chair for Youth Aliyah. A graduate of Boston University, she holds a master's degree in human resource development from Villanova University. Benita and husband, Michael, are the proud parents of three sons and grandparents of five granddaughters and two grandsons. She is the third of a five-generation Life Membership family with four-generations of Hadassah Associates.

Anne Rothenberg inherited her love of writing from her mother, a published author. A former Hadassah president, her mom encouraged Anne to lead her own 1600 member chapter. In 2005, Anne became president of Hadassah Capital District, but "bulletin editor" is her favorite and current portfolio. A Jewish educator by profession, Anne taught in Hillel Academy of Broome County, New York, the Hebrew Academy of the Capital Region, and several Hebrew schools. Currently, she and her husband split their time between their homes in Jerusalem and Albany, New York.

Bonnie Saban was born and raised in the Midwest. Her parents always enriched her life of Judaism with teachings, values, music, and traditions. She participated fully in all that was offered in their small Jewish community. After graduating from Northwestern University in 1964, she traveled to Israel to see the land and learn the language. She remained in Jerusalem for fourteen years. She married, had three children, and survived two wars. When she returned to the United States in 1979, she continued teaching Hebrew, loving Israel, and forever appreciating Hadassah Hospital.

Joan W. Sacarob of Annandale, Virginia is a former National Vice President and has been on the National Board for nearly forty years. She is known locally and nationally as an activist. Her activities besides Hadassah include the JCCNV, JCRC, and Chr. of the Free Wallenberg Committee, George Mason School of Public Policy, and The Sy Kenen Society (AIPAC) Federation of

Greater Washington. She has been honored by numerous organizations for her passionate leadership, inspiration and effective advocacy for Israel and civil rights. She is married to Donald Sacarob, a vice president of Hadassah Associates. They belong to the Circle of Founders.

Wendy Salkin of River Edge, New Jersey, has been a member of Hadassah since 1977 and a Life Member since 1980. She rose through the ranks of her local chapter and has been serving as co-president since 2006. A retired social worker, she and her husband Barry are the proud parents of daughter Stacey, married to Michael; son, Leon, married to Lori, and proud grandparents of Chloe. They are all part of a very supportive Five Generation Life Member family.

Joyce Saltman has been a Life Member since she was a child, as has her daughter, Beth, and granddaughter, Sophia. She was installed as president of her chapter in Connecticut by her mom, a former president of the Miriam Group in Brooklyn, whose meetings became her most vivid Hadassah connections. Joyce is a professor emeritus of special education as well as an international lecturer on "Laughter: Rx for Survival." She has two brilliant grown children, and a wonderful husband, Sol Hitzig.

Paige Sass received undergraduate and graduate degrees in administrative science from The Johns Hopkins University. After a career in health care administration at the same institution, Paige and her husband retired to Alabama in 1999. Paige's Hadassah portfolios include chapter treasurer, chapter president, Southern Region Area vice president and Southern Region Organization vice president. She continues to serve as Unit Service co-facilitator. Paige is married to Dr. Neil L. Sass, and they have one daughter. Paige's family connections with Hadassah include her mother-in-law, sister, daughter, and great-niece—all Life Members—and her husband is an Associate. Paige and her husband live on Dauphin Island, Alabama, where they continue to be involved with volunteerism, family, and friends.

Gertrude Schloff is a native of Portland, Maine. After reading Henrietta Szold's biography in 1944, she became president of Junior Hadassah and is still an active member at the age of eighty-eight. After "the courtship" in 1946, Gertrude and Milton were married and moved to New Jersey. Gertrude is a proud mother of two, "grams" to three granddaughters, and great grandmother to Emma Irene. Her high school valedictory speech was entitled, "Light in a Dark World," exactly what she feels Hadassah brings to many lives.

Sharon Schneider is part of a four-generation Hadassah family and is a second-generation National Board member. She is currently the National Chair of The Centennial Path. Sharon was the youngest member of the National Board when she served as president of Lower New York State Region in 1986. Her favorite national portfolio was Youth Aliyah chair. Sharon is a member of the Rockland County JCC Board of Directors. She received a bachelor's from New York University and a master's from Lehman College.

Millie Fain Schneir, age ninety-four, has had a strong commitment to Hadassah and Israel all her adult life. She has been a dynamic president of the L'Chayim-Plantation Chapter for a total of twenty years so far. She is very proud to have instilled her love of Hadassah to her family; her three daughters, four granddaughters and two great granddaughters are all Life Members of Hadassah, who are proud of her many accomplishments.

Jan Secunda was born in Brooklyn, New York in 1952. After graduating from college with a bachelor's in psychology, she moved to New Mexico where she earned a master's in special education. She taught special education for twenty-seven years while raising a family. For the last eight years, she has been the principal of a private school for special needs students. When Jan's youngest son was an active member in Young Judaea, she became the youth commissioner for the Albuquerque Chapter of Hadassah. She has been on the board ever since in one capacity or another and is currently the president of the Hadassah of Greater Albuquerque Chapter.

Betty (Batya) Samuels Seidel has been a proud multi-generational Hadassah member since July 10, 1956—her membership card signed by Rebecca Shulman, President. At the age of fifty, she received a Johns Hopkins University master's in adult education and has advocated lifelong learning and keeping active in mind, body, and spirit. A highlight of her life was the honor of reading the Declaration of Israel's Independence in 1948 at a Baltimore citywide celebration. Joy unbounded!

Shelley Sherman currently serves as a National Hadassah Vice President and as Coordinator of the Executive Division. She previously served as the Young Judaea Coordinator and in Hadassah's Development Division. Shelley graduated from George Washington University with a degree in Political Science and a minor in Russian Studies, and from Hofstra University School of Law. She practiced public service law for many years before becoming a full-time Hadassah lay leader. Shelley has two children who were Young Judaeans.

Iris Shur, who always loved to write, lives in Naples, Florida where she is a past-president of Collier County Hadassah. She writes a column, for fun, in the Naples Daily News called "The Shur Thing" telling stories about herself and her family. She is a member of the Naples Writers Forum. Iris is a retired audiologist. She has three sons and two grandchildren. Iris was born in Buffalo, New York, but lived in Concord, Massachusetts for many years before retiring to Florida.

Faye Sidder (born Faye London in Detroit) was surrounded by three brothers. Her father owned movie theaters. Her mother was a dedicated volunteer for Jewish National Fund. She attended the University of Michigan and managed a theater during World War II. She married Herbert Schnaar. They raised two sons. Herb died in 1986. Today, Faye and her husband, Richard Sidder, live in West Bloomfield, Michigan. They enjoy their large, combined family.

Renee Sidman was born in Seattle, Washington and has lived in Colorado Springs, Colorado for over thirty years. She is a Life Member and past president of the Colorado Springs Chapter. She has two adult children, an Associate and a Life Member, living on each coast, as well as a child still at home and in middle school. She has been married to Michael Sidman, an Associate, for thirty years. In her spare time she enjoys tennis, hiking, and yoga.

Leah Bassan Silver has been a member of Hadassah for the fifty years that she has lived in Highland Park, New Jersey. She has been editor of the Raritan Valley Chapter's Bulletin as well as its president. She is on the board of the Southern New Jersey Region working for IZAIA, the Israel, Zionist and International Affairs committee. She monitors the local news media for unbalanced reporting on Israel and writes letters to the editor to correct the imbalance.

Jacqueline Silverberg was born in England and was educated at Lycee Français de Londres, St. Martins School of Art. She emigrated to the United States in the late 1950s. She married and has two sons. She has served as the president of Southern Seaboard Region of Hadassah. She has been Co-Chair of National Young Leaders & Career Women. She was appointed to the Virginia

Commission for the Arts. She also served as chair on the United Jewish Appeal and Art For Collectors. She has been a part of Hadassah International since the inception of chair of Young Leaders of Europe and a liaison of Hadassah United Kingdom for fifteen years. She has lived in five places including the Virgin Islands, Connecticut, New York City, Florida, and London, England.

Belle Simon is a former National Vice President and member of the Executive Committee, deputy chair of Hadassah International, and National Ethics Chair. She has been a member of the National Board of Hadassah for twenty-nine years. Belle has served as Chair of the Hadassah Medical Organization, as Education Coordinator and as Coordinator of Operations. She received her bachelor's and master's degrees from Brooklyn College. Belle is a link in a four-generation Life Member family. Her husband Arthur, their sons and grandsons are all Associates. Belle and Arthur are members of the Society of Major Donors and Keepers of the Gate.

Barbara Sofer is a prize-winning journalist, author, and speaker who lives in Jerusalem. She is a graduate of the University of Pennsylvania and Hebrew University of Jerusalem. Her byline has appeared in many publications, and she has written six books. Sofer writes a Friday column, "The Human Spirit," for the *Jerusalem Post*. Inspired by Young Judaea, she moved to Israel after college. As the Israel director of public relations for Hadassah, she has witnessed and documented the drama of Jerusalem's biggest medical center. Sofer is married to a scientist/writer, Gerald Schroeder. Together they have five children.

Ronnie Jo Sokol leads river cruises for the Chicago Architecture Foundation. She hiked in Jane Austen's England and contributed a chapter on film adaptations in *Pride and Prejudice in Nineteenth Century Women at the Movies*. For thirty-three and a half years, Ronnie Jo taught teenagers with special needs and chaired Holocaust Remembrance activities. In Israel, Ronnie Jo volunteered at the Shikmah Home in Raanana, spent three summers on army bases with Volunteers for Israel, studied Hebrew at Ulpan Akiva in Netanya and volunteered half a year with abused children at Neve Hanna Children's Home in Kiryat Gat. She is president of Ketura-Hadassah.

Barbara Spack, from Edison, New Jersey, is a member of the National Board and past National vice president. Life achievements include committee member, JAFI Board of Governors; secretary, World Confederation United Zionists; Board Member JCPA, Jewish National Fund, No. Middlesex JCC; and life trustee, Middlesex County Jewish Federation. Barbara is fulfilled by three graduate Young Judaean daughters, the oldest of whom made Aliyah twenty-five years ago. A five-generation Life Member, thanks to her granddaughter, she is proud of family Associates—husband Eliot, sons-in-law Jeffrey and Michael, and four grandsons.

Sharyn Miller Spitzer, wife, mother and grandmother grew up in Elmont, New York. She studied public speaking at SUNYA, where she was Hillel president, and at Penn State. She resided in Wayne, New Jersey, and Warren, Ohio, where as a Life Member she served as Hadassah President and was a Jewish educator. In Montreal, she served with the Jewish Education Council. She worked as information officer in the Consulate of Israel in Montreal. Today, she lives in Jerusalem.

Binnie Stein moved from her native Brooklyn, New York, in her youth, to Woodmere, Long Island, and she still lives there. After graduating from NYU, she worked as a laboratory technologist at Memorial Sloan-Kettering Cancer Center. Having worked with UJA Young Leadership and the Israel Day parade, she joined Hadassah in 1972 and became a group president in 1977. Under her leadership, the unit was revitalized and exceeded all goals. Since then, she has served on the Nassau Region Board and was Region Legislative Chairman for Breast Cancer Awareness in 1988. Today, she is chapter bulletin editor, and program and media chairman.

Phyllis Perlman Stern was born on February 15, 1911 in Eveleth, Minnesota. Phyllis graduated from the University of Wisconsin in 1932 with degrees in English and French. After marriage to Herbert Stern, they relocated to Connecticut where she raised three children—and now has seven grandchildren and eleven great grandchildren. Phyllis worked as a teacher for public and Hebrew schools and devoted her life to her Jewish activism by serving as president of her Hadassah chapter and working for many other Jewish causes.

Jane G. Strom was born and raised in Stamford, Connecticut. Jane used degrees in French and Spanish from Brown University, a master's in TESOL, and a degree in school administration to teach French, Spanish, and English as a Second Language. She and Joel settled in Dix Hills, New York, where Jane served twice as president. Resettled in Tampa, as president of the Florida Central Region, she joined her sister, Nancy G. Wiadro, on the National Board in 2009. Including her five grandchildren, she's part of a five-generation Life Member/four-generation Associate family. Jane interviews for Brown and is on the Board of Directors of the Florida Orchestra.

Bernice S. Tannenbaum is a visionary leader who served as National President of Hadassah from 1976–1980. She proposed the creation of The Hadassah Foundation and now serves as its liaison to the National Board. She founded Hadassah International and became its first Chair in 1983. She brought Hadassah's history into book format, and the first edition of *It Takes a Dream* was published in 1997. From 1982–1992, she Chaired the World Zionist Organization (American section), and also served as National Vice President of AIPAC. In 2003, Bernice was honored with Hadassah's prestigious Henrietta Szold Award and was the inaugural recipient of Hadassah International's Woman of Distinction Award in London, United Kingdom.

Lucille Tarant lives in Florida with her husband, Herb. She has four children. Lucille taught perceptually impaired students in New Jersey. She received her master's degree as a learning disability teacher consultant. Lucille is a Life Member of Shira Hadassah in Delray Beach. Her major project is raising money to purchase incubators for Hadassah Hospital. A plaque to honor her generosity was presented by Shira's Board for Placement in Israel. Lucille also volunteers at the nonprofit association for community counseling in Delray Beach.

Jeanette Thorner was born in Cochabamba, Bolivia in 1945, where her parents settled after their fortunate escape from Germany in 1938. When she was six years old, her mother died, and soon after that they left for New York City where they had family. Her father remarried when she was nine and once again she had a wonderful mother. She went to Queens College and in 1965, she married. Eventually, they moved to Denver, Colorado. They are the proud parents of two daughters, a son, and five amazing grandchildren. They are the joy of their lives.

Bonnie Juran Ullner lives in Cincinnati, Ohio with her husband, Jon. She has two daughters; Toria Perrin, twenty-two, and Jessa Perrin, nineteen. Since Jessa's illness, Bonnie has further committed herself to Jewish causes including Hadassah, JNF, Adath Israel Sisterhood, and the Jewish Federation. Her mother, Sue Juran, and late maternal grandmother, Bernice Waxberg, were life-long Hadassah members. Her maternal grandfather's first cousin was Charlotte

Jacobson, Hadassah's National president from 1964–1968. Her mother-in-law, Lila Ullner Menowitz, was very active in the Cincinnati Hadassah chapter. Her brother, Richard Juran, was a Young Judea counselor. Bonnie hopes that Jessa's miraculous story will inspire others to become involved with and donate to Hadassah.

Ruthanne Warnick's Hadassah career began with the Huntsville Alabama Chapter. After moving to Atlanta with her family in 1996, Ruthanne served as president of the Nes Harim Group and the Greater Atlanta Chapter. She now proudly serves as president of the Southeastern Region. Ruthanne is passionate about helping women develop leadership skills and empowering them to make a difference. She is the Founder of Creating the Journey, and she and her husband, Larry, have two grown children, Naomi and Mitchell.

Teddy Weinberger, Ph.D., writes a bi-weekly column on life in Israel for several American Jewish newspapers. He is also a certified tennis coach. Teddy made Aliya with his family in 1997 from Miami, where he was an assistant professor of religious studies. He and his wife, Sarah Jane Ross, live in Givat Ze'ev. Ezra, now twenty, is the fourth of their five children. The others are: Nathan, twenty-four; Rebecca, twenty-three; Ruthie, twenty-two; and Elie, eighteen.

✦✦✦ HADASSAH CENTENNIAL ✦✦✦
THIN THREADS COMMITTEE

Melanie Nasberg follows her mother's example as an active Hadassah volunteer. She is a member of the National Board and currently serves as National Grassroots Fundraising Vice-Chair. During her terms of office as Sharon Chapter co-president and New York Region president she was thrilled to have raised millions of dollars for Hadassah's projects. The dedicated and caring women she has met through Hadassah have become her dearest friends. Melanie is proud of her three daughters, all Hadassah life-members, as they follow on the path of volunteering in their communities as does her husband, Stanley, a Hadassah associate. Currently a Centennial Founder and Keeper of the Gate, she is extremely pleased to be able to support Hadassah's youth projects and the amazing research conducted at Hadassah Hospital.

Marlene Edith Post of New York, New York is a distinguished leader and prominent member of the Jewish community in the United States and in Israel. Her 40-year volunteer career working on behalf of a myriad of humanitarian causes has placed her at the pinnacle of vital new initiatives for the 21st century. Mrs. Post is a past National President of Hadassah and past President of Hadassah International. She is currently a National Honorary Vice President, Co-Coordinator of the Hadassah Centennial and Chair of the Missions Department.

Mrs. Post, a passionate Zionist, has led more than 300 trips to Israel, where she is widely recognized for her leadership, pace-setting and humanitarian activities and unwavering support of Israel.

Frieda Unger Rosenberg of Merrick, New York, is the National Co-Coordinator of Hadassah's Centennial Celebration, National Grassroots Fundraising Chair, National Board member, and Executive Committee member. She has held many portfolios within Hadassah including Nassau Region President, Merrick Bellmore Chapter President, Dayan Lilah President, and Junior Hadassah President in Long Beach, New York. Frieda is part of a four-generation Life Member Family, a four-generation Associate Family and a three-generation Hadassah Presidents Family with her grandmother Gertrude Mandel, her mother Alyce Unger and her sister Leslie Rappaport. She and her husband, Alex, are the proud parents of Aaron, an attorney and Jessica, a family practice physician. Frieda and Alex are Centennial members of the Circle of Founders and Keepers of the Gate. An attorney, Frieda considers Hadassah the career of her heart.

Roselle Ungar of New Orleans, Louisiana is a former National Vice President and is a member of the National Board of Hadassah. She currently serves on the Executive Committee.

Roselle has held many portfolios within Hadassah including: 2011 National Business Meeting Co-Chair, Young Judaea Development Chair, Southeast Area Development Center Chair, Southern Region President, and New Orleans Chapter President. She is a Certified Fundraising Executive (CFRE) and a graduate of the Association of Fundraising Professionals (AFP) Faculty Training Academy. She is currently employed as Director of Community and Philanthropic Affairs for Crescent Bank & Trust.

Roselle has been to Israel seventeen times. She and her husband Stanley are Circle of Founders donors. They are a six-generation Life Member family and a four-generation Associate family.

✦ ✦ ✦

✦ ✦ ✦ CO-EDITORS ✦ ✦ ✦

STACEY K. BATTAT is an inspirational speaker, the creator of the *Thin Threads* book series, co-founder of Kiwi Publishing, and most significantly a wife, mom, friend, and Zionist. She is a Life Member of Hadassah. Stacey has merged her passions by putting together this centennial celebration book, as she marks her own half-century.

Beginning with her first move (Aliyah) to Israel with her very brave parents and three siblings in 1971, all of Stacey's "paths" have led to Jerusalem. As a young adult, Stacey returned to Jerusalem for university studies and later to work as a monthly contributor and field producer for the cable television show, "Hello Jerusalem," wherein she captured the life stories of some of Jerusalem's most colorful inhabitants. In 1990, Stacey "captured" her own life changer, marrying her Hadassah-Jerusalem-born partner, Eitan.

Stacey graduated from the University of Florida with a degree in Journalism/Broadcasting and later pursued graduate work in education and counseling. Stacey served as dean of students, curriculum developer, and instructor for the Hebrew High School at The Jewish Federation of New Haven for ten years. She sings at community events and in community musical theatre, and has always used her voice to warm and enlighten her audiences. Over the last twenty years, Stacey has inspired thousands of women and youth through her programs and presentations. She has volunteered in a wide array of both Jewish and urban community service venues, ranging from women's shelters and programs for disadvantaged youth, to creating Jewish educational programming for a number of Synagogues, to her current volunteer work on the residential life committee for a large assistant living facility in New Haven. Stacey's title at Kiwi, "Director of Inspiration," captures her goal to inspire people by eliciting and sharing stories. She begins each day anticipating a surprise, a story or a new thin thread connection, and looks forward to the next stage of her journey, creating more paths back to Jerusalem!

———— ✦ ————

ELLIN YASSKY, Ph.D., is a third-generation Life Member, with her children, Max, and Zoe, bringing in the fourth generation. Her earliest memories are working alongside her mother, Rhoda, at the Hadassah Thrift Shop in Fair Lawn, New Jersey. This early education was priceless.

For the past twenty years, while raising her two children as a working, single mother in Connecticut, Ellin has devoted herself to volunteering in her Jewish community where she served on many boards, taught at the evening Hebrew high school, was a founding trustee of the new Jewish High School of Connecticut, and created and directed the Kladno Torah Research and Rededication Project at Congregation Beth El in Fairfield.

Professionally, Ellin spent the last quarter century producing and editing more than seventy major books on art, Judaica, and Jewish cultural history. In 2012, she decided to return to the lessons learned as a young girl in the Hadassah Thrift Shop—those of *pekuah nefesh* (saving lives, one person at a time), and made *Aliyah* in order to work at the Emunah Children's Center in Afula, Israel.

Ellin is proud to have worked with Stacey Battat on this important book, celebrating 100 years of the largest and most important women's organization on the planet.

✦ ✦ ✦

100 Years of HADASSAH

A CHRONOLOGY IN WORDS AND PICTURES

✦ ✦ ✦

A Century of Distinguished Leadership

HENRIETTA SZOLD, FOUNDER ✦ *1912–1921, 1923–1926*

ALICE SELIGSBERG ✦ *1921–1923*

IRMA LINDHEIM ✦ *1926–1928*

ZIP SZOLD ✦ *1928–1930*

ROSE JACOBS ✦ *1930–1932, 1934–1937*

ROSE HALPRIN ✦ *1932–1934, 1947–1952*

JUDITH EPSTEIN ✦ *1937–1939, 1943–1947*

TAMAR DE SOLA POOL ✦ *1939–1943*

ETTA ROSENSOHN ✦ *1952–1953*

REBECCA SHULMAN ✦ *1953–1956*

DR. MIRIAM FREUND-ROSENTHAL ✦ *1956–1960*

LOLA KRAMARSKY ✦ *1960–1964*

CHARLOTTE JACOBSON ✦ *1964–1968*

FAYE SCHENK ✦ *1968–1972*

ROSE MATZKIN ✦ *1972–1976*

BERNICE TANNENBAUM ✦ *1976–1980*

FRIEDA LEWIS ✦ *1980–1984*

RUTH POPKIN ✦ *1984–1988*

CARMELA KALMANSON ✦ *1988–1991*

DEBORAH KAPLAN ✦ *1991–1995*

MARLENE POST ✦ *1995–1999*

BONNIE LIPTON ✦ *1999–2003*

JUNE WALKER ✦ *2003–2007*

NANCY FALCHUK ✦ *2007–2011*

MARCIE NATAN ✦ *2011–*

HADASSAH SINCE 1912
PARTNERS WITH ISRAEL FOR LIFE

1912

Hadassah is born. At a meeting at Temple Emanu-El in New York City on February 24, Henrietta Szold together with other Zionist women propose to the Daughters of Zion study circle that they expand their purpose and embrace practical Zionism, proactive work to help meet the health needs of Palestine's people. Because the meeting is held around the time of Purim, the women call themselves The Hadassah chapter of the Daughters of Zion, adopting the Hebrew name of Queen Esther. Henrietta Szold becomes the first National President.

Above: Temple Emanu-El in New York City, as it looked in 1912.

1913

Within a year, Hadassah has five growing chapters in New York, Baltimore, Cleveland, Chicago and Boston. Its charter articulates twin goals: to begin public-health initiatives and nurses training in Palestine, and to foster Zionist ideals through education in America. Thanks to a gift from Nathan and Lina Straus, Hadassah is able to send two American nurses, Rose Kaplan and Rachel (Ray) Landy, to Palestine. The nurses set up a small public-health and welfare station in Jerusalem to provide maternity care and treat trachoma, a dreaded eye disease then rampant in the Middle East.

Right: When patients did not come to the settlement house, Rose Kaplan went into Jerusalem neighbor-hoods to treat them.

Far right: Rae Landy, Eva Leon and Rose Kaplan at Hadassah Nurses' Settlement, Jerusalem. Photograph by Ya'akov Ben Dov.

1914

Eight of ten existing Hadassah chapters attend the first National Convention, held in Rochester, New York. After several votes and lengthy discussion, the group officially adopts the name "Hadassah" in place of "Daughters of Zion" and establishes the tradition of holding conventions annually.

The first *Hadassah Bulletin*, a precursor to today's Hadassah Magazine, is printed and distributed nationally to chapters, and by 1915 to each member.

Above: Hadassah voted at their first annual National Convention to publish a national newsletter, originally titled, "Bulletin No.1" and later, "Hadassah Bulletin"

1915

The core of future Hadassah education programs emerges when Jessie Sampter founds The Hadassah School of Zionism in New York. The school requires chapter leaders to take courses, institutes a correspondence course and inspires other Hadassah chapters to create their own Schools of Zionism. Sampter publishes "A Course in Zionism", a collection of facts, essays, and reading lists financed by prominent American Zionist, Judge Louis D. Brandeis.

Right: "Monthly Statistical Report of the District Work in Palestine", sent by Rae Landy. Both Rae Landy and Rose Kaplan sent frequent letters and monthly reports to Henrietta Szold and Alice Seligsberg for distribution via the Bulletin to Hadassah members. This report is from the March 1915 issue, shortly after Rose Kaplan had departed for New York for medical care.

MONTHLY STATISTICAL REPORT OF THE DISTRICT WORK IN PALESTINE

Month of December, 1914—

Home visits to patients	92	Letters			6
Total applicants to Settlement	248	Number of nurses on duty			2
Patients treated at Settlement	107	Midwives, permanent			3
Persons otherwise assisted at Settlement	141	Midwives, not permanent			4
Visits of co-operation	39	Probationers doing trachoma treatments in schools			2
Treatments in schools	7,633				

	Total	Adults	Children
Patients under treatment 1st of month	9	8	1
Number of new patients	28	28	..
Readmissions	2	2	..
Total number of patients treated	39	38	1

Patients remaining on file last of month.. 4

Classification of dismissed patients—		Diagnosis	
Improved and recovered	31	Maternity cases	29
Cured	4	Malaria	2
Patients receiving extra nourishment	39	Dysentery	2
Duration of care—		Pneumonia	1
1–14 days	34	Nephritis	1
1–3 months	1		

1916

Hadassah establishes the Palestine Purchasing and Supplies Department (later the Hadassah Supplies Bureau) to buy and ship items unavailable in the yishuv, the pre-state Jewish community in Palestine.

Right: Pamphlet describing the need for garments and linens for the clinics and for the Jewish Orphans in Palestine.

1917

Although Hadassah's first two nurses were compelled to return to America in 1915, the physicians with whom they had co-operated as well as the midwives and probationers were able to carry on their work.

Below: On November 2, Great Britain issues the Balfour Declaration, which supports "the establishment in Palestine of a national home for the Jewish people." Hadassah responds with new educational initiatives.

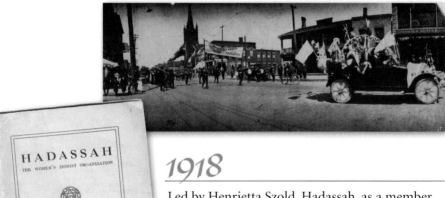

1918

Led by Henrietta Szold, Hadassah, as a member of the American Zionist Federation and at the behest of the World Zionist Organization, forms the American Zionist Medical Unit (AZMU, the Unit).

Left: Pamphlet describing Hadassah's work in America and in Palestine.

Comprised of 45 doctors, nurses, dentists and sanitary engineers, the Unit is set up to combat the intolerable health conditions of postwar Palestine and to create permanent health and welfare programs. From the beginning, it establishes a principle that it will serve all with equal care, regardless of race, creed, ethnicity or nationality.

Led by Alice L. Seligsberg, the Unit sails for Palestine in June, bringing desperately needed drugs, medical instruments and supplies, linens and clothing.

Over the next few years, the Unit, based in the old Rothschild Hospital in Jerusalem, initiates American-style health and welfare programs with intensive campaigns to wipe out malaria, cholera, trachoma and scalp diseases in many Jewish communities in the yishuv. The Unit organizes a sanitation program and founds Hadassah hospitals in Jaffa, Tiberias and Safed. The Nurses' Training School opens at the Rothschild Hospital in Jerusalem. In 1924 the Unit's name is changed to Hadassah Medical Organization.

Right: Hadassah pamphlet announcing the formation of the American Zionist Medical Unit in response to the urgent need for medical relief in Palestine.

Below: Nurses of the AZMU and members of Hadassah's Central Committee on New York City pier before sailing, June 1918.

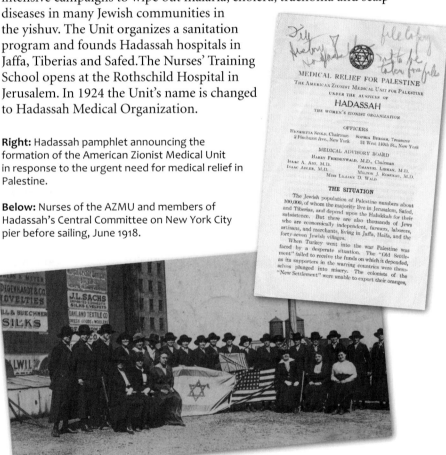

1919

The Unit organizes Palestine's first School Hygiene Department, which gives routine health examinations to Jerusalem school children. Many members of the Unit depart Palestine for home after the end of their one-year contracts, but many stay permanently.

Right: Hadassah nurses treat schoolgirls for trachoma and check their height and weight.

Below: Dr. Louis Ungar treats dental patient, 1919.

Bottom right: Female ward in Rothschild Hospital, 1919.

1920

The British Mandate of Palestine Begins. (1920–1948) Back in New York, Alice Seligsberg forms Junior Hadassah, providing innovative programs for young women who want to participate in Hadassah's Zionist mission. Henrietta Szold moves to Palestine to lead the medical work started by the Unit. She remains based in Jerusalem for the rest of her life, involved in medical and youth work in the yishuv.

Right: Mothers and children outside infant welfare station in Jerusalem, 1920s.

1921

Hadassah nurse, Bertha Landsman, creates Palestine's first permanent infant welfare station, Tipat Halav (drop of milk), in Jerusalem. Overwhelming success inspires Hadassah to expand the program, delivering fresh milk to needy families by "donkey express."

Hadassah opens a hospital in Tel Aviv, that city's first house of healing. Under Hadassah's philosophy of "devolution," it initiates and develops a number of facilities and projects and then transfers them to the appropriate municipalities. Hadassah transfers administration of this hospital to the Tel Aviv municipality in 1931.

The first 22 young women graduate from Hadassah's Nurses' Training School. Each receives her diploma from Henrietta Szold.

Left: Henrietta Szold surrounded by first graduates of Hadassah's Nurses' Training School.

1922

Hadassah is first incorporated, as Hadassah, Inc.. Hadassah Hospital opens in Haifa (devolved to the municipality in 1931).

Right: In the children's ward of the Hadassah Hospital in Haifa.

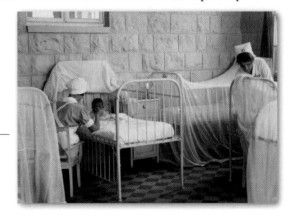

1923

Hadassah institutes a school lunch program to teach nutrition and serve healthy meals to children and teenagers in Palestine. Pennies are collected by American Hebrew school students to fund this project, which is devolved to the Israeli government in 1950, with Hadassah's support ending in 1954.

Left: Children preparing a school lunch for their classmates (PR photograph).

Right: Yemenite boys at Hadassah-provided school lunch.

1924

Nathan Straus contributes $10,000 with which Hadassah develops its Infant Welfare Stations into a complete network, extending from Jerusalem to Tiberias. Pamphlets were distributed to all Hadassah chapters for five cents each.

Left: This pamphlet publicized the enlargement of Hadassah's Infant Welfare work throughout Palestine and introduced the slogan for the Milk Bottle Campaign: "The future of the Holy Land lies in the cradle."

1925

Junior Hadassah assumes sole support of the Meir Shfeyah Children's Village, a youth village housing World War I orphans and socially disadvantaged children (devolved to the Israel Ministry of Agriculture in 1953, with Hadassah continuing limited financial support).

Right: Bakers at Meir Shfeyah Children's Village.

1926

Hadassah forms a partnership with the Jewish National Fund (JNF), also known as Keren Keyemeth LeYisrael (KKL), an organization established in 1901 by the Fifth World Zionist Congress to purchase and transform land in Palestine for Jewish farming, housing, roads and recreation. JNF immediately becomes, and has remained, a major Hadassah project in Israel.

Hadassah opens Palestine's first tuberculosis ward in its Safed hospital, which becomes the region's tuberculosis center in 1935 (devolved to the Israeli government in 1957).

Right: Children participate in JNF Arbor Day planting.

1927

The cornerstone is laid at a solemn ceremony for the Nathan and Lina Straus Health Center in Jerusalem, conceived as a model for future health centers in Palestine, with funding from Nathan Straus. According to Dr. E. M. Bluestone, then Director of the Hadassah Medical Organization, this center would serve as the headquarters of the Health Welfare Department of the Hadassah Medical Organization, with space devoted to new health activities. Through the decades many preventive health programs were housed in this building—a dental clinic, children's exercise programs, and Nathan Straus' milk pasteurization plant among others.

Left: Henrietta Szold speaking at the cornerstone ceremony of the Nathan and Lina Straus Health Center.

1928

Hadassah's urban recreational activities program begins with the supervision of the Guggenheimer Playgrounds, with funds from the estate of Bertha V. Guggenheimer. By 1950, when the playgrounds were devolved to the Israel Government's Department of Education, the program had grown to fifty playgrounds throughout the country where urban children had a safe, sanitary place to play.

Above: Children playing in the Guggenheimer Playground

1929

Hadassah Medical Organization (HMO) opens the Nathan and Lina Straus Health Center to serve Jerusalem's growing population, made possible by a large gift from the Straus family. (Operates today as an outpatient facility in downtown Jerusalem).

1930

Britain issues a White Paper restricting Jewish immigration into Palestine and land sales to Jews. In the United States, Hadassah joined the men's Zionist organizations in a political demonstration. According to National Hadassah President Zip Szold, cousin

Right, top: Nathan and Lina Straus. Hadassah Medical Organization opened the Nathan and Lina Straus Health Center to serve Jerusalem's growing population in 1929. It operates today as an outpatient facility in downtown Jerusalem.

Right, middle: Preparing to anesthetize a patient prior to abdominal surgery (probably at the Straus Health Center.)

Right, bottom: National President Zip Szold.

of Henrietta Szold, this was "the first time that Hadassah took part in a political act when a group went to Washington with Rabbi Israel Goldstein as the spokesman to encourage the government to stop the riots in Palestine."

1931

Beit Hadassah Clinic in Hebron reopens. Nathan Straus dies.

Hadassah enters America for Palestine Campaign through Jewish Agency and agrees to help raise 2.5 million dollars.

100 Junior Hadassah members at Midwinter Conference in New York vow to carry on work in Palestine.

Top: Henrietta Szold returned to Palestine from America at the insistence of the yishuv leaders to organize the social services of the incipient Jewish nation.

Right: Recha Freier.

1932

Recha Freier had the vision to bring Jewish youth from Germany to Palestine.

1933

Recha Freier begins Youth Aliyah (Jugendaliyah, Aliyat Hano'ar) in Berlin, working with German youth leaders to resettle Jewish children in Palestine. Henrietta Szold is appointed the

Above: Henrietta Szold greeting first Youth Aliyah arrivals.

first Director of Youth Aliyah by the governing council of the Yishuv, the Va'ad Le'umi.

1934

Youth Aliyah's first 43 wards arrive in Haifa. In what becomes a lifelong practice, Henrietta Szold greets them at the dock and accompanies them to Kibbutz Ein Harod.

The cornerstone is laid on Mount Scopus for the Rothschild-Hadassah University Hospital (RHUH) and new quarters for Hadassah's Nurses' Training School.

Top: Henrietta Szold inserting the scroll into the cornerstone on Mount Scopus.

Left: Youth Aliyah pamphlet.

1935

Spearheaded by National President Rose Jacobs, Convention delegates accept Youth Aliyah as an official Hadassah project and establish Hadassah as its sole American sponsor.

Palestine's first social-service programs begin when Hadassah opens the Nettie Lasker Social Service Department in Jerusalem.

Right: Henrietta Szold wielding pick-axe at Groundbreaking on Mount Scopus. Behind her are Hebrew University President Judah Magnes in white suit and Hadassah Medical Organization Director Chaim Yassky.

1936

In honor of Henrietta Szold's 75th birthday, the name of the nursing school is officially changed during graduation ceremonies to the Henrietta Szold-Hadassah School of Nursing.

October 21 is the Groundbreaking ceremony for the Hadassah-Hebrew University Hospital and Medical School on Mt. Scopus, attended by Henrietta Szold, David Ben-Gurion, hospital architect Erich Mendelsohn and others

Young Judaea, the oldest Zionist youth movement in the U.S. (founded 1909), joins the Hadassah family when Hadassah agrees to provide partial funding for the movement.

Right: Construction site of Mount Scopus Hospital.

1937

Hadassah's 25th anniversary is designated the Silver Jubilee, with membership and fundraising activities throughout the year.

1938

Youth Aliyah activities intensified following Kristallnacht in Germany.

Above: Refugees arriving in Palestine.

1939

The Rothschild-Hadassah University Hospital on Mount Scopus, the first teaching hospital and medical center in Palestine, opens on May 9. New Scopus quarters for the celebrated Henrietta Szold-Hadassah School of Nursing are also dedicated.

When World War II begins in Europe on September 1st, Hadassah begins war emergency shipments of medical supplies, equipment, food, drugs and clothing to Palestine. Hadassah began the Palestine Supplies Bureau in the 1920s.

Top: A small crowd gathers to dedicate the opening of the Rothschild-Hadassah University Hospital on Mount Scopus.

Left: Henrietta Szold with HMO director Chaim Yassky and director of Hadassah School of Nursing Shulamit Cantor.

1940

Hadassah and the Zionist Organization of America (ZOA) form the American Zionist Youth Commission, establishing Hadassah as Young Judaea's co-sponsor.

Hadassah forms an American Affairs Committee, the core of today's American Affairs and Advocacy programs, reflecting Hadassah's concern with the ideals of democracy, freedom and justice in the U.S. and in the yishuv. War relief and defense of democracy are two immediate committee projects.

Former Hadassah national president Rose Jacobs starts the Committee for the Study of Arab-Jewish Relations to promote "Zionism's unfinished agenda," co-existence between Palestine's two major populations.

Above, left: Young Judaea logo. **Above, right:** Rose Jacobs, national president 1930-1932 and 1934-1937.

1941

At age 81, Henrietta Szold establishes the Child and Youth Welfare Organization to coordinate the activities of public and voluntary child and youth welfare services. Hadassah, the Va'ad Leumi and the Jewish Agency fund the project. In 1945, after her death, the organization is renamed the Henrietta Szold Foundation for Child and Youth Welfare. In 1948 it becomes autonomous, with Hadassah participating on the board of directors. In 1960, on the centennial of Szold's birth, the Israeli government, together with Hadassah and the Jewish Agency, undertake to contribute to the budget of the foundation, now renamed Machon (or Mosad) Szold, the Szold Institute.

Above: Hadassah sends an American neurosurgeon, Dr. Henry Wigderson, to Palestine to create the Hadassah Medical Organization's first Department of Neurosurgery.

1942

After the U.S. enters World War II, Hadassah immediately mobilizes to support the American war effort. Members establish blood banks, sell war bonds, volunteer in their local communities, while National Hadassah continues to ship food, drugs and medical supplies to Palestine.

Left: Hadassah members support the American war effort by selling war bonds

Above: Pattern-making at the Alice L. Seligsberg Trade School for Girls

At the behest of Henrietta Szold, Hadassah begins its vocational education initiatives, later called the Hadassah Vocational Education Services (HVES), by establishing the Alice L. Seligsberg Trade School for Girls, the first school of its kind in Palestine; 35 girls enroll. It opened on the grounds of the recently vacated Rothschild Hospital alongside the already established Judge Julian W. Mack Workshops and School. This compound became known as the Louis D. Brandeis Vocational Center.

1943

Due in part to Hadassah's relentless efforts, the Teheran Children, a group of more than 800 young Polish Jewish refugees, arrive in Haifa, after four years of wandering from Poland through the Soviet Union to a squalid refugee camp outside Teheran. Youth Aliyah accepts these young Holocaust survivors and helps them adjust to their new lives.

Hadassah welcomes its 100,000th member.

Above: Teheran children arriving in Palestine.

1944

Hadassah opens the Apprenticeship Department at the Brandeis Vocational Center, named in honor of Supreme Court Justice Louis D. Brandeis. The Fine Mechanics Workshop is joined two years later by the Apprenticeship School of Printing.

Opening of the Hadassah Vocational Guidance Bureau in Jerusalem (later, the Hadassah Vocational Guidance Institute, renamed Hadassah Career Counseling Institute [HCCI] in 1989).

Youth Aliyah observes its tenth year of youth rescue.

Above: Young boy learning tools of the trade.

Right: Henrietta Szold and others broadcasting a skit on the occasion of the tenth anniversary of Youth Aliyah.

1945

Henrietta Szold, age 84, dies of pneumonia on February 13 (30 Shevat 5705) at the Rothschild-Hadassah University Hospital. Her funeral is attended by

some of the thousands of Youth Aliyah children and nursing students whose lives she touched. She is mourned throughout the world.

Hadassah and the American Friends of Hebrew University initiate a $4 million fundraising campaign to build the Hebrew University-Hadassah School of Medicine.

Above: Henrietta Szold's funeral at the cemetery on the Mount of Olives.

Hadassah is awarded a citation recognizing the sale of $200 million worth of U.S. government defense bonds during World War II.

Hadassah becomes the Jewish Agency's official "health arm" and prepares to meet the postwar needs of Palestine's people and an anticipated flood of war refugees.

1946

David and Paula Ben Gurion are each patients at Hadassah Hospital on Mount Scopus in April.

Opening of Occupational Therapy Department at Rothschild Hospital.

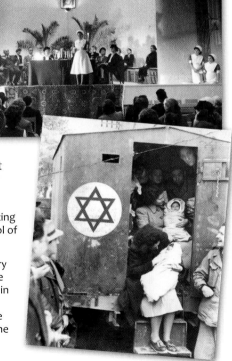

Right, top: Silver Jubilee of the first graduating class of the Henrietta Szold Hadassah School of Nursing.

Right: Hadassah had moved a "night delivery room" into town by this time because of the danger in getting ambulances up to Scopus in the dark. Loaded into this ambulance were mothers and babies who had given birth the night before, headed up to the hospital in the morning.

1947

In the wake of the UN partition plan of November 29, which calls for the establishment of independent Jewish and Arab enclaves in Palestine within a year, travel to and from Mount Scopus becomes increasingly dangerous. Hadassah and Hebrew University personnel are compelled to commute by armed convoy.

Part of the process in making their decision involved a visit by members of the United Nations Special Committee on Palestine (UNSCOP) to various facilities throughout Palestine, including the sophisticated Rothschild-Hadassah University Hospital on Mount Scopus.

Top: Mount Scopus staff boarding armored ambulance in town for ride up to hospital.

Right: United Nations Special Committee on Palestine visiting hospital on Mount Scopus.

1948

While attempting to reach Mount Scopus on April 13, a convoy of Hadassah and Hebrew University doctors, nurses and other personnel are ambushed. Besieged and under fire for hours, in the end 78 people are killed, among them HMO Director Dr. Chaim Yassky.

Unable to guarantee the safety of its patients or staff, Hadassah evacuates all its facilities on Mount Scopus, relocating all departments to five makeshift hospitals in temporary quarters around Jerusalem. Hadassah's access to Mount Scopus is lost for the next 19 years.

Above: Ambush enroute to Mount Scopus, April 13.
Right: Chaim Yassky, Director of HMO from 1928-1948.

The State of Israel is born. Israel is invaded, igniting the War of Independence.

HMO tends the thousands of wounded soldiers pouring into Jerusalem, plus the usual high numbers of civilians seeking aid. By the cessation of the fighting in 1949, HMO has treated more than 5,000 war casualties.

Above: Establishment of Camp Tel Yehudah.

1949

As "Operation Magic Carpet" rescues and brings 45,000 Yemenite Jews to Israel, HMO creates an emergency hospital in Rosh Ha'ayin for the care of new immigrants, as requested by the new Israeli government.

Youth Aliyah opens Ramat Hadassah Szold Youth Village near Haifa as a reception center and to receive refugee children from Arab countries, Turkey, Hungary and elsewhere. Today it serves Israeli-born and immigrant children, ages 11 to 15, who require intensive remedial education programs.

Hadassah establishes the Henrietta Szold Award as its highest honor, to be presented annually. Eleanor Roosevelt is named the first honoree for her efforts on Hadassah's behalf, most notably as World Patron of Youth Aliyah.

The Hebrew University-Hadassah Medical School, Israel's first, opens with 50 students in temporary buildings in Jerusalem.

Right, top: Former First Lady Eleanor Roosevelt receives the first Henrietta Szold Award.

right: First class of students at the Hebrew University-Hadassah Medical School.

The National Board establishes Hadassah's national life membership program, piloted by the Boston Chapter in 1935.

1950

Two years after the evacuation of Mount Scopus, the Hadassah National Board votes to build a new, state-of-the-art medical center on the hillside above Ein Kerem, a small village west of Jerusalem. A fundraising campaign for this medical complex begins in 1953.

As part of its continuing policy of devolution, Hadassah transfers its Nutrition Department, including the school lunch program, to the Israeli government.

Above: Dr. Kalman Mann, Director-General of HMO, points out the site of the new Medical Center.

Right: First Young Judaea Summer Course students departing for Israel.

1951

Young Judaea sponsors its first summer course program in Israel.

1952

Hadassah transfers its network of 134 health welfare stations throughout Israel to the Israeli government, retaining its 32 stations in Jerusalem and surroundings, which it devolves to the government in 1963.

Together with the Jewish Agency, Hadassah's Vocational Education Department establishes a Rural Center for Vocational Education at Kfar

Vitkin to teach agricultural and domestic science. (The village is renamed Hadassah-Neurim in 1965.)

The Hebrew University-Hadassah School of Medicine graduates its first class of physicians.

The groundbreaking is held for the new Medical Center at Ein Kerem.

Hadassah's educational youth programs in Israel, previously grouped under Hadassah Youth Services, changes name to Hadassah Vocational Education Services.

Above: YAL/1952 Opening ceremony at Kfar Vitkin/Rural Vocational Center.

1953

Hadassah participates in "Operation Reindeer," a U.S. government program to alleviate food shortages within Israel, particularly within immigrant populations.

HMO pilots the Family and Community Health Center at the multi-ethnic immigrant settlement of Kiryat HaYovel, under the leadership of HMO Director-General Kalman Mann (today the Sally and Philip W. Lown Kiryat HaYovel Community Health Center, Jerusalem). The center becomes a model for community health throughout Israel.

The Hebrew University-Hadassah School of Dental Medicine, founded in cooperation with the Alpha-Omega Dental Fraternity, opens. Students train at HMO's Jerusalem dental clinic.

Above, top: Denise Tourover at right helps distribute surplus food in "Operation Reindeer"

Above: Kiryat HaYovel Community Health Center in Jerusalem.

1954

HMO pilots Ya'al, the "Helping Hand of Hadassah," a volunteer auxiliary of women who serve in Hadassah's medical facilities. This innovative Israeli "first" becomes a model for volunteerism in Israel.

HMO opens Israel's first cardiac surgical unit and its first Department of Psychiatry at the Hebrew University-Hadassah School of Medicine.

1955

Youth Aliyah begins its day center program with services for youth from Israel's rural and development areas. The program rapidly expands to encompass urban youth as well.

The national headquarters of HWZOA moves into its first "house," a Hadassah owned and occupied building on East 52nd Street in New York City.

Right, top and middle: Children study, learn and are nurtured in Youth Aliyah day centers.

Right, bottom: First Hadassah House head-quarters in New York City at 65 East 52nd Street (1955-1976)

1956

HMO pilots a community health station in the Arab village of Abu Ghosh.

Young Judaea opens its first Year Course in Israel for high school graduates.

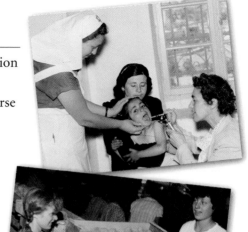

Right , top: Hadassah nurse examines child at community health station set up by Hadassah in Abu Ghosh.

Right: Young Judaeans.

1957

HMO is assigned responsibility for mass Salk polio vaccine immunizations in the city of Jerusalem and the Jerusalem corridor.

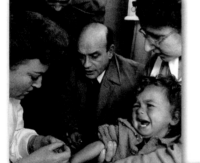

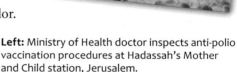

Left: Ministry of Health doctor inspects anti-polio vaccination procedures at Hadassah's Mother and Child station, Jerusalem.

1958

The site of the new Hadassah-Hebrew University Medical Center at Ein Kerem is officially named Kiryat Hadassah and is incorporated into the city of Jerusalem; construction of the Medical Center accelerates.

First Hadassah pilgrimage to Israel.

Left: Dr. Mann and Florence Pearlman with hospital model.

1959

HMO introduces open-heart surgery to Israel, installs the cobalt bomb for cancer therapy and graduates the first ten Israel-trained dentists from the Hebrew University-Hadassah School of Dental Medicine.

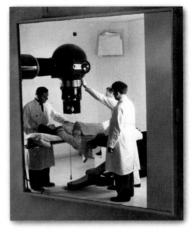

Above: HMO installs the "cobalt bomb" for cancer therapy .

As part of Israel's ongoing commitment to aid developing nations, the Hebrew University-Hadassah School of Medicine begins training African and Asian doctors in cooperation with the World Health Organization and Israel's Foreign Ministry. The initiative later expands to include South American doctors.

1960

Hadassah-Hebrew University Medical Center is dedicated on August 3.

Left: Prime Minister Ben-Gurion at the dedication: "May the memory and life's work of Henrietta Szold be a light to guide your path. She gave herself to our country."

1961

Hadassah-Ein Kerem opens on June 6 with a joyous moving day. Supervised by HMO senior staff, the Israeli Army meticulously and efficiently transports every patient in each of Hadassah's five temporary hospitals to a preassigned bed at the new medical center.

Right: On Moving Day , patients on stretchers are transferred to the new medical center.

1962

Hadassah turns 50 and celebrates its golden jubilee year.

The Fannie and Maxwell Abbell Chapel (synagogue) at Hadassah-Ein Kerem is dedicated. Marc Chagall's magnificent 12 stained glass windows, each representing one of Israel's 12 tribes, grace the synagogue. Former National President Dr. Miriam Freund-Rosenthal is responsible for enlisting the noted artist and seeing the project to completion.

National President Lola Kramarsky remarks during the Golden Jubilee Year: "Hadassah has become a tested, skilled instrument of service, viewing its role as that of faithful steward of the Jewish heritage and responsible partner in the shaping of Jewish destiny... Hadassah appraises its practical program from time to time, shifting its work-a-day emphasis as current needs change

Above: Marc Chagall and architect Joseph Neufeld, admiring the magnificent stained glass windows.

and capacity and experience increase. But the motivation and objectives are constant, and in this constancy lies the uniqueness of Hadassah."

1963

October 18th, one month before his assassination, President John F. Kennedy records remarks in the White House Cabinet Room to be played at Hadassah meeting in Washington, D.C. The President discusses voluntary public service, Hadassah programs, and how Hadassah's efforts in America and Israel contribute to the advancement of civil rights and the protection of civil liberties.

Right: Hadassah's nursing program for young women from Malawi.

Right: Dedication of the new mother and child pavilion.

Far right: Behind the scenes at the new mother and child pavilion.

1964

The Hebrew University-Hadassah School of Dental Medicine moves into its new quarters at Hadassah-Ein Kerem.

Chaim Gross' bronze "Mother and Child" sculpture is installed near the entrance to Hadassah-Ein Kerem.

Right: Children play on "Mother and Child" sculpture

1965

The U.S. Agency for International Development (AID) announces its first grant to Hadassah: $335,000 for Hadassah-Ein Kerem and the Alice L. Seligsberg High School. Today Hadassah continues to receive generous AID grants earmarked for HMO.

The Hebrew University-Hadassah School of Medicine moves to new building facilities at Hadassah-Ein Kerem.

1966

The Alice Seligsberg Vocational High School is renamed the Alice Seligsberg Comprehensive High School, reflecting evolving educational needs in Jerusalem.

An HMO surgical team completes Israel's first successful two-valve open-heart operation.

Right: Young women studying chemistry at the Alice Seligsberg Comprehensive High School.

1967

Hadassah Associates is founded as the fundraising arm for American men who want to provide support for Hadassah's work.

Rebecca Shulman, the only National Board member in Israel during the Six-Day War, is given a seat in the first Hadassah Medical Organization car to travel to the hospital on Mount Scopus immediately after the war ends. For the first time since 1948, the Hadassah flag was raised at the damaged hospital buildings.

At the end of the Six-Day War, National President Charlotte Jacobson and HMO Director-General Dr. Kalman Mann travel to Mount Scopus to receive the keys to Hadassah's hospital. At the request of the Israeli government, Hadassah agrees to rebuild its first "hill of healing" as a state-of-the-art general hospital for the surrounding community.

Hadassah accepts sole sponsorship of an expanded, co-educational Zionist

Left: National President Charlotte Jacobson receives the keys to Mount Scopus from Commander Scharfman; Dr. Kalman Mann is in suit.

Youth Movement. Young Judaea and Junior Hadassah are merged as Hashachar (the Dawn) for ages 9–18. Young adults, ages 18–25, become members of Hamagshimim (the Fulfillers). The movement as a whole is referred to as "Young Judaea."

HMO performs Israel's first successful kidney transplant.

Above: Youngsters prepare for Maccabiah games at Camp Tel Yehuda.

Hadassah Vocational Education Services changes name to Hadassah Israel Education Services.

1968

The official restoration of Hadassah-Mount Scopus begins when Hadassah plans a 260-bed hospital for the entire community and agrees to build a state-of-the-art rehabilitation center within.

Fundraising Campaign for the restoration of Hadassah-Mount Scopus.

HMO pioneers 24-hour emergency units at Hadassah-Ein Kerem for acute respiratory and coronary care, burns and trauma.

At the first National Board Mid-Winter meetings held in Israel, ground is broken at Hadassah-Ein Kerem for the Siegfried

Above: The official restoration of Hadassah-Mount Scopus begins.

Right: Ground breaking for the Siegfried and Irma Ullman Building for Cancer and Allied Diseases.

& Irma Ullman Building for Cancer and Allied Diseases, which will house the Moshe Sharett Institute of Oncology (opens 1976).

1969

Garin Hamagshimim, a group organized by and comprised of former Young Judaeans, arrives in Israel under the auspices of the Hadassah Zionist Affairs Department's Aliyah Committee. They settle in Neve Ilan, a moshav shitufi [cooperative moshav] outside Jerusalem.

Above: Young families settle in Neve Ilan.

1970

Hadassah establishes a youth center on Mount Scopus, for Young Judaeans participating in Israel programs, in the building that was intended for the Nurses' Training School before 1948. The building, where Henrietta Szold lived during her final illness, the first on Mount Scopus to be renovated, is renamed the Judith Riklis Building (Beit Riklis).

Right, top: Hadassah Medical Center at Ein Kerem.

Right: Students on the steps of Beit Riklis.

✦ 437

Hadassah establishes the Hebrew University-Hadassah School of Occupational Therapy, housed in the Edith and James Ross building on Hadassah-Mount Scopus.

The Hadassah Community College, Israel's first American-style community college, opens in the Brandeis Vocational Center complex with 124 day and 84 evening students (renamed Hadassah College Jerusalem [HCJ] in 2006).

Above: The Hebrew University-Hadassah School of Occupational Therapy. Pauline Mack and Dr. Kalman Mann greet guests.

The Alice Seligsberg Comprehensive High School merges with Brandeis (see 1944) to become the co-ed Hadassah Seligsberg-Brandeis Comprehensive High School (devolved to the Jerusalem municipality in 1988).

1971

First graduation of the International Course in Public Health and Social Medicine.

1972

The Hadassah Community College graduates its first class with Golda Meir as guest of honor. Hadassah incorporates the high school, the college and the guidance center under one project, named Hadassah Israel Education Services (HIES).

Middle: Graduation ceremony.   **Bottom:** Graduation, with Golda Meir as guest of honor.

1973

Graduates of the Young Judaea Year Course in Israel lead a group of olim ("new immigrants") and native-born Israelis and establish Kibbutz Ketura in the Arava region of the Negev.

HMO medical teams rapidly mobilize, treating more than 4,000 casualties during the Yom Kippur War.

During and after the war, HMO concentrates on the rehabilitation of the severely burned and wounded, relying heavily on pace-setting rehabilitation services offered through its newly opened Trauma Unit.

Top: Judy Kleinman holds dedication scroll at Kibbutz Ketura.

Above: Chagall windows are boarded up during the 1973 war.

Left: Helicopter with wounded soldiers at Hadassah Ein Kerem landing pad.

Bottom: Rose Matzkin Youth Aliyah Day Center.

1974

In honor of Youth Aliyah's 40th anniversary, Hadassah allocates more than $1 million to provide new residential and innovative day centers for Youth Aliyah.

After Congress passes legislation, which helps tens of thousands of Soviet Jews to immigrate to

Israel during the 1970s and '80s, the National Board allocates $1 million to retrain Russian doctors, nurses and other health professionals at HMO.

1975

On October 21 Hadassah rededicates the rebuilt and refurbished Hadassah University Hospital at Mount Scopus.

Above: Mezuzah ceremony of rededication of Hadassah University Hospital on Mount Scopus; from left: Charlotte Jacobson, Fanny Yassky, Rose Matzkin, Zip Szold and Dr. Kalman Mann.

The Arab bloc succeeds in passing Resolution #3379 in the U.N. General Assembly, "Elimination of All Forms of Racial Discrimination", better known as the "Zionism Equals Racism" resolution. Hadassah works passionately for its repeal, and it is ultimately rescinded in 1991.

Hadassah introduces the Bachelor of Nursing Sciences program at the Henrietta Szold Hadassah-Hebrew University School of Nursing, Israel's first four-year degree program in nursing.

Hadassah pledges to help Youth Aliyah absorb 3,000 disadvantaged Israeli youth and allocates $200,000 to build new dormitory space, its first program to focus exclusively on native-born Israelis. This program continues today as Youth Aliyah's Children at Risk.

1976

Hadassah welcomes its 100,000th Life Member.

The newly reopened Hadassah-Mount Scopus hospital receives its first 100 patients in April, almost 28 years after the convoy massacre of 1948.

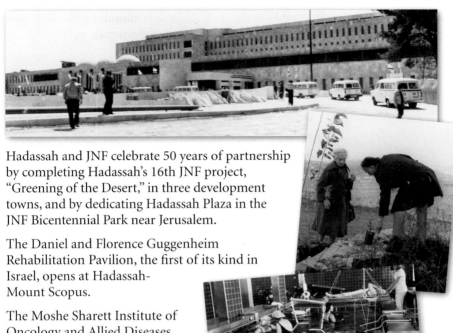

Hadassah and JNF celebrate 50 years of partnership by completing Hadassah's 16th JNF project, "Greening of the Desert," in three development towns, and by dedicating Hadassah Plaza in the JNF Bicentennial Park near Jerusalem.

The Daniel and Florence Guggenheim Rehabilitation Pavilion, the first of its kind in Israel, opens at Hadassah-Mount Scopus.

The Moshe Sharett Institute of Oncology and Allied Diseases opens in the Siegmund and Irma Ullman Building at Hadassah-Ein Kerem.

Hadassah moves its national headquarters from West 52nd Street to 50 West 58th Street, New York.

Top: 1976 convoy to Mount Scopus with first patients since 1948.

Middle: Tree planting in JNF Bicentennial Park near Jerusalem.

Above: Physical therapy at Mount Scopus.

Bottom: A doctor uses the EMI scanner at HMO's Radiology Department.

1977

Hadassah installs Israel's first EMI scanner at HMO's Radiology Department and opens the Rosalie

Goldberg Neonatal Intensive Care Unit, Israel's first NICU, at Hadassah-Mt. Scopus. The NICU soon receives its first one-pound baby.

The Aleen and Lawrence Schacht-Hadassah Day Care Nursery opens at Hadassah-Ein Kerem to care for 100 preschool-age children of hospital personnel.

Above: Schacht-Hadassah Day Care Nursery.

1978

Hadassah Community College opens Israel's first two-year dental technicians' course, in cooperation with the faculty of the Hebrew University-Hadassah School of Dental Medicine.

HMO performs Israel's first successful bone marrow transplant.

In the euphoria following the previous year's visit of Egyptian President Anwar el-Sadat to Jerusalem, Hadassah convenes its 64th National Convention—its first in Israel—bringing 2,500 participants to Jerusalem. Hadassah establishes a tradition of holding periodic National Conventions in Israel.

Jacques Lipchitz's sculpture, "Tree of Life", is unveiled at Hadassah Mount Scopus.

Middle: Students studying dental technology at Hadassah Community College.

Above: "Tree of Life" by Jacques Lipchitz.

1979

Hadassah's Aliyah Department, organizes Israel Family Live-In programs for work-study-travel participants.

National and local Hadassah leaders march for Soviet Jewry in the Solidarity Sunday parade in New York.

Left: Past National Presidents and members of the National Board march for Soviet Jewry.

1980

The Joseph and Belle Braun Hebrew University-Hadassah School of Public Health and Community Medicine opens at Hadassah-Ein Kerem.

Right: School of Public Health and Community Medicine opens.

1981

Youth Aliyah welcomes its 200,000th ward.

The Israel Nursing Association prize is awarded to the Henrietta Szold Hadassah-Hebrew University School of Nursing for its contribution to the teaching of nursing.

1982

HMO receives casualties by helicopter and ambulance convoy throughout the first war with Lebanon. Despite the war, Hadassah holds its 68th National Convention in Israel, the organization's second Israel convention.

Above: Ambulance loads wounded from helicopter.

Right: Past national presidents at dedication of presidents' memorial garden on Mount Scopus; from left Bernice Tannenbaum, Miriam Freund, Frieda Lewis, Charlotte Jacobson and Rebecca Shulman.

Hadassah-Ein Kerem becomes one of five world centers capable of performing test-tube conception. A year later, Jerusalem's first test-tube baby (a girl) is born there to a "high risk" mother.

Far left: Dr. Niri Laufer with researcher in the test-tube laboratory.

Left: Professor Joseph Schenker visits Nina Calderon, mother of the first triplets made possible through Hadassah's test-tube baby conception program.

1983

Hadassah International (HI) is established as Hadassah's global arm to advance and enhance HMO's lifesaving work. Membership is open to men and women, Jews and non-Jews. This new branch of the organization, which will grow to encompass more than 30 countries, is the

Right: 2 millionth-visitor to the Chagall windows in the Abbell Synagogue at Hadassah Medical Center, Ein Kerem.

Above: Ethiopian Jews arrive in Israel.

inspiration of Former National President Bernice S. Tannenbaum.

1984

Youth Aliyah celebrates its 50th anniversary.

Young Judaea celebrates its 75th anniversary.

As "Operation Moses" evacuates 7,000 Ethiopian Jews to Israel, Youth Aliyah creates and adapts specific programs geared to help the newest arrivals adjust to Israeli society.

1985

The Lithotripter, a revolutionary kidney stone crusher, using sound waves to eliminate the need for invasive surgery, is presented to Hadassah.

Right, top: Kinetic sculpture "The Beating Heart" by renowned Israeli artist Yaacov Agam, is dedicated at Hadassah, Ein Kerem.

Right: Ina and Jack Kay, and National President Ruth Popkin at opening of Ina and Jack Kay Hospice, Jerusalem's only hospice.

1986

The Ina and Jack Kay Hospice, Jerusalem's only Jewish hospice, opens at Hadassah-Mount Scopus, in response to a critical need by Jewish patients.

HMO opens a regional AIDS testing center at Hadassah-Ein Kerem.

The Israel National Skin Bank, located at Hadassah University Medical Center in Ein Kerem, is founded by the IDF and the Ministry of Health. It is the world's largest skin bank.

1987

HMO initiates its two-year, full-time, fully funded program to teach Palestinian physicians from the West Bank and Gaza how to improve medical care in their communities.

HMO surgeons perform the first heart transplant in Israel.

Disregarding a major loss in revenue, Hadassah Magazine stops accepting tobacco ads, in keeping with Hadassah's mission as a health organization.

Right, top to bottom: First heart transplant surgery, 1987; Heart transplant recipient after surgery; Heart transplant patient after one month.

SURGEON GENERAL'S WARNING: Smoking Causes Lung Cancer, Heart Disease, Emphysema, And May Complicate Pregnancy

We will never print this warning again

HADASSAH MAGAZINE is clearing the air. Starting with this issue, we will no longer accept advertisements for tobacco products. We are quitting cigarette ads cold turkey, with a discomfort similar to that left by smokers who have just quit; the main withdrawal symptom will be the loss of 20 percent of our annual ad revenue. Our reason for quitting cigarette ads is also the same as that of the smoker—to promote health. We won't be printing the Surgeon General's warning again because there will be nothing in our pages to warn against.

Left: Hadassah Magazine issue announcing the new "no tobacco ads" policy.

1988

At the invitation of U.S. AID, HMO medical staff members help plan, construct and open a hospital in Kinshasa, Zaire.

Hadassah advocates for increased health services for those infected with

Left: Hospital in Zaire opens with the help of HMO staff members.

HIV/AIDS and adequate funding for AIDS research in the U.S.

The Hadassah Seligsberg-Brandeis Comprehensive High School is devolved to the Jerusalem municipality and relocates to East Talpiot. Expansion of Hadassah Community College begins.

Left: Aids symposium.

1989

At a historic pro-choice rally of 300,000 in Washington DC, Hadassah marches with women and men from across the U.S.

With the end of the Cold War and the gradual collapse of the Soviet bloc, hundreds of thousands of Soviet Jews begin to leave for Israel; Hadassah prepares to meet their needs and to absorb many of them as employees.

HIES is restructured: Hadassah Community College is renamed the Hadassah College of Technology (HCT), then

Right, top: Hadassah women march in pro choice rally.

Right: Orientation for Soviet Jews.

Israel's foremost technology institute (now called Hadassah College-Jerusalem). The Hadassah Vocational Guidance Bureau is renamed Hadassah Career Counseling Institute (HCCI).

The city of Jerusalem honors Hadassah by dedicating Hadassah Square, a small city square on Rehov Ha-Melekh George (King George Street), near Agron Street.

Above: National President Carmela Kalmanson with Mayor Teddy Kollek at dedication of Hadassah Square in Jerusalem.

HMO's Complementary (alternative) Medicine Department opens in downtown Jerusalem (moves to Hadassah-Ein Kerem in 2001).

1990

As "Operation Exodus" brings waves of Jews to Israel from the dissolving Soviet Union, Hadassah takes part in these ways: 1. HMO begins to absorb and retrain groups of health- care professionals. 2. HCT becomes the first institution in Israel to retrain the immigrants by using both Russian and Hebrew courses in dental and laboratory technology, and translating its materials into Russian. HCCI trains Russian career counselors and offers Russian-language occupational materials to immigrants. 3. Youth Aliyah starts its first ulpan (Hebrew language program) for Soviet students. 4. Young Judaea invites Soviet teen immigrants living in the U.S. to attend its leadership camp, Tel Yehudah.

Middle: Russian immigrant at HMO lab.

Above: Russian students at HCT.

Hadassah meets an additional JNF pledge to replace 100,000 trees destroyed by arson, and pledges to provide JNF recreational facilities in a Galilee development plan.

Within one two-week period in a remote area of Kenya, HMO eye surgeons operate on 400 blind people, giving sight to many for the first time.

1991

During the Persian Gulf War ("Operation Desert Storm," 1991), Iraqi Scud missiles assault Israel. HMO treats casualties and helps distribute health information and gas masks to the population. Despite the risks, 45 National Board members, led by National President Carmela E. Kalmanson, travel to Israel on their scheduled mission, demonstrating Hadassah's solidarity with Israel's besieged people.

"Operation Solomon" brings thousands of Ethiopian Jews to Israel; 14,500 arrive within a single day. Hadassah contributes $3 million to Youth Aliyah over three years, enabling it to adapt its programs to meet the needs of this newest group of olim.

HMO installs a positron emission tomography (PET) unit in the Department of Medical Biophysics and Nuclear Medicine, allowing researchers to observe the functioning of human organs.

Top: Hadassah's Solidarity Mission to Israel during the Persian Gulf War.

Above: National President Deborah Kaplan standing with newly arrived Ethiopian children

As thousands of Soviet Jews continue to arrive in Israel, Hadassah creates special retraining programs and tries to find employment for them. The National Board allocates an additional $1 million for HMO, Young Judaea and HIES emergency programs.

Israel President Chaim Herzog presents Hadassah with the Shazar Prize for Excellence in Jewish Education.

To meet the needs of a growing tourism boom, Hadassah opens Dvir Hotel Management School, which became part of Hadassah College-Jerusalem. (Earlier, in 1950, Hadassah had founded the Hadassah Hotel Management School, devolved to the government in 1956.)

Right: Hotel Management.

1992

Ivrit la Hadassah, Hadassah's innovative, peer-led Hebrew education program, successfully debuts in the U.S.

Hadassah establishes its Curriculum Watch program to help guarantee the factual correctness of TV and radio programs, novels, textbooks and other school materials relating to Judaism, anti-Semitism, the Holocaust and Israel.

HMO opens its Rapid Response Trauma Unit—Israel's first—to treat victims of accidents and terrorism.

HMO formally opens two major interdisciplinary units for liver disease and diabetes, both with state-of-the-art inpatient wards, outpatient clinics, laboratories, and facilities for day care, patient education, teaching and research.

Kiryat HaYovel opens a special clinic to extend care to 700 Ethiopian immigrants.

Hadassah initiates Hadassah Cares, an ongoing breast health awareness and education program for American women of all ages. This program includes Hadassah's award-winning Check It Out program for high-school girls, and today offers testicular cancer education for teenage boys.

Left: Hadassah Check it Out program for breast health awareness.

1993

HMO performs Israel's first successful heart-lung transplant.

Right, top: Israeli Prime Minister Yitzchak Rabin, PLO Chairman Yassir Arafat with U.S. President Bill Clinton at the White House.

Right: Hadassah launches a national campaign to secure the release of Israeli soldiers missing in action in Lebanon.

Raise your voice for Israeli MIAs!

Ron Arad
DATE OF BIRTH: MAY 5, 1958
COUNTRY OF BIRTH: ISRAEL

Zvi Feldman
DATE OF BIRTH: DECEMBER 29, 1956
COUNTRY OF BIRTH: ISRAEL

Zachary Shlomo Baumel
DATE OF BIRTH: NOVEMBER 17, 1960
COUNTRY OF BIRTH: U.S.A.

Yehuda Yekutiel Katz
DATE OF BIRTH: JULY 15, 1959
COUNTRY OF BIRTH: ISRAEL

1994

Hadassah, WZOA, receives the approval of the Zionist General Council for special status as a member of the World Zionist Organization, ensuring that Hadassah will be granted participation in all activities of the World Zionist Organization, as well as in every Congress, with a fixed delegation of 32 members.

1995

Congress passes the Violence Against Women Act, creating programs and greater legal recourse for survivors of domestic abuse. Hadassah, an early advocate on behalf of victims of domestic violence, intensifies its programs on domestic abuse, both in the U.S. and in Israel.

The National Committee of Hadassah Associates is formed to encourage men to take a more activist role in its membership enrollment and fundraising activities for the benefit of the Hadassah Medical Organization.

Reflecting the world's high hopes for peace in the Middle East, Hadassah honors Prime Minister Rabin and Foreign Minister Peres with the Henrietta Szold Award, presented at the national annual convention held in Jerusalem.

Hadassah dedicates its $23 million, state-of-the-art Mother and Child Center at Hadassah-Ein Kerem during the annual National Convention. Comprised of the Julia Goldwurm Maternity Pavilion and the Wolfson Children's Pavilion, the center is built with the physical, mental and social well-being of the sick child in mind. It offers the latest care to its patients, in a child friendly atmosphere.

Above: Mother and Child Center at dedication.

Above: Relief drive for war-torn Bosnia.

1996

Elsie Roth galvanizes her Hadassah Nurses' Council colleagues to spearhead a relief drive for war-torn Bosnia. Hadassah members collect over 100 tons of supplies. Roth and fellow volunteer, Sherry Hahn, personally deliver them to Bosnia's people.

Hadassah's National Commission on American Jewish Women publishes Voices for Change: Future Directions for American Jewish Women, a landmark study that directly questions Jewish women about their needs, hopes, and desires.

Hadassah initiates grassroots community service with READ*WRITE*NOW!, a U.S. volunteer literacy program.

Hadassah transforms its historic 19th-century Villa Rosemarie in Jerusalem's German Colony into Merkaz Hamagshimim, an absorption/community center and residence for young adult olim from English-speaking countries.

1997

In honor of Hadassah's 85th Anniversary, Hadassah's first Women of Distinction Awards are presented in Israel (January) and in the U.S. at Purim (March) at Temple Emanu-El, where Hadassah's first meeting was held in 1912.

Hadassah joins a broad-based national coalition lobbying for federal legislation to prevent genetic discrimination by health insurance carriers and employers.

The Henrietta Szold Hadassah-Hebrew University School of Nursing forms a historic partnership with the University of Maryland School of Nursing to create a clinical master's program at Hadassah. Future projects include graduate programs in trauma/critical care, geriatric nursing and oncology nursing.

Young Judaea forms ATID (future, in Hebrew), an educational and action partnership with Israel's Tsofim (Scouts) and Britain's Federation of Zionist Youth (FZY), its sister movements.

Impelled by Voices for Change, Hadassah founds the International Research Institute on Jewish Women at Brandeis University, now known as the Hadassah-Brandeis Institute (HBI).

Above: National President Marlene Post with Shulamit Reinharz, Director of the Institute.

1998

In honor of Israel's 50th Anniversary 1) Hadassah allocates $3 million to make JNF's American Independence Park Israel's first completely handicapped-accessible park. Eight more such Hadassah-funded parks are scheduled for necessary renovation. 2) Hadassah's Jewish Education

Department publishes "Zionism: The Sequel", examining the state of the Zionist movement and Israel, its greatest creation. 3) Hadassah sponsors a special Miracle Mission to Israel, led by former National President Ruth W. Popkin.

Hadassah initiates the Hadassah Leadership Academy (HLA), which then pilots its first multi-year program in Jewish women's history, Zionism and Israel, community leadership, and social advocacy.

Hadassah's National Board formally establishes the Hadassah Foundation with a $10 million dollar endowment to

address societal needs in Israel and the U.S., outside the traditional Hadassah project framework.

The Goldyne Savad Institute of Gene Therapy is established at Hadassah-Ein Kerem, enabling HMO to become a leader in genetic therapy and gene research.

The Young Judaea Alumni Study, undertaken to gauge the youth movement's long-term impact on participants, reveals that active membership in Young Judaea exerts a powerful positive influence upon adult Jewish identity and increases Jewish involvement.

HMO health professionals Professor Dan Engelhardt and Professor Yoel Donchin, activated IDF reservists, bring medical equipment and eight tons of medical supplies to Macedonian field hospitals to assist refugees from a devastated Kosovo.

Top: Former National President Ruth Popkin and National President Marlene Post accompany handicapped man at handicapped-accessible JNF park.

Above: Youth Aliyah's Meier Shfeyah Children's Village receives the Israel Prize in Education.

1999

At National Convention in Washington, D.C., 2,000 Hadassah delegates from across the United States visit Capitol Hill, bringing Hadassah voices to their senators and representatives— Hadassah's largest "Day on the Hill" ever.

Above: Hadasssah members participate in Day on the Hill program at Convention in Washington, D.C.

2000

The Hadassah College of Technology turns 30 and graduates its first academic class.

Hadassah introduces Pikuah Nefesh—To Save a Life, a program created to increase awareness of the need for organ and tissue donations.

In support of stricter gun control legislation, Hadassah members and friends join the Mother's Day Million Mom March in Washington D.C. and around the United States.

The Al-Aksa intifada erupts on the Temple Mount on September 28. Violence engulfs the territories and the entire land of Israel. HMO mobilizes to treat the wounded, while HWZOA provides new programs, speakers, materials and action alerts for its members in the United States.

Above: Hadassah at the Million Mom March.

Hadassah partners with Birthright Israel, a philanthropic initiative to foster connections with Israel by giving every Jewish youngster/student between the ages of 18 and 26 a free, first-time trip to Israel; some programs are to be provided through Young Judaea.

Hadassah hospitals at Mount Scopus and Ein Kerem are declared smoke-free zones in accordance with Hadassah's mission to protect and promote health.

2001

Hadassah is approved by the U.N. Economic and Social Council (ECOSOC) as a non-governmental organization (NGO), enabling Hadassah to lend its medical and social expertise to the international body.

As JNF celebrates its centennial, Hadassah, its partner for 75 years, designates $3 million to help improve Israel's water situation with a new reservoir in the Jordan Valley.

The Esther Gottesman Center for Technology, housed within HCT's restored "Arches" building, is dedicated. It includes the new Henrietta Szold Center for students with special needs and challenges.

Top: Young Hadassah International holds a World Wide Walk in major world cities to raise awareness and funds for pediatric cancer research at HMO.

Above: After September 11, National Board members present gifts to local fire department for distribution to families of fallen firefighters at holiday time in New York City.

2002

In response to the growing need for state-of-the-art trauma medicine, Hadassah launches a major fundraising program to expand the Center for Emergency Medicine at Hadassah-Ein Kerem.

Right, top: Former Director General of Hadassah Medical Organization Shmuel Penchas.

Right: National President Bonnie Lipton at work site of Center for Emergency Medicine.

2003

The Hadassah Human Embryonic Stem Cell Research Center is established.

The Mother and Child Center is renamed the Charlotte R. Bloomberg Mother and Child Center in honor of New York City Mayor Michael Bloomberg's mother.

2004

With many months of recovery and reconstruction work needed to repair the devastation left by Hurricane Charley on the southwest coast of Florida, Hadassah launches a special appeal to raise assistance funds.

Researchers at HMO show that human embryonic stem cells can improve the functioning of a laboratory rat with Parkinson's disease. The research team is headed by Prof. Benjamin Reubinoff, director of Hadassah's Center for Human Embryonic Stem Cell research at the Goldyne Savad Institute of Gene Therapy and the Department of Gynecology, and Prof. Tamir Ben-Hur, senior physician in Hadassah's department of Neurology, the Agnes Ginges Center for Human Neurogenetics.

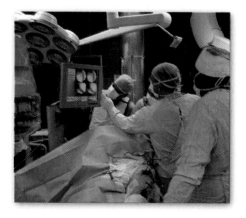

Right: First computer guided hip replacement surgery in the world.

The research was funded in part by the National Institute of Neurological Disorders and Stroke (NINDS), a component of the National Institute of Health (NIH) in the United States.

2005

Hadassah dedicates its newest facility, the Judy and Sidney Swartz Center for Emergency Medicine at Ein Kerem. The $50 million center has the capacity to treat 100,000 to 120,000 patients annually, an increase of 41 percent above previous use, and includes an expanded trauma and resuscitation unit, an acute and critical care facility, adult and pediatric emergency units, and an observation unit.

Hadassah, nominated for the 2005 Nobel Peace Prize for its ongoing initiatives to use medicine as a Bridge to Peace, conducts a wide variety of training programs for medical personal and students from the Palestinian Authority, Egypt, and Jordan as well as ninety countries throughout the world.

Top: Professor Reubinoff.

Above: JNF Chair, Deborah Kaplan, at Hadassah Dedication Center of Hadassah's Tirzah Reservoir Project in the Jordan Valley.

Young Judaeans organized the caravan to provide relief supplies to hurricane Katrina victims.

Hadassah launched SOS: State of Stem Cells; in a period of six weeks, Hadassah delegations visited all 50 state capitols to address the issues with their legislators.

Right: Left to right: National President June Walker, Past National President Bonnie Lipton, Campaign Chairs Sidney and Judy Swartz, Assistant HMO Director General and Head of Medical Services Dr. Yair Birnbaum, and HMO Director General Professor Shlomo Mor Yosef.

2006

Hadassah staff from the Hadassah-Hebrew University Medical Center in Jerusalem volunteer to travel the 112 miles north to Katyusha-struck Nahariya every weekday during the missile bombardment during the summer.

Above: Youngsters at Young Judaea Summer Camp.

More than 500 Young Judaea Year Course participants volunteered during the 2006 War with Lebanon. They bagged supplies for soldiers, entertained children who had to leave their homes in the south, and conducted fundraisers to help the war effort.

2007

Henrietta Szold, founder of Hadassah, is inducted into the National Women's Hall of Fame in Seneca Falls, NY, the birthplace of the American women's movement.

As Young Judaea's Year Course in Israel celebrates its fiftieth year, a new Year Course track includes travel to and study about four extraordinary communities with deep-rooted connections to the Jewish people—Marranos in Portugal, the Lemba of Southern Africa, Bene Israel and Bnei Menashe communities in India, and the Abayudaya Jews of Uganda.

Inspired by its historical imperative to continue building the medical infrastructure of Jerusalem, Hadassah raises the first $164

Above: National President Nancy Falchuk addresses Hadassah Foundation meeting.

Left: Hadassah College students in laboratory.

✦ 459

Left: Hadassah Young Women/ Young Leaders Mission visits Hadassah-Mount Scopus.

Middle: Model of the new Hospital Tower.

million needed to begin construction of the new Sarah Wetsman Davidson Tower on the campus of Hadassah Medical Center in Ein Kerem; Judy and Sidney Swartz, Campaign Chairs; Professor Shlomo Mor-Yosef, Director General of Hadassah Medical Organization.

2008

Nancy Falchuk, National President of Hadassah, is part of the Bush Delegation celebrating the 60th Anniversary of the State of Israel.

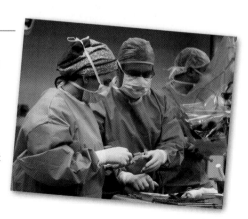

Right: Hadassah Hospital treats every individual who requires medical attention without regard for race, religion, gender, ethnicity, or political persuasion.

Above: The school at Meir Shfeyah won the President's Prize for education.

Research at HMO shows that transplantation of human embryonic stem cells into the brains of mice with multiple sclerosis (MS) significantly slows the clinical symptoms and pathological manifestations of the disease.

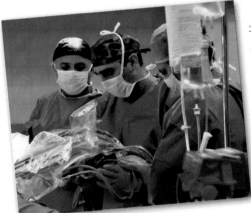

2009

56 Young Judaeans of high school age give up their vacations to volunteer for YJ's Alternative Winter Break in New Orleans, where they work with families, children and community organizations still struggling in the aftermath of the 2005 Hurricane Katrina.

2010

Conducting more than half of the hospital research in Israel, Hadassah physicians have pioneered innovative and unique medical treatments, introducing them to Israel and many areas of the world. Their clinical and research achievements have gained fame throughout the world, garnering Hadassah an international reputation for excellence.

Above: Use of the surgical robot "da Vinci" launches the Hadassah University Medical Center in Jerusalem into the elite group of the world's leading medical centers that uses this advanced technology.

Israel is among the first responders to the post earthquake crisis in Haiti, sending IDF rescue troops, medical personnel from Hadassah and other hospitals, and Hadassah medical clown David Barashi. The clown uses humor to ease the pain of earthquake victims and to cheer their caregivers.

Above: Hadassah clown in Haiti.

2011

The state of the art Marlene Greenebaum Multidisciplinary Breast Center, at Hadassah-Ein Kerem, is dedicated.

Above, left: Construction of the new Sarah Wetsman Davidson Hospital Tower accelerates.

Above, right: Four sets of newborn twins at Charlotte R. Bloomberg Mother and Child Center.

2012

Hadassah celebrates its Centennial with the dedication of the Sarah Wetsman Davidson Hospital Tower, Hadassah's Centennial gift to the people of Israel.

HADASSAH SINCE 1912
PARTNERS WITH ISRAEL FOR LIFE

Above and left: The new Sarah Wetsman Davidson Hospital Tower soars above the Judaean Hills, changing the skyline of Jerusalem and changing the future of medical care in Israel and around the world.

Far left and left: Moving in day. (Left) National President Marcie Natan and Professor Ehud Kokia, Director General of Hadassah Medical Organization.

Above: Hadassah 2012 National Board.

ADDITIONAL INSPIRATIONAL THIN THREADS® TITLES FROM KIWI PUBLISHING.

Order on line at www.thinthreads.com for your special
Hadassah discount of **20%**

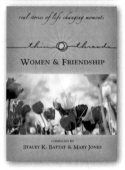

Use product HAD20 to receive your discount.

(not including the Hadassah Centennial Edition, or the Collector Edition)